Transitions from Education to Work

Labour markets are becoming more dynamic in response to pressures from globalisation, new technologies and trade agreements, as well as cross-border migration, inter-generation differences, changing education imperatives and employer expectations. By focusing on several Asia Pacific countries, this book explores the differences in their workforces: ageing, or abundant in labour but lacking in skilled employees. One similarity these countries share is the difficulty in attracting and retaining employees with the required skillset and capabilities, and these constraints can stymie national economic growth and long-term development.

This book brings together national and international perspectives on employability challenges faced by selected countries in the Asia Pacific region. While the region is forecast to enjoy high growth in the coming decade, a recurring challenge is addressing skill shortages and ensuring effective transition from training colleges and universities into employment. Consequently, the book focuses on the roles of multiple stakeholders, primarily: governments, education providers and employers – in more effectively addressing these key socio-economic challenges.

Roslyn Cameron is Associate Professor and Head of HRM Discipline at the Australian Institute of Business. She is also Co-Convenor of the Mixed Methods Special Interest Group (MMR SIG) of the Australian and New Zealand Academy of Management (ANZAM).

Subas P. Dhakal is Lecturer at Curtin Business School in Curtin University. He is a management academic with expertise in the theory and practice of sustainable development.

John Burgess is Professor of Management at RMIT University, Australia. His research interests include HRM practices of multinational enterprises, the relationship between working time and health and work in care sectors.

Routledge Advances in Management and Business Studies

For a full list of titles in this series, please visit www.routledge.com/series/SE0305

Transitions from Education to Work

Workforce Ready Challenges in the Asia Pacific

Edited by Roslyn Cameron, Subas Dhakal and John Burgess

Routledge
Taylor & Francis Group

LONDON AND NEW YORK

First published 2018 by Routledge

2 Park Square, Milton Park, Abingdon, Oxon OX14 4RN
605 Third Avenue, New York, NY 10017

Routledge is an imprint of the Taylor & Francis Group, an informa business

First issued in paperback 2021

Publisher's Note

The publisher has gone to great lengths to ensure the quality of this reprint but points out that some imperfections in the original copies may be apparent.

British Library Cataloguing in Publication Data
A catalogue record for this book is available from the British Library

Library of Congress Cataloging-in-Publication Data
A catalog record for this book has been requested

ISBN: 978-1-138-69175-9 (hbk)
ISBN: 978-0-367-85961-9 (pbk)

Typeset in Galliard
by Apex CoVantage, LLC

Contents

Figures

Tables

Contributors

Vipapone Aphayvanh is Project Manager at Indochina Research Laos. Her work involves working with research consultants on various projects, including rural development, evaluation study on public health system and skill needs assessment in the food-processing sector in Lao PDR.

Azad Singh Bali is Lecturer and Research Fellow at Murdoch University, Australia. His research focuses on comparative social policy in Asia, economic development in India and economic policy in Singapore.

Kerry Brown is Professor of employment and industry at the School of Business and Law in Edith Cowan University. She is Director of the Centre for innovative Practice at ECU and executive board member and founding fellow of the International Society of Engineering Asset Management.

John Burgess is Professor of Management at RMIT University, Australia. His research interests include HRM practices of multinational enterprises, the relationship between working time and health and work in care sectors.

Roslyn Cameron is Associate Professor and Head of HRM Discipline at the Australian Institute of Business. She is also Co-Convenor of the Mixed Methods Special Interest Group (MMR SIG) of the Australian and New Zealand Academy of Management (ANZAM).

Kwok-Mow Chan is Lecturer at Curtin University, Malaysia. He is Chair of the Industry Engagement and External Relations Committee.

Julia Connell is Research Development Advisor of UNHAS, Makassar, Indonesia, and Visiting Professor at the Graduate School of Research in the University of Technology Sydney, and Adjunct Professor of at Curtin Business School.

Subas P. Dhakal is Lecturer at Curtin Business School in Curtin University. He is a management academic with expertise in the theory and practice of sustainable development.

Jude C. Emelifeonwu is Senior Lecturer at Curtin University, Malaysia. He has over fifteen years of industry experience in the field of human resource management. His area of expertise includes employee voice, employee engagement, industrial relations in Africa and employability in Asia.

Sanjeev Kumar is Associate Professor at the Department of Management Studies in Graphic Era University, Dehradun, India. His major research areas are in service quality, work-readiness challenges and retailing and marketing analytics.

Noorziah Mohd Salleh is Senior Lecturer at the Business and Management Faculty in the Universiti Teknologi MARA, Kota Kinabalu, Malaysia. Her research fields include human resource management, strategic management and entrepreneurship.

Alan Montague is Senior Lecturer at RMIT University, Australia. He was previously a senior manager with a federal government department with expertise in government employment programs.

Barbara Mumme is PhD candidate at the University of Western Australia and currently teaches in the School of Management at Curtin University. Her primary research areas include graduate work-readiness, employability, the employment relationship and the effect of the Fourth Industrial Revolution on these topics.

Alan R. Nankervis is Adjunct Professor of Human Resource Management at Curtin University, Australia. He was formerly research director in the School of Management at Curtin University, director of the Graduate School of Management at Western Sydney University and the head of Human Resource Management at RMIT University.

Nguyen Ba Ngoc is Senior Researcher at the Institute of Labour Science and Social Affairs. He is also head of technical team of the National Wage Council.

Verma Prikshat is Lecturer (Management/HRM) at Australian Institute of Business. His key expertise is in the fields of Management, Human Resource Management, Organisation Change & Development, Leadership and Organisation behavior. He has presented his research findings in numerous international conferences, and his major areas of research interest are in human resource competencies and graduate work-readiness challenges in the Asia-Pacific region.

Soegeng Priyono is Director of DevOne Consulting in Jarkarta, Indonesia. He specialises in strategy and planning, turnaround management and human capital development.

Parinita Raje is PhD candidate at Monash University. Her research looks at ways to enhance graduate employability through the development of employability skills.

Christopher Vas is Associate Professor and Deputy Dean at Murdoch University, Singapore, and Director of the university's first offshore R&D centre – Singapore Centre for Research in Innovation, Productivity and Technology (SCRIPT).

Peter Waring is Dean of Murdoch University, Singapore. He is also a qualified lawyer and holds degrees in Commerce and Management. His research and teaching interests include the business and law fields of employment relations, human resource management, corporate governance and labour law.

Jonathan Winterton is Professor of Employment and Executive Dean of the Faculty of Business and Law at Talyor's University, Malaysia.

Part I

The issues and the challenges

1 Introduction

Applicant work-readiness and graduate employability challenges in the Asia Pacific

John Burgess, Roslyn Cameron, Subas Dhakal and Kerry Brown

The purpose of the book

This book outlines and examines a contemporary labour market policy challenge for many countries, both developed and developing, in the Asia Pacific region. The transition of recent graduates from education to employment is a key issue in building sustainable communities and resilient economies. However, graduates are finding increasing difficulty in attaining post-qualification employment.

The smooth transition from education to work has been impeded for many young job seekers. Relatively high youth unemployment rates have persisted across nearly all countries. Reasons for this persistence includes supply factors, such as the lack of work experience and skills of young people. On the demand side, employers perceive inexperience as a barrier, the costs of training as not justifying investments and there is also a raft of attitudinal issues around the commitment and behaviour of graduates. The irony is that while many countries face considerable challenges linked to population ageing and a shortage of skilled labour, new graduates have difficulties in accessing employment. Another irony is that in the context of extensive technological change and the emergence of global industries based on information and communication technology (ICT) platforms, the most advanced group of graduates in terms of skills and familiarity with new ICT platforms cannot access employment. What factors explain these conundrums? The ILO (2013, p. 1) *Report on Global Employment Trends for Youth* stated that:

> The global youth unemployment rate, estimated at 12.6 per cent in 2013, is close to its crisis peak. As many as 73 million young people are estimated to be unemployed in 2013. At the same time, informal employment among young people remains pervasive and transitions to decent work are slow and difficult. The economic and social costs of unemployment, long-term unemployment, discouragement and widespread low-quality jobs for young people continue to rise and undermine economies' growth potential.

The inability of young people to achieve secure employment erodes the ability of countries to establish sustainable growth. The prospect of poor employment outcomes for the newest generation of workers creates long-term social and economic dislocation and diminishes community resilience to further economic shocks.

The report (ILO 2013, p. 1) discussed the challenge of youth unemployment in terms of skills mismatch:

> Skills mismatch on youth labour markets has become a persistent and growing trend. Overeducation and over-skilling coexist with undereducation and under-skilling, and increasingly with skills obsolescence brought about by long-term unemployment. Such a mismatch makes solutions to the youth employment crisis more difficult to find and more time consuming to implement.
>
> (ILO 2013, p. 1)

The mismatch of skills and increasing youth unemployment creates an increasingly 'wicked problem' (Clarke and Stewart 1997) that is persistent and resistant to policy imperatives that attempt to provide programmatic solutions to the increasingly large gap between young people's expectations of attaining post-qualification jobs and their ability to achieve employment, especially in their chosen field. The ILO Report (2013) outlined the challenges of transition from education to stable and secure employment. Globally it appears that youth are experiencing long periods of unemployment and under employment, with many youth finding part-time, temporary and insecure jobs for which they are over-qualified. Yet, what this volume reports on is an apparent under-supply of certain skills by graduates; that is, they do not have the qualifications or the competencies that employers are seeking.

Skill requirements and the skill content of jobs are constantly changing. This means that at any one time, the provision of skills will lag behind the requirement for skills. There will be ongoing and unanticipated changes in trade, workplaces and technology that will generate changes in the skills required to carry out a job. It also seems that these changes in skills are ongoing and extensive. Keogh et al. (2015, p. xx) state that

> the context of the workplace is quite different from the formal learning context in which professional knowledge, skills and competence are acquired. The 21st Century Graduates should be supported in their transition to the world of work by being equipped with the resources to assimilate the activities of their host rapidly, to assess how their particular role is situated, supplied, and constrained, and appreciate its associated expectations, risks and consequences.

Transitioning from graduation to work is becoming a greater challenge in the light of profound structural changes occurring that impact on work. The World Economic Forum Human Capital Report (2016) highlighted the changing nature of jobs and the dramatic impact of technological change on jobs. Technological developments not only transform the labour market in terms of skills and occupations that are in demand; they also transform how education and training can be delivered through such arrangements as online learning. Extensive technological change not only impacts on the demand for labour, but it also transforms how skills and education can be accessed. The World Economic Forum's Future of Jobs Report (2015) suggests that around 60 percent of children entering primary school may work in jobs that do not exist at the moment.

The OECD (2016, p. 129) highlighted the significance of the skills matching challenge:

> Ensuring a good match between the skills acquired in education and on the job and those required in the labour market is essential if countries want to make the most of their investments in human capital and promote strong and inclusive growth. It is also a desirable outcome for individuals who have, themselves, invested in education. A mismatch between workers' skills and the demands of their job has potentially significant economic implications. At the individual level, it affects job satisfaction and wages. At the firm level, it increases the rate of turnover and may reduce productivity. At the macro-economic level, it increases unemployment and reduces GDP growth through the waste of human capital and/or a reduction in productivity.

An investigation into the readiness to meet industry skills requirements undertaken on behalf of the National Centre for Vocational Education Research (NCVER) found that job mismatch and the gap between skills acquired in education and those skills required for employment was widening over time (Beddie et al. 2014).

Further the OECD Report (OECD 2016, p. 130) commented that:

> some level of mismatch is inevitable. Requirements regarding skills and qualifications are never fixed. The task content of jobs changes over time in response to technological and organisational change, the demands of customers, and in response to the evolution of the supply of labour. Young people leaving education and people moving from unemployment into employment, for example, may take jobs that do not necessarily fully match their qualifications and skills. Thus, for a number of reasons, some workers are likely to be employed in jobs for which they are too qualified and others may be in jobs, at least temporarily, for which they lack adequate schooling.

The chapters in this book examine one aspect, albeit important, of youth unemployment. As suggested by the above international reports, the transition from graduation to regular employment represents a major challenge across countries. Those who have invested in human capital acquisition through formal education (technical and university) anticipate that completing their programs and receiving their formal qualifications will serve as a formal pathway into job entry. Indeed, the formal qualifications around many trade and technical training programs are designed to meet the formal entry conditions into those trade occupations. However, the evidence presented in this book is that graduates are finding it increasingly difficult to transition from tertiary education qualifications into a regular job. Many obtain jobs, but not in the occupations for which they received their qualifications. Others transition into those occupations for which they are qualified but cannot access an ongoing or full-time job (ILO 2013). The key questions are: why do there appear to be major problems in moving from graduation into regular employment? What is the nature of these obstacles? What explains these obstacles? Are these obstacles persistent, or are they linked to significant structural adjustments, such as technological change and globalization? How can policy makers and key institutions linked to the training and education system address these challenges? What are the views of the key stakeholders in the labour market as to the reasons for difficulties in transitioning from tertiary education to employment? Finally, how are these challenges being addressed through public policy in each of the countries represented in this volume? This book seeks answers to these questions for selected countries in the Asia Pacific region.

The Worlds Economic Forum's Human Capital Report (2016, p. 14) indicates that

> the learning and employment landscape of the Fourth Industrial Revolution will increasingly be shaped not only by technology-enabled education but also by the emergence of digital talent platforms, amplifying people's potential to develop and deploy their skills and experience beyond geographic boundaries while enabling employers to engage and integrate a globally dispersed workforce. Moreover, as both the demand and supply of skills and jobs migrate to a digital environment, there is a new horizon for understanding Learning and Employment.

Matching between graduates and jobs is context specific and subject to shocks (such as a recession) and structural change. The ILO (2013) highlights it is not only a matter of matching between graduates and jobs, but it also includes redundant and unused skills. One of the problems to consider is not only possessing too few skills to access jobs, but also having the wrong skills or not utilizing the skills that are possessed. Graduate work-readiness challenges are not only linked to unemployment but to under-employment, suggesting an over investment in skill acquisition.

What is graduate work-readiness?

There are various terms used to describe the ability, capacity and credentials of graduates to fill job vacancies. Terms include "job ready", "work ready", "skills mismatch" and "graduateness". The terminology is often not defined, and in many cases, it refers to a check-list of attributes that graduates are required to possess in order to transition to employment. What is clear is that despite the growing participation in tertiary education and the growing numbers of graduates, graduates are having difficulties accessing regular employment. Work-readiness suggests that graduation is itself a sufficient but not necessary qualification to enter into employment. The definition of graduate work-readiness, or job readiness, is not clear cut. It suggests that formal qualifications are only one of several attributes that are required to access employment. The term also suggests that the nature of these attributes is embodied in the jobs that graduates seek and that the formal process of education as an instrument for preparing graduates to transition into work has to consider what attributes or competencies can be accessed through the formal education process.

Cabalerro et al. (2011, p. 42) state that:

> As a construct . . . work-readiness is still in its early stages of development and there appears to be a lack of clarity and consensus, first, regarding what is meant by work-readiness, and second, with respect to the general skills and attributes that indicate work-readiness.

Tran (2015, p. 60) in a review of the literature on employability suggests that it is largely a check-list of attributes that graduates should possess in order to access employment; "employability is defined as the types of skills, knowledge, attributes or understandings." After reviewing a number of definitions Tran (2015, p. 61) indicates that "these definitions all relate employability to a set of skills and/or attributes that are necessary for any graduate to move into the employment market, to find and retain jobs and to develop his/her career".

The list of skills and attributes is extensive. There are a range of technical skills, soft skills and desirable attitudinal traits.

> While technical skills often refer to discipline-based skills and capacity, generic skills . . . cover such areas as coping with uncertainty, working under pressure, planning and strategic thinking, reliability, communications and interpersonal interactions, teamwork and networking, writing and speaking, information technology skills, creativity, self-confidence, self-management and time-management, willingness to learn and acceptance of responsibility.
>
> (Tran 2015, p. 61)

The list of attributes, while extensive, varies from job to job, occupation to occupation and industry to industry. An important question is how these attributes should be evaluated. Is it through the programs that graduates complete; is it through the examination of the professional qualifications and competencies that are acquired on graduation; or is it through testing the individuals who have graduated? Presumably required skills and competencies are listed for job vacancies and are used to assess and rank job applicants. However, the ordering and weight of the attributes would again vary across jobs. Equally challenging is the evaluation process – how is possessing the attributes demonstrated? Possible processes include thorough resume processing, interviewing and various forms of testing. The process of attribute certification is linked to the validation through certification of competencies. These would for example include language proficiency, IT skills and numeracy. However, how do you evaluate attitudes and behavior traits such as commitment, team working, independent decision-making ability and trust before job entry?

The conceptualization of graduate job readiness is important since given the public policy significance of the topic, it is surprising that job readiness largely remains undefined and flexible, nor is it fully integrated or contextualised within a learning process. If job readiness is about achieving a given set of attributes, then how are those attributes embedded within a learning process that allows new graduates to be better prepared for the job market? The ambiguity and fluidity of the definitional and conceptualisation structures of job readiness extend beyond industries and occupations. There are differences across regions and in the context of this volume, and there are major differences across countries. Hence the first challenge to address in the volume is what is graduate work-readiness? What attributes make up graduate work-readiness? How does the concept vary across different jobs and countries?

There is public recognition of the challenge and an attempt to address some of the skills deficits identified as being linked to job readiness. Many universities now have graduate work-readiness programs that are incorporated into formal study programs that provide graduates not only with formal technical qualifications but accredited skill attributes that were accessed through the teaching and learning environment. Universities are addressing graduate employability as a means of attracting new entrants and being competitive in a sector that is being privatised and globalised; the issue is also being addressed in response to the demands and funding rules applied by key stakeholders and public authorities that graduates have more than a degree on graduation. Since extensive public funding of tertiary institutions are involved, it is natural that governments are linking funding to graduate employment outcomes across the globe (Tran 2015). There are a range of national programs (UK, USA, Canada, Australia) for assessing and international systems linked to graduate attributes (see the Bologna agreement in the EU) and accreditation systems associated with particular programs (such as AACSB for business faculties) that assess programs in terms of their ability to impart an array of skills and attributes to graduates (Tran 2015).

The terminology is flexible, as is the meaning, and in this volume the terms graduate work-readiness and job readiness are used interchangeably. The focus is on graduates (in the 18 to 25 years age range) who have completed tertiary education programs. In terms of work-readiness, the discussion is around pre-job entry; training and on-the-job programs that may be provided post-job entry are not addressed in this study. While it is recognised that skills are temporary and that training and skill development extend beyond formal education, the book will not examine adult education and lifelong learning programs. Chapter 2 discusses the definition and conceptualization of job readiness and identifies the attributes and competencies that contribute to developing job readiness.

The Asia Pacific context for the book

The countries included in the study share proximity as they are part of the world where growth rates have been high, and they are characterised by large movements of cross border trade, labour and capital. More recently there have been large flows of students across borders to access tertiary qualifications. In discussing job readiness, the presence of large numbers of international students means that job readiness is not only about preparation for national jobs, but more about those generic skills that are needed to access jobs globally. Within the region, Australia, Singapore and Malaysia have large numbers of international students. Across these three countries, there are over one million students from abroad studying for university degrees.

Labour migration in and out of the ASEAN (Association of South-East Asian Nations) region is extensive. The ILO estimates that there are over 10 million migrant workers in ASEAN countries, two-thirds of whom are from those countries. An estimated 20 million ASEAN workers are employed outside of the region (ILO 2013). ASEAN countries with high labour outflows are the Philippines, Indonesia, Thailand and Vietnam. Countries with high migrant labour inflows include Singapore, Brunei, Malaysia and Thailand. Outside of ASEAN, India has large numbers of nationals working abroad, especially in the Middle East, and Australia has a large migrant inflow. Migrant labour ranges from unskilled labourers and domestic workers through to highly paid executives. The issue of job readiness is part of the labour migration flows as many job seekers may turn to other countries if they cannot access employment in their home country, and domestic businesses may turn to international labour if they cannot access skills in their home country.

In this volume the countries included are Australia, India, Indonesia, Laos, Malaysia, Nepal, Singapore, Taiwan and Vietnam. Chapter 2 provides an overview of the regional context of the book, reviewing the economic, demographic and cultural and institutional factors relevant to the framing of the study which has informed this volume. The comprehensive background details of each country will be addressed in the relevant country chapters in the volume. The list is not exhaustive for the region, as there are obvious omissions including China, the Philippines and Thailand. Apart from proximity and trade links, the countries differ according to wealth and stages of development, size, industry structure, demographic and skills profiles, culture and religion. However, they all face the challenge of graduate work-readiness, albeit in very different contexts.

The World Economic Forum 2016 Human Capital Index combines over 40 different indicators of human capital to assess the extent to which individual countries are developing their human capital potential. The Human Capital Report (2016) provides an overall ranking across 130 countries, and it reports on the scores across different demographic profiles of the population. The index reports on the learning and employment outcomes that are scaled from 100 (the best performer) to 0 (the worst performer) across the population and across 5 different age groups.

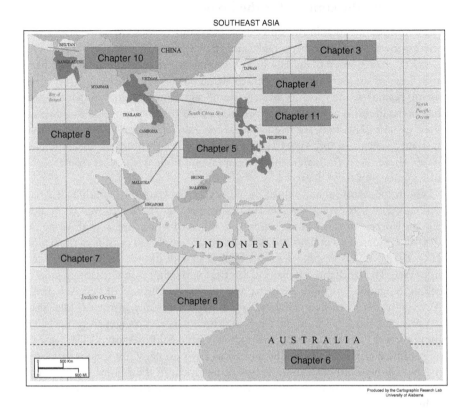

Figure 1.1 Geographic location of countries included in the study

The Human Capital Index ranks 130 countries on how well they are developing and deploying their human capital potential. The index assesses learning and
employment outcomes on a scale from 0 (worst) to 100 (best) across five distinct
age groups to capture the full demographic profile of a country. In the context of
this volume, the 15 to 24 age group encompasses the majority of graduates who
are transitioning into the labour market. The Report (2016) states that

> in the 15–24 age group, for whom the Index emphasizes factors such as
> workplace relevant skills and a successful education-to-employment transi-
> tion, countries have on average only leveraged 66% of young people's human
> capital potential, pointing to a disconnect between learning and employment
> in many economies around the world.
>
> (p. 14)

The Report provides a regional overview,

> Asia and the Pacific, the world's most populous region, scores towards the
> middle of the range of the Human Capital Index results, with an overall

Table 1.1 Human capital index for participating countries

Country	Human Capital Index	World Ranking
Australia	88.87	6
Singapore	75.96	22
Vietnam	74.99	29
Malaysia	74.85	30
Indonesia	67.35	65
Nepal	61.62	84
Laos	59.06	92
India	57.50	98

Source: World Economic Forum (2016) (Taiwan not included)

average score of 67.83. The gap between the best and worst performers in the Asia and the Pacific region is the second largest of any region, reflecting in part the different stages of development of the 22 countries from the region covered in the Index, but also the varying degrees of human capital outcomes even between countries with similar income.

(p. 9)

For those countries included in this study the results for the 15 to 24 years age group are reported in table 1.1.

The points to note from Table 1.1 are the diversity of scores in the region, that all countries score over 50 in the index and that 4 countries score 0.75 and above in the index. The index incorporates graduate work-readiness, but it also incorporates other indicators, such as unemployment rates, labour force participation and educational attainment. That is, it provides an extensive snapshot of human capital development for the age group most affected by the challenges to transitioning from education to work.

In the context of the overall country index scores, the Human Capital Index scores are on average higher for the 15 to 24 years group than for the total population. The region in general has far better scores for the under 15 and the 15 to 24 years group than it does for the population. This outcome reflects the heavy investment in schooling and education, and the increased participation in schooling and education in the region. By implication the regional challenge is to translate these investments into improved outcomes in terms of employment, productivity and incomes for graduates and for national economies.

Who are the key stakeholders in improving graduate work-readiness?

While tertiary institutions as the providers of education and employers as the recipients of those who have graduated from educational institutions are the two most prominent stakeholders, there are a range of groups implicated in preparing young people for their working careers. Developing an understanding of graduate work-readiness is only part of the process of developing workable programs to address the challenges that are identified. A central issue is responsibility, not in terms of assigning fault, but in terms of identifying who are the parties who have input, a vested interest and ownership of the issue. An investment in a tertiary qualification requires a large resource commitment and opportunity cost in terms of time and money. Individuals, families, communities, organisations and governments all invest heavily in tertiary education programs with the expectation that there will be a combination of private and social returns from such investments. The international contexts detailed in this book demonstrate the variety of those groups with an interest in the work-readiness of graduates and the different country contexts illuminate the differing weight of those influences across national contexts. For example, Jackson (2012) supports a multi-country comparative study to understand work-readiness attributes and understanding of the different roles of stakeholders in different national contexts.

This is particularly imperative in the Asia and Pacific, where countries that are the focus of this book are at varying stages of economic development. According to the recent World Bank's (2017) Gross National Income (GNI) based classification, Nepal is considered low-income economy whereas Australia, Singapore and Taiwan are categorised as high-income countries. The other main point of distinction is that the population in high-income economies are ageing significantly, whereas the low and lower middle economies – India, Nepal, Vietnam and Indonesia – have amongst the youngest populations and labour markets in the world. As a result, there are substantial variations in terms of changing vocational and higher education imperatives as well as graduate and employer prospects.

The World Economic Forum (2015) acknowledges the difficulty in preparing graduates for the world of work in the present, as future skills must be anticipated:

> Above all, the transition from education to employment has become fraught with uncertainty around the world. There is a pressing need to break down the divide between ministries of labour and education, and between the global education and employment conversations. Business has a critical role in stepping up investment in education, as well as clearly spelling out desired curriculum outcomes. As today's economies become ever more knowledge-based, technology-driven and globalized, and because we simply don't know what the jobs of tomorrow will look like, there is also a growing recognition that we have to prepare the next generation with the capacity for lifelong learning. The idea of a one-time education providing people with a lifelong skillset is a thing of the past.
>
> (World economic Forum 2016, p. 1)

The inability of graduates to find regular jobs in the careers for which they received their degree or the non-use of skills and competencies acquired through completing a program results in not only smaller individual and social returns from the investments, but also loss of value of the investments. On the demand side of the market, there will be potential losses in terms of output and productivity if required skills cannot be accessed by employing organisations.

In terms of a human capital investment process, the key stakeholders in this transaction are the graduates and their families and communities; the relevant public funding agencies; employers and the education agencies that provide the programs. However, the stakeholder interests extend beyond this. Around this core there are other key stakeholders, such as professional bodies that set entry and competency conditions for job entry; there are industry bodies that also set conditions around job entry; there are those job search and placement agencies that intermediate between bob seekers and employers; there are accreditation bodies that assess, rate and certify programs. The list goes on. There are pre-tertiary education programs in secondary schools that are linked to basic skills around numeracy, literacy and IT skills. Tertiary education graduation is the end of a long-term and major individual and public investment in education.

There is an extensive range and positioning of stakeholders in the graduate work-readiness framework. Across countries there will be different funding arrangements and different stakeholders who have input into the work-readiness process. The country stakeholder differences will be addressed in each of the country chapters. Chapter 2 provides a more detail around analytical framework for identifying and positioning stakeholders in the job transition process.

What will be clear from the book is that the scale of the challenge requires the key stakeholders to effectively communicate and co-operate. Universities cannot meet the different skill requirements of tens of thousands of individual businesses. However, peak business groups can identify and communicate to universities the core skill and competency requirements of their constituencies. These business associations are critical links between higher education providers and businesses employing graduates. Formal ties through advisory boards and committees are one avenue for taking into account the perspectives of business, but other informal relationships including reference groups, industry forums and workshops are important ways of supporting knowledge transfer and learning.

In recognition of the job-ready challenge universities are undertaking quality audits of degrees that includes skills and competencies deemed necessary for job entry. The ASEAN university network includes 30 universities that have a quality assurance process that includes graduate employment rates and employer reviews of curricula (Tran 2015). The Australian Quality Framework (AQF 2015) is applied to programs and tertiary education providers and includes graduate employment. The AQF relies on an approach that attempts to standardise the levels of student educational attainment and offers a comprehensive way of ensuring that those employing graduates with degrees can do so with the assurance that their qualifications meet regulatory requirements for skills and knowledge acquisition, and consequently, capability.

Policy responses to the challenges of work-readiness

Finally, what can be done to address the problem? Chapter 3 and the country chapters outline the responses and policies that are being implemented in each country to improve graduate work-readiness. There are six broad approaches to improving the matching process. First, having accurate and reliable information on future job needs and the skills and competencies required for those jobs is critical. There are issues around accurate labour market forecasting and effective communications between the key stakeholders. Since investments in education are based on future labour market conditions, there will always be a degree of uncertainty around the accuracy of such data. However, using more reliable data acquisition software and adopting more sophisticated interrogation methodologies goes some way to ameliorate problems of information lag and incomplete understanding of labour markets and future requirements. Second, linking funding and accreditation of tertiary institutions to graduate employment outcomes is a key activity. This strategy is already occurring in many countries through graduate surveys and program audits. Third, greater co-operation and networking between tertiary education institutions and employers and professional organisations should be encouraged. This could include extended industry and professional involvement in curriculum and pedagogy. Fourth, employers also can be more pro-active through providing scholarships, internships and induction programs. Anticipating skill needs and skill shortages would mean seeking potential employees before they graduate. In some countries in the region, skills shortages are addressed through employing migrant labour. Fifth, graduates can seek additional skills and competencies prior to graduation. Again, providing accurate labour market information, including the types of skills and competencies required, would allow graduates to build up in-demand competencies and resumes that are effective in supporting job seeking prior to graduation. Finally, governments need to ensure that the funding of education is sufficient to meet current and future skill needs, and this requires that there is sufficient funding and resources to fully develop those required skills.

Of course, there are complexities and complications in all labour markets. Not all graduates get jobs in those areas for which they are trained. Not all graduates can access a regular job, nor do they utilise the skills they acquired in their path to gaining qualifications and work experience. Structural changes in organisations, such as outsourcing and contracting out, and in technology, have a major impact on the content, task requirements and number of jobs available. Recessions increase the challenge of graduate employability. This is not a national problem. The large numbers of international students and large numbers of migrant workers in the region indicates that national responses have to keep in mind what is happening in the wider region.

How the book is organised

The book is structured in three Parts.

> *Part A: The Issues and the Challenges* contains two chapters: an introduction to the book followed by a comprehensive literature review of job readiness and the presentation of a theoretical framework which is central to the volume.
>
> *Part B: Country Studies* consists of nine comprehensive country chapters (Chapters 3 to 11), each with a summary box at the end which encapsulates

the key demographic and economic contexts of each country and their respective tertiary education systems. The important and fundamental employability challenges and policy initiatives are also given a brief overview.

Part C: Comparative Analysis and Conclusions contains the remaining two chapters, with Chapter 12 undertaking a country comparative of those countries in Part B of the volume. The last chapter, Chapter 13, concludes the volume and provides a synopsis of the issues and initiatives across the multiple stakeholders and the Asia Pacific region before presenting a research agenda around work-readiness and graduate employability for the future.

References

Australian Quality Framework. 2015, *Australian qualifications framework*, Canberra: AQF.

Beddie, F., Creaser, M., Hargreaves, J. and Ong, A. 2014, *Readiness to meet demand for skills: A study of five growth industries*, Adelaide: NCVER.

Caballero, C., Walker, A. and Fuller-Tyszkiewicz, M. 2011, 'The Work-readiness Scale (WRS): Developing a measure to assess work-readiness in college graduates', *Journal of Teaching and Learning for Graduate Employability*, Vol. 2, no. 2, pp. 41–54.

Clarke, M. and Stewart, J. 1997, *Handling the wicked issues: A challenge for government*, in INLOGOV Discussion Paper, University of Birmingham, UK.

International Labour Organisation. 2013, *Report on global employment trends for youth*. Available at: www.ilo.org/wcmsp5/groups/public/@dgreports/@dcomm/documents/publication/wcms_212423.pdf.

Jackson, D. 2012, 'Testing a model of undergraduate competence in employability skills and its implications for stakeholders', *Journal of Education and Work*, Vol. 27, no. 2, pp. 220–242.

Keogh, J., Maguire, T. and O'Donoghue, J. 2015, 'Graduate work-readiness in the 21st century', *Higher Education in Transformation Conference*, Dublin, Ireland, pp. 385–395.

OECD. 2016, *Skills matter: Further results from the survey of adult skills*, OECD skills studies, Paris: OECD Publishing. Available at: http://dx.doi.org/10.1787/9789264258051-en www.theewf.org/uploads/pdf/OECD%20Skills%20Studies.compressed.pdf.

Tran, T. T 2015, 'Enhancing graduate employability and the need for university-enterprise collaboration', *Journal of Teaching and Learning for Graduate Employability*, Vol. 7, no. 1, pp. 58–71.

World Bank. 2017, *Gross national income per capita*. Available at: http://databank.worldbank.org/data/download/GNIPC.pdf.

World Economic Forum. 2015, *Human capital index*. Available at: http://reports.weforum.org/human-capital-report-2015/the-human-capital-index/.

World Economic Forum. 2016, *Future of jobs*. Available at: www3.weforum.org/docs/WEF_Future_of_Jobs.pdf.

World Economic Forum. 2016, *The human capital report* 2016. Available at: www3.weforum.org/docs/HCR2016_Main_Report.pdf.

2 Graduate work-readiness in Asia Pacific economies

A review of the literature

Alan Nankervis, Verma Prikshat and Roslyn Cameron

Introduction

This chapter provides an overview of the relevant literature on the challenges faced by many Asia Pacific nations with respect to graduate 'work-readiness' in their labour markets, and their impacts on future economic growth and social development strategies. It was compiled from a thorough exploration of global and regional scholarly articles on 'work-readiness', together with recent industry, media and consultant reports. It begins with a brief exploration of the demographic and socio-economic contexts of the regional countries included in this book, followed by a discussion of the nature, extent and causes of the work-readiness challenges across the region, with a specific focus on graduate capabilities. It presents several explanations and models of work-readiness, together with a discussion of stakeholder theory as an analytical framework for an examination of the key players associated with its antecedents and consequences. Finally, a range of actual and potential strategies and solutions to the identified issues are considered.

Regional contexts

It is generally acknowledged that not only are the economic structures of countries changing in response to globalism, the influences of new technologies and new trade agreements; but also that labour markets are increasingly dynamic in response to these pressures as well as to cross-border migration, inter-generational differences, changing vocational and higher education imperatives and employer expectations (Brown et al. 2011; Bruni 2013; Galagan 2010; Jackson & Chapman 2012; OECD 2011). As Bruni (2013) suggested, 'the pace of economic growth and the typology of development will determine the amount of labor force that will be needed and the competencies and skills that will be required' (p. 3). An OECD report (2011) agreed, suggesting that skills shortages or mismatches between the required and available skills 'lower the potential for growth and waste resources' (p. 7).

Whilst there are commonalities in economic growth and social development across the Asia Pacific region, there are also significant differences in relation to stages of growth; industry structures; demographic profiles; labour markets;

vocational and higher education systems; employer expectations, and employee conditions, including salaries, benefits and union representation (Bruni 2013; Burgess and Connell 2013; OECD 2011). As explained in the International Labour Organisation's (ILO's) *World Employment and Social Outlook – Trends 2015 Report*, the post-global financial crisis (GFC) world has to date been characterised by an uneven and fragile job recovery. The report estimated that there were 61 million fewer people in employment globally in 2014 than there would have been had pre-crisis employment growth trends continued. The Asia-Pacific region accounts for 37 percent of this global jobs gap (ILO 2015). Whilst Australia has become primarily a service economy, with significant declines in the agricultural, manufacturing, mining and retail sectors, as Singapore has always been; Vietnam maintains its robust manufacturing sector (at both low skill, and increasingly high technical levels), alongside healthy agricultural, retail and (focused) service sectors; while India's economy is rooted in agriculture, which has slowly declined in importance, and the services and industrial sectors are now the largest and fastest-growing parts of the economy, contributing more than 50 and 30 percent to GDP respectively. Malaysia aims at high-tech manufacturing, but retains successful agricultural, mining, retailing and service industries, as does Indonesia, whilst Taiwan's success depends on high-tech services complemented by retailing and service sectors, and to a lesser extent, agriculture (CIA 2015; ILO 2013; OECD 2011).

With respect to country demographic profiles and associated labour markets, the populations of Australia, Singapore, Taiwan and to a lesser extent Malaysia, are ageing significantly, whilst India, Nepal, Vietnam and Indonesia have amongst the youngest populations and labour markets in the world (Bruni 2013; CIA 2015; di Gropello and Kruse 2011; Galagan 2010; ILO 2014; Montague 2013). Illustrations of the above characteristics include the proportion of elderly or younger people in the population (for example, Singapore has 27 percent elderly with 17.5 percent young people, whilst Malaysia has 14.5 percent elderly and 30 percent young people – Bruni 2013, p. 16). The median age of Vietnam's population is only 27.8 years (Montague 2013, p. 211). It can be inferred from the available data that the working populations of Singapore, Australia, Taiwan and Malaysia are primarily middle-aged, with significantly younger working-age populations in India, Vietnam and Indonesia. However, whilst countries such as Australia, Singapore, Malaysia and Taiwan are experiencing significant skills shortages due to their ageing workforces; in India, Vietnam and Indonesia there is 'an over-supply of available labour but an under-supply of qualified and skilled employees' (Montague 2013, p. 209).

A report by the McKinsey Global Institute analysed the economies of seventy nations in relation to their emerging global labour market positions. The analysis grouped these nations into eight clusters with common attributes based on the age and educational attainment of their labour forces (Dobbs et al. 2012). The clusters are represented on a continuum with the lowest average ages and lowest educational attainment commencing with the 'young developing' nations and the highest average ages and educational attainment culminating with the 'aging advanced' end of the cluster continuum. Table 2.1 provides a summary of these

Table 2.1 Eight clusters of global labour markets

Attributes	Young Developing	Young Middle-Income	India	China	Young Advanced	Russia and CEE	Southern Europe	Aging Advanced
Workers (million)	322	640	469	783	290	141	60	145
GDP per capita	<3,000	3,000–20,000	3,000	7,000	25,000–50,000	10,000–20,000	20,000–30,000	30,000–45,000
Countries	Bangladesh Pakistan Nigeria Tanzania Kenya Uganda Morocco Ghana Mozambique **Nepal** Cote d'Ivoire	Brazil **Indonesia** Mexico **Vietnam** Philippines Thailand Iran Turkey Egypt Columbia South Africa Argentina Algeria Peru Venezuela Saudi Arabia Sri Lanka Chile UAE Kazakhstan	**India**	China	US UK France S Korea Canada **Australia** Norway	Russia Ukraine Poland Romania Czech Republic Hungary Slovakia	Italy Spain Portugal Greece	Japan Germany Belgium Netherlands Sweden Switzerland Austria Denmark Finland

Source: Adapted from Dobbs et al. (2012)

eight clusters. India and China have their own cluster, Australia is categorised as 'Young Advanced', whilst Vietnam is considered Young Middle-Income. Not all countries represented in this book have been covered by this report; nonetheless the eight clusters assist in categorising the current and future global labour markets at a macro-level.

The scope and extent of work-readiness challenges across the Asia Pacific

All countries explored in this book are experiencing difficulties in attracting and retaining employees with the required portfolio of qualifications, vocational skills and personal capabilities (Galagan 2010; ILO 2013, 2014; India Skills Report 2015; Manpower 2015; OECD 2011). As Bruni (2013) explained, these labour market deficiencies which constitute the 'knowledge structure' of these economies are primarily 'the result of past formal learning processes inside the education and vocational training systems and of the training on the job provided by the production structure' (p. 38). Their effects include significant constraints on national economic growth, future production structures and long-term socioeconomic development.

In almost all these, particular concerns have been expressed regarding the quality of graduates, and these are often exacerbated by high levels of graduate unemployment. In Malaysia, according to the Ministry of Higher Education, 25 percent of graduates remained unemployed six months after they had graduated (Cheong et al. 2015), whereas youth unemployment has reached almost 25 percent in Indonesia (compared with 5 percent for the overall population) and is particularly high for secondary school graduates (Indonesia Skills Report 2010). The Indonesian Ministry of Manpower and Transmigration data also demonstrated that the number of people seeking jobs far exceeded job opportunities/vacancies available for graduates of higher education institutions (UNESCO 2012). Moreover, graduate supply is out of sync with emerging labour market requirements: only 16 percent of graduates studied engineering, manufacturing and construction (OECD/ADB 2015), and the country has a severe shortage of skilled labour due to the migration of skilled workers to other countries, and the lack of industry capacity to provide training (DCR Trendline 2015). The challenges of graduate work-readiness are chronic in Nepal, where university graduates are three times more likely to be unemployed than uneducated youths (Serrière and CEDA 2014). Similarly, Vietnamese graduates outnumber the requirements of industry, but many end up unemployed or underemployed, and employers still complain about the lack of graduates with appropriate workplace knowledge and skills (Pham 2010; Tran 2010b).

The Indian economy is witnessing a divergent trend within which both critical levels of graduates' unemployment and serious skill shortages coexist (Srivastava and Khare 2012; The Economist 2014). It is asserted that the Indian education system has prepared graduates poorly for the labour market (Khare 2014), and that Indian vocational and higher education graduates lack the required workplace skills, thus making them unsuitable for the competitive market (Srivastava and Chatterjee 2014). In Taiwan, the dramatic expansion of the number of higher educational institutions as part of the government's controversial education reforms launched in the mid-1990s in a bid to popularise tertiary education, has contributed significantly to the growing unemployment rate of university graduates (Ho 2015; Lee 2015).The unemployment rate for such university graduates was 5.26 percent in 2013, which was much higher than the unemployment rate of 4.11 percent for individuals who only held a high school diploma, and 3.53 percent for those who had only gained an elementary school diploma (Ho 2015). Another survey conducted in 2015 found that 35 percent of Taiwanese graduates had yet to find full-time work, up six percentage points from the previous year (Vanderklippe 2016).

According to the latest *Talent Shortage Survey* by the Manpower Group (2015), a lack of appropriately talented candidates is most likely to be a concern in Singapore, as the number of employers reporting talent shortages has risen sharply in Singapore (to 40 percent), with other noteworthy increases in Taiwan (up 12 percentage points to 57 percent) (Manpower Group 2015). Although underemployment has yet to become a significant concern in Singapore, if the economy and job market take a turn for the worse, underemployment could quickly turn into outright unemployment and a resultant graduate glut situation with 'over-educated and underemployed' workers, as witnessed in Taiwan (Boon 2014). Australia is also going through a difficult phase, as job prospects for new university graduates are the worst they have been since the 1980s, with only 68 percent of new graduates in full-time work within four months of finishing their course, down from more than 80 percent before the GFC (Norton 2014). The same report observed that in early 2013, the proportion of university graduates looking for full-time work, including those with part-time or casual work, was 29 percent, but in 2014 it reached almost 32 percent, causing growing concerns regarding diminished job prospects for graduates (Norton 2014).

According to a survey conducted by Grant Thornton (2013), about 62 percent of companies in Malaysia found it difficult to source skilled workers. It further observed that in the ASEAN region, the shortage of technical skills was the most significant impediment for businesses development. This was also the case in Vietnam (affecting 86 percent of businesses), followed by Malaysia (68 percent), and Singapore (66 percent – Grant Thornton International Business Report, 2013). The World Bank Report (2014) reconfirmed the high rates of Malaysian graduate unemployment observed in its previous report (2013), citing Ministry of Higher Education 2013 statistics that of the 220,527 graduates in 2012, 25.6 percent had failed to secure a job six months after graduation (Malaysia Economic Monitor, December 2014, p. 34). A study by Indonesia's Investment Coordinating Board (BKPM) projected that over the next fifty years the country's population will experience a 'demographic bonus' in which 60 to 70 percent of the population will be within the working age of 15 to 64, but ironically it is also projected that by 2020, Indonesia will only have 56 percent of the middle managers that companies need to run their businesses (DCR Trendline 2015). In order to support the growth of an evolving economy, Indonesia is in dire need of qualified and work-ready graduates. As examples, the World Bank found that 84 percent of employers in manufacturing report difficulties in filling management positions, and 69 percent report problems in sourcing other skilled workers (Indonesia Skills Report 2010). This problem is further complicated due to the fact that the number of foreign workers in Indonesia is increasing in line with the increase in foreign direct investment. In January 2005, there were 21,255 foreign workers in Indonesia; in June 2009, the figure rose to 46,226, an increase of 121 percent in five years or an annual increase of 25 percent. The fact that most of the foreign workers in Indonesia occupy highly skilled positions becomes a deterrent factor for Indonesian graduates to secure these jobs as they lack basic competencies and employability skills (UNESCO 2012).

Similar to Indonesia, India's youngest segment of the working-age population (15–64 years) is likely to increase significantly, from around 749 million to 962 million between 2010 and 2030 (CRISIL, 2010). With an ever-increasing population, and India's forecasted status as one of the 'youngest' countries in the world by 2020, it is imperative that India effectively meets its graduate employability challenges, for economic, productivity, growth and competitiveness purposes. In Nepal, the 2011 survey of over 4,000 manufacturing establishments revealed that a majority (60.3 percent) of businesses identified a lack of skilled manpower as one of the main problems facing the sector (CBS 2014). Although Vietnam is one of the fastest-growing economies in the world with an abundant and youthful (but largely unskilled) labour force, these characteristics create a different set of problems altogether (Cox 2013). Vietnam has experienced a continuous and serious shortage of skilled workers since the advent of *doimoi* ('opening up' – UNESCO 2014), despite significant growth in the educational system. For example, the number of students enrolling in higher education increased more than sixteen times between 1987 and 2010, from about 130 thousand to more than 2.1 million students (General Statistics Office of Vietnam 2012). The shortage of skilled workers, the lack of work-related competencies in graduates and the high level of unemployment among graduates signify the mismatch between employer needs and educational outcomes (Institute of International Education 2004; Oliver 2002). It is estimated that nearly 85 percent of the workforce has no formal post-secondary qualifications; with only 6 percent having university qualifications (Nguyen 2013), and only 60 percent of these are able to secure employment, whilst many 'do not work in areas of their major, or need to be retrained' (Pham and Tran 2013, p. 8).

In contrast with the prolonged economic downturn in most Western countries and China's ageing population, India's economy has grown faster than its pool of skilled workers, posing an immense challenge to its long-term sustainability (Chatterjee et al. 2014). As an example, a recent survey revealed that 83 percent of Indian educational institutions reported that they believed that their graduates were ready for the market, but only 51 percent of employers agreed (Mourshed, Farrell & Barton 2012, p. 40). Finding work-ready graduates to match job requirements has thus become a significant problem for many Indian employers

(India Skills Report 2014). Given the current pace of economic growth, India is likely to face an unimaginable skills gap in the future in which between 75 and 80 percent of university graduates lack the skills for the growing labour market (India Skills Report 2014, p. 13). This is evident across all industry sectors (India Skills Report 2014), representing a paradox in which the country will have more than enough formally qualified people, but an insufficient quantity of work-ready or employable job candidates, according to industry requirements (Goldin 2015).

In Taiwan, the increase in the number of universities has paradoxically resulted in the conundrum that as more graduates are produced, the value of their degrees has been diminished (Chung 2016). An excess of universities and a shortage of students – with 164 institutions of higher learning enrolling some 1.46 million students – have resulted in the degradation of the overall quality of education (Chien et al. 2013; Ferry 2015). Many graduates have no choice but to take up jobs with salaries far lower than their expectations in the wake of too many graduates seeking graduate-level jobs (Lee 2015). According to a Directorate General of Budget, Accounting and Statistics (DGBAS) Report, there were 445,000 unemployed graduates in July 2015, up 14,000 from the preceding month, and among them, 11,000 were first-time job seekers. The month-on-month rise in unemployment was driven by the entry of fresh graduates to the labour force and not by Taiwan's economic slowdown (Lin 2015).

Even in booming Singapore, which is importing highly skilled workers to stem a talent shortage, graduate unemployment rose from 3.6 to 3.9 percent in 2014, higher than the average unemployment rate in Singapore of around 2 percent (Ministry of Manpower 2014). The number of unemployed university graduates was higher than for groups of any other educational level in 2014, as figures showed that 18,600 degree holders were unemployed, making up close to a third of the overall 59,800 (Aspire 2014). The 2015 Talent Shortage Survey (Manpower Group 2015) reported the most noticeable increase (40 percent) in talent shortages in Singapore of the 29 countries studied. In Australia, university graduate employment was at twenty-year high in 2015. Statistics released in 2014 revealed that more than 11 percent of students graduating with a bachelor degree failed to find employment and were still looking for full-time work four months after graduation. This figure was the highest since 1995 and had more than doubled since 2008. Moreover, in 2015 the number of job vacancies listed by the Australian Department of Employment had almost halved to 159,400, resulting in job seekers outnumbering job vacancies by a ratio of eleven to one (AIM Network 2015).

The nature of graduate work-readiness challenges

Malaysia has become a growing global hub for growth industries such as gaming, content and cloud IT services, but in reality further growth is being hampered by its significant talent shortage (Grant Thornton 2013; Hays 2016). Malaysian employers reported that graduates lack the critical thinking, communication skills, language proficiency (especially in English), positive character, attitude or personality skills, that do not match the industry requirements (Chew 2013; Hariati and Lee 2011; MoHE 2012). Similarly, while analysing trends in skills demand, gaps and supply in Indonesia, the Indonesia Skills Report (2010) observed that while unskilled positions are relatively easy to staff, finding the right profile for senior management and professional jobs is perceived to be difficult by between 60 and 80 percent of respondents respectively. Greater difficulties were found in recruiting staff for the manufacturing, exporting and service sectors, and the widest gaps were observed across professional profiles for lack of English proficiency and computer skills, followed by thinking and behavioural skills, in addition to theoretical and practical knowledge of the job (Indonesia Skills Report 2010). Further, a lack of linkages between employers and training organisations, skills mismatches, training and job creation programs for young people are some of the key skill issues to date in the Indonesian workforce (ILO 2016).

The extent of the graduate work-readiness challenge in Vietnam has been highlighted by recent research by Montague (2013) who noted that Vietnam has an over-supply of available labour but an under-supply of quality skilled employees. This dilemma can be attributed to the current educational infrastructure at both vocational and university levels, as it suffers from an over-emphasis on theory rather than practice ('a failure to combine theoretical learning with practical or behavioural skills' – EIU 2012, p. 9), a societal preference for university rather than vocational education and outdated curricula (Truong 2013, p. 17). Moreover, the number of university students has increased sixteen times, whereas the number of teaching staff increased only slightly more than three times in the same period (General Statistics Office of Vietnam 2012). The growth in the Indian education sector, buoyed by more than a 7 percent per annum GDP growth in the last decade, has witnessed a deficient array of haphazard policies that lack strategic and systemic planning (Sanghi et al. 2012). This has resulted in the vast majority of education service providers not being in a position to produce students equipped with a desirable skill-set for the job market (Khare 2014; Srivastava and Chatterjee 2014). Consequently, graduate unemployment is four times (33 percent) higher than the total country unemployment (8.5 percent) (The Economist 2014, p. 10).

Similarly, with the exponential rise in the number of higher education institutions in Taiwan and less emphasis on quality, the graduate programs fail to instil in their students the practical knowledge that employers seek in their prospective workers, resulting in a large portion of 15- to 29-year-olds – 64.5 percent, compared with 59 percent for the total workforce in 2014 – having to settle for low-paying, low-skilled work in the service sector (Chung 2016). Many employers are struggling to find enough qualified job candidates, lamenting that university graduates no longer possess the knowledge and skills necessary for career success (Ho 2015). Australia has different graduate challenges as compared to the other six countries, as the field of study affects full-time job prospects more than the type of university attended. Compared to science graduates, graduates with education degrees are marginally less likely to find themselves unemployed, but graduates with society and culture or creative arts qualifications are about 2.5 times more likely to be unemployed (ABS 2014). Moreover, 'poor or inappropriate academic qualifications or results' consistently ranks high as an issue in graduate recruitment. The key graduate work-readiness issues for Australian employers are interpersonal and communication skills, attitude and work ethic, and motivation. In 2013, around 22 percent of employers reported that they would have recruited more graduates had a larger number of better candidates been available (GCA 2014, p. 6).

In Singapore some recent studies have suggested that the quality of polytechnic graduates (79 percent) was higher than university graduates (48 percent), and that they possess stronger work ethics and greater ability to work with information technology and learn new skills. There appears to be limited evidence of up-skilling and training of the workforce by employers, and very limited use of management development practices for senior management. To address these perceived deficiencies, the government has implemented a program called *Skills-Future*, which, according to Singapore's deputy prime minister, aims to 'create a new environment for lifelong learning. It is critical to our future. It will develop the skills and mastery needed to take our economy to the next level'. This and other initiatives are further discussed in chapter 8.

Thus, it is clear from the above discussion that in all eight Asia Pacific economies mere graduation and a high grade point average alone do not guarantee employment, but that graduates increasingly need to be work-ready in terms of the qualities most sought after by their potential employers. These are what some researchers have classified as "++ factors", and they are discussed in considerable detail in the following section of this chapter. Each country has its own particular issues and labour market characteristics within their respective economies. These include undersupply, oversupply and graduate employability skills, across country-specific industry sectors, which reflect the positioning of these economies and their relative stages of economic development. With the establishment of the Association of Southeast Asian Nations (ASEAN) Economic Community (AEC) in late 2015, all these countries will be facing increased regional competition, and therefore countries which can establish a robust mechanism for enhancing the work-readiness of graduates will stand to gain and others will face serious consequences.

Concepts of 'work-readiness' and associated challenges

These notion of 'work-readiness' reflects the need for graduates to possess a range of generic skills and attributes, over and above their formal qualifications, that make them 'prepared' or 'ready' for both general and more specific workplaces (ACNielsen Research Services 2000; Casner-Lotto et al. 2006; Goldin 2015). Different terms are used in the literature to describe the notion of work-readiness, including "employability", "job-readiness", "work preparedness", "graduate employability", "transferable skills" and "generic attributes" (O'Neil 2014). Some of these terms focus more on employer or graduate expectations, whilst others reflect both. According to Connell and Burgess (2006), 'employability – not employment – is said to be the new workplace reality, whereby many of the generation Y population . . . will not expect full time jobs with career ladders' (p. 498). This view represents the perspectives and expectations of generation Y school-leavers, vocational and higher education graduates who, it is reported, are reluctant or unwilling to commit themselves to long-term employment or traditional career patterns due to their desires for fulfilling jobs and adequate work-life balance opportunities. However, it presents only one side of the coin with respect to work-readiness. Many employers in most Asia Pacific countries have been reported as being critical of the actual knowledge, skills, work experience and/or personal qualities of applicants for both basic and higher-level occupations.

A recent Manpower report (2015), for example, revealed that 38 percent of employers in the region expressed their inability to fill key positions due either to the quantity or quality of applicants, notably in skilled trades, sales representative, engineer, technician, accounting, information technology and managerial categories. The report also found that whilst a third of the employers had experienced difficulties due to an absence of applicants, the remainder complained of either deficient technical skills, a lack of work experience and/or undeveloped workplace competencies. Similar studies in China, India and Vietnam found similar, if not greater, skills gaps in most of the same occupations and industry sectors (Galagan 2010; Montague 2013; Nankervis et al. 2012). Brown et al. (2011, p. 24) argued that 'only 13% of university graduates from the twenty eight low-wage Asian nations were suitable for jobs', whilst Galagan's study revealed that the industry sectors most seriously affected by work-readiness skills deficits in the Asia Pacific region were the education and health, leisure and hospitality, trade, transportation, banking and finance, professional and business services and government sectors (Galagan 2010, p. 47).

Drawing on this and other associated research, several definitions of the concept of work-readiness have emerged. Mason et al. (2006) described work-readiness as 'possession of the skills, knowledge, *attitudes and commercial understanding* that will enable new graduates to make productive contributions to organisational objectives *soon after commencing employment*' (our italics – p. 2). Nilsson (2010) regarded it as 'both hard and soft skills, including formal and actual competencies, interpersonal skills and personal characteristics' (p. 540). The OECD's definition is simpler but more direct – namely, 'the right skills mix not only for the present but also for the *future needs of dynamic labour markets*' (our italics – OECD 2011, p. 11). Connell and Burgess (2006, p. 498) added the dimensions of employee 'capacities' and 'willingness to be proactive *in a diversity of jobs*' (our italics). Finally, the Australian Qualifications Framework (AQF) defines the non-technical skills required of effective work-ready graduates, whether from vocational or higher education, as:

> transferable, non-discipline specific skills (which) a graduate may achieve through learning that has application in study, work and life contexts. The

four broad categories in the AQF are: fundamental skills; people skills; thinking skills and personal skills.

(AQF 2015)

Whilst it is generally acknowledged that many job applicants throughout the Asia Pacific region appear to lack work-readiness skills or aptitudes, the specific deficiencies require some exploration. Montague (2013) categorised them into two types – namely, 'vocational skills' and 'capabilities', where vocational skills refer to formal qualifications at both technical or higher education levels, and capabilities are represented by the so-called 'soft' skills. Other authors have divided work-readiness into four competencies – namely, 'key', 'core', 'transferable' and 'generic' – where the latter two are considered to be amongst the most deficient in many applicants (Mason et al. 2006, p. 2). There is some evidence that these deficiencies exist at secondary, vocational and higher education levels:

> almost one third of secondary education graduates are considered to be below average or very poor, and most of the rest are just fair. Although tertiary education graduates have a somewhat better reputation, the majority are considered only fair, and just a very small proportion are rated very good.
> (di Gropello et al. 2011, p. 21)

Other researchers have noted the irony that a growth in the number of educational institutions in the Asia Pacific region may have in fact added to the work-readiness problem by reducing the quality and applicability of higher education qualifications – 'the education "explosion" in the supply of college-educated workers. . . (is) a problem because widening access to a college education lowers the value of credentials in the competition for jobs' (Brown et al. 2011, p. 7). Additional contributing factors to work-readiness challenges include deficiencies in both vocational and higher education standards due to the commercialisation of education, emphases on theory at the expense of professional practice (including the removal of work-integrated learning, student placements or internships), the replacement of experienced teachers with doctorate-qualified researchers, the quality of teaching facilities, the currency of curricula and pressures to streamline courses and to provide more facile assessment systems. One study of the Indonesian education system, for example, found that secondary education often suffers from poor teaching-learning quality, inadequate teaching facilities and unresponsive curricula; whilst tertiary education has often failed to provide students with appropriate practical skills, capacities for adaptability and innovation, and effective links to industry. Although informal training providers tended to be 'reasonably responsible to labour market needs' (OECD 2011, pp. 22–25). Similar criticisms have been made about the Australian, Malaysian, Vietnamese, Taiwanese and Indian education systems (Nankervis et al. 2012). Accordingly, some researchers have suggested that 'a supply push is required to increase the relevance of secondary and tertiary education to the needs of (industry)' (OECD 2011, p. 18).

Together with the failure of some regional education systems to provide industry with the professional and technical skills and thus to enhance their immediate productivity, perhaps the most cited work-readiness challenges are in the
area of applicant 'capabilities', whether of secondary, vocational or higher education graduates. Numerous researchers have attempted to identify the particular
components of this work-readiness skills component, and it is generally agreed
that national governments, educational systems and employers (separately and
together) share the responsibility for nurturing and developing them. Thus,
Mason et al. (2006) suggested that numeracy, literacy, information technology,
general communication, problem-solving and teamwork; together with 'learning
how to learn' and 'understanding the world of work' were key competencies for
all new job applicants (p. 3). Mitchell et al. (2010) distilled the specific associated skills sets as general communication, oral communication, written communication, general ethics, teamwork, diversity time management and organisation,
problem-solving, customer service, leadership and 'business etiquette' (p. 48–9).

Andrews and Higson (2008), on the other hand, listed professionalism, reliability, abilities to cope with uncertainty, working under pressure, planning and
strategic thinking, written and verbal communication, self-confidence, good
self-management and willingness to learn as key work-readiness competencies
(p. 413). Di Gropello et al. (2011) elaborated these skills further, with special
reference to the services and export-oriented sectors in Indonesia – job-specific
skills plus behavioural skills (communication and leadership), client orientation,
teamwork, innovation, information technology and managerial competencies
(services); thinking, negotiation, IT and language skills (export-oriented sectors);
plus creativity, critical thinking, communication technological skills, pro-activity,
curiosity and effective understanding of company and industry operations (p.
6–10).

An OECD report (2011) further categorised them as basic foundation skills
(literacy and numeracy), higher level cognitive capabilities (problem-solving
and analytical), interpersonal skills (communication), teamwork and negotiation, technological flexibility, learning skills, creativity and entrepreneurship (p.
14–15). However, the most comprehensive taxonomy of the 'soft' or 'non-
technical' competencies required by but often lacking in job applicants across the
Asia Pacific region is provided by Jackson and Chapman (2012, pp. 548–551).
Following an extensive study of undergraduate business programs in universities
in Australia and the United Kingdom, they compiled a thorough listing of graduate competencies required 'to successfully and innovatively *apply* disciplinary
knowledge in the workplace' (p. 541), which has implications for government
policy, higher education service providers and employers alike. Table 2.2 summarises these twenty competencies and associated behaviours.

Finally, the Victorian Department of Education – Australia (2006) designed its
Employability Skills Framework based on two pillars – namely, skills and attributes. The former includes many of the competencies included in earlier studies but
added a set of necessary graduate 'attributes', or personal characteristics – loyalty,
reliability, commitment, honesty and integrity, enthusiasm, personal presentation,

Table 2.2 Taxonomy of "soft" graduate competencies

Competency	Behaviour name	Competency	Behaviour name
C1: Business principles	Use of business concepts	C11: Self-awareness	Meta-cognition Lifelong learning
C2: Core business skills	Numeracy Technology	C12: Self-discipline	Self-regulation Stress tolerance Work – life balance
C3: Critical thinking	Pattern recognition and conceptualisation Evaluation	C13: Innovation	Entrepreneurship Change management
C4: Problem solving	Analytical/ convergent reasoning Diagnosing	C14: Leadership	Project management Performance management Meeting management Developing others
C5: Decision management	Lateral thinking/ creativity Information management Decision making	C15: Formal communication skills	Public speaking Meeting participation Written communication
C6: Political skills	Influencing others Conflict resolution	C16: Performance	Efficiency Multi-tasking Autonomy
C7: Working with others	Task collaboration Team working Social intelligence Cultural and diversity management	C17: Organisational skills	Goal and task management Time management
C8: Oral communication	Verbal communication Giving and receiving feedback	C18: Environmental awareness	Organisational awareness Commercial awareness
C9: Personal ethics	Personal ethics	C19: Professional responsibility	Social responsibility Accountability
C10: Confidence	Self-efficacy	C20: Work ethic	Drive Initiative

commonsense, positive self-esteem, motivation, adaptability, ability to deal with pressure and a balanced attitude to work and home life (pp. 1–3). There are several concepts used to describe work-readiness ("employability", "job-readiness", "work preparedness", "graduate employability", "transferable skills" and "generic attributes") and these are further broken down into skills, capabilities and competencies. The next section provides an overview of some of the key models and taxonomies for work-readiness.

Models and taxonomies of work-readiness

Given the extensive, if largely congruent, lists of specific work-readiness skills and competencies discussed above, it is useful to consider the various thematic models or taxonomies which have been derived from them in order to provide analytical frameworks as foundations for future empirical research. Wickramasinghe and Perera (2010) suggested that there are three key purposes of work-readiness – namely, the ability to gain employment, the ability to maintain employment and importantly, the ability to 'make transitions between jobs and roles' (p. 226). In pursuit of these goals, they divide the pertinent skills requirements into two categories – subject skills and transferable skills, thus associating the latter with graduate career paths. Heckman and Kautz (2012) explained that 'soft' skills are also categorised as personality traits, non-cognitive skills, non-cognitive abilities, 'character' and socio-emotional skills (p. 4), whilst Nilsson (2010) proposed that work-readiness encompasses 'individual, contextual and relational' capabilities, including social/interpersonal, cultural capital (social networks) and symbolic capital (formal qualifications) elements (p. 548). Eisner (2010) simply divided them into interpersonal, conceptual and 'informational' capabilities, plus 'drive and adaptability' (p. 29).

The above literature review involved searching the management and social science databases. Five research databases were searched for publications from 2006 through to the present (2016), with the key articles being obtained from Pro-Quest, Informit and Emerald journals, together with internet resources (Google and Google Scholar). In order to ensure that relevant studies were covered, the search terms remained broad. These were 'work-readiness competencies', 'graduate competencies', 'work ready graduates' and 'work-readiness skills'. Studies were eligible for consideration in this review if: (a) the focus of the study was work-readiness/employability or unemployability of graduates; and (b) there was at least mention of words 'work-readiness skill' or 'work-readiness competencies'.

From these searches, the ten most important work-readiness skills and competencies were listed along with their dimensions and were ranked in order of their frequency. These are shown in Table 2.3.

Finally, Figure 2.1 distils the key work-readiness themes as the framework for this book.

Having discussed the scope, extent and nature of the broad work-readiness challenges facing many (if not all) Asia Pacific economies and some underpinning conceptual frameworks, this chapter now briefly reviews the literature on stakeholder theory as a means of understanding the roles of governments, industry, educational systems and graduates in designing integrated strategies to address these graduate work-readiness dilemmas.

Stakeholder theory

Stakeholder theory suggests that all labour market policies and strategies involve multiple stakeholders, with similar and diverse interests, and that the key role in their management is to continually balance these interests in order to achieve the

Table 2.3 Frequency of work-readiness skills and competencies in literature review

	Skills and competencies	Dimensions	Literature	Frequency
1	**Teamwork and political skills**	Working with others, Influencing others, Conflict resolution, Diversity management, Political skills, Interpersonal orientation, People skills	Caballero et al. 2011; Carrier and Gunter 2010; City & Guilds Centre for Skills Development(UK),(CSD 2010; Fong et al. 2014;Connell and Burgess 2006; di Gropello et al. 2011;Jackson and Chapman 2012; Mason et al 2006; Mitchell et al 2010; Nilsson 2010; OECD 2011;Rosenberg et al. 2012	12
2	**Cognitive capabilities**	Problem-solving and analytical, Planning and strategic thinking, Learning skills	Caballero et al. 2011;City & Guilds Centre for Skills Development(UK),(CSD 2010; di Gropello et al. 2011; Fong et al 2014;Mason et al 2006; Mitchell et al 2010; OECD 2011; Jackson and Chapman 2012; Mitchell et al 2010; Rosenberg et al 2012	9
3	**Core business skills**	Performance management, Organisational management, Professionalism and a strong work ethic	Andrew et al 2008; Caballero et al 2011; Carrier and Gunter 2010; City & Guilds Centre for Skills Development(UK),(CSD 2010; di Gropello et al 2011; Jackson and Chapman 2012; Mason et al. 2006; Mitchell et al. 2010	8
4	**Information technology skills**	ICT literacy, ethical issues surrounding the technology	Caballero et al. 2011; Carrier and Gunter 2010; City & Guilds Centre for Skills Development(UK),(CSD 2010; di Gropello et al. 2011; Fong et al. 2014; Mason et al. 2006; OECD 2011; Rosenberg et al. 2012	8
5	**Self-management**	Meta-cognition, Lifelong learning, Self-regulation	Andrew et al. 2008; Caballero et al. 2011;Carrier and Gunter, 2010; City & Guilds Centre for Skills Development(UK),(CSD 2010; Connell and Burgess 2006; Impetus 2014; Jackson and Chapman 2012; Mitchell et al. 2010; Nilsson 2010; Victorian Department of Education 2006	7

	Skill	Description	References	
6	General communication	Written & verbal communication, languages skills, giving and receiving feedback	Andrew et al. 2008; di Gropello et al. 2011; Fong et al. 2014; Jackson and Chapman 2012; Mason et al. 2006; Mitchell et al. 2010; OECD 2011	7
7	Foundation skills	Numeracy, Literacy	Andrew et al. 2008; City & Guilds Centre for Skills Development(UK),(CSD 2010;Jackson and Chapman 2012; Mason et al. 2006; Nilsson 2010; OECD 2011; Rosenberg et al. 2012	7
8	Leadership abilities	Leadership skills, Logical thinker, Visionary, Influencer, Developing people, Managing relationships, Taking charge	City & Guilds Centre for Skills Development(UK),(CSD 2010;di Gropello et al. 2011; Fong et al. 2014;Jackson and Chapman 2012; Mitchell et al. 2010; Rosenberg et al. 2012	6
9	Innovation and creativity	Entrepreneurship, Change-management, Ability to cope with uncertainty	Andrew et al. 2008; di Gropello et al. 2011; Fong et al. 2014; Jackson and Chapman 2012; OECD 2011	5
10	System thinking skills	Big picture, Fixing recurring problems, Solving difficult problems, STS, Social/Psychological outcomes	City & Guilds Centre for Skills Development (UK), (CSD 2010), Rosenberg et al. 2012	2

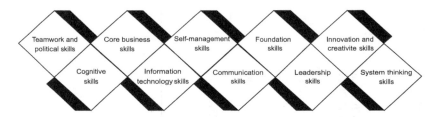

Figure 2.1 Common work-readiness themes

greater good, whether the primary objective is profitability or merely survival and growth. As Fontaine et al. (2006) explained, such policies and strategies encompass 'groupings of stakeholders, and (the role of management) is to manage their interests, needs and viewpoints'. Stakeholders are variously identified as 'those groups who are vital to survival and success' (Freeman et al. 2004, cited in Fontaine et al. 2006); 'committed value-chain partners to create outstanding performance' (Freeman et al., 2008, p. 365); or 'those persons or interests that have a stake, something to gain or lose as a result of the activities' (Clarkson 1998, cited in Buchholz and Rosenthal 2005, p. 137). These definitions combine input, process and outcomes components, suggesting that different stakeholders have diverse roles, motives and expectations, and that conflict between them is inevitable from time to time. They further imply that their relative influence or power varies, whether overall or in particular circumstances. As Reynolds et al. (2006, p. 288) explained, 'relative saliency can vary based upon the power, legitimacy and urgency of the stakeholders' claims'.

The 'relative saliency' view is central to considerations of effective stakeholder management, as it highlights the comparative importance of different stakeholder groups at different times, or with respect to diverse projects, and emphasises the need to dynamically balance their interests. This is particularly evident amongst the key stakeholders associated with graduate work-readiness challenges in Asia Pacific economies, which include national, provincial and local governments; a plethora of industry sectors and a blend of public and private organisations; multinational corporations, local large, medium and small organisations; secondary, vocational and higher education institutions; professional associations; graduates themselves and their families. Agle et al. (2008, p. 154) argued that there is a need for 'stakeholder-focused management that does no harm to (particular) interests while also benefiting a larger constituency', whilst Buchholz and Rosenthal (2005, p. 138) advised

> taking the interests and concerns of these various groups and individuals into account in arriving at decisions, so that they are all satisfied *at least to some extent, or at least that the most important stakeholders with regard to any given issue,* are satisfied (our italics).

Given the broad range of interested stakeholders associated with the work-readiness challenges, and their relative power and influence, effective and integrated stakeholder management is likely to be inherently problematic. However, as Buchholz and Rosenthal (2005) suggested, addressing the challenge is not only to 'serve and coordinate' stakeholder interests, but it also represents a 'moral obligation'.

Most authors would agree, however, that stakeholder management is complex, and usually requires situational leadership. Ideally, stakeholder management should aim to 'develop relationships, inspire their stakeholders, and create communities where everyone strives to give their best to deliver the value' (Freeman et al., 2008, p. 364). In fact, the concept of 'shared value' is a common theme in the literature, reflected in such hyperbolic expressions as 'a relationship of mutual enrichment, and nurturing rather than either domination and control or "external tolerance"' (Buchholz and Rosenthal 2005, p. 147). In reality, stakeholder management is more challenging, multi-faceted and problematic than such prescriptions would suggest, and involves the balancing of a myriad of diverse and sometimes conflicting vested interests. It can be argued that the foundations of effective stakeholder management lie in the strategic perspectives of stakeholder 'engagement', which may be adversely affected by factors such as a limited understanding of stakeholder expectations, a lack of reinforcement of 'shared' values and contested definitions of the 'public good'.

Strategies & stakeholder responsibilities in enhancing job applicant work-readiness

As discussed above, a range of stakeholders are responsible for the effective short- and longer-term management of the identified mismatches between potential employees' skills and capabilities and employers' dynamic requirements. National governments are responsible for the design, funding, regulation and evaluation of appropriate economic, social and human capital development strategies and policies; state or provincial governments are charged with their implementation; vocational and higher educational systems and their institutions are responsible for the effective design and evaluation of appropriate qualifications; industries and their associated organisations have imperatives to attract, retain and develop qualified and skilled employees; and prospective employees and their families have a key interest in facilitating the development of the necessary competencies and capabilities. As Connell and Burgess (2006) pointed out, there are only

> six possible sources of funding for skills acquisition – the family, individuals, the firm, the industry, the community and the state – (and) the allocation of funds toward skill development depends on the transferability, recognition, application and returns from time and money invested.
>
> (p. 498)

With respect to *governmental* imperatives, Bruni (2013) cited a joint statement from the 17th ASEAN Summit, held in Hanoi in 2010 – 'human resource development should be an integral part of a country's development strategy . . . HRD correlates with productivity and higher productivity leads to higher economic growth' (p. 9). She argued that such government human capital development strategies and associated policies should contain both short-term objectives – 'a correct response to the local labour demand in terms of skills' – and long-term goals – 'to endow the incoming generation with the knowledge and skills necessary to move the national production structure towards high quality products' (p. 46). A subsequent ILO report (2014) spelt out the key priorities of such government strategies, including employment creation, labour productivity, investments in school-training-work programs and wages growth and policies which support industry structural change and quality employment and improve workplace gender equality (p. 4).

Under this umbrella, government policies are required which encourage industry to improve its skill utilisation; disseminate information and advice which assist the matching of skills; formulate national skills assessments and qualifications frameworks; provide flexible recognition of prior learning (RPL) opportunities; and influence the demand for higher-level skills (OECD 2011, pp. 20–23). Remedial approaches such as improving skills measurement techniques; addressing unsatisfactory quality indicators in secondary, vocational and higher education systems; establishing multiple pathways for skills development; developing specialised approaches to youth skills acquisition; and dealing with labour market constraints to skill-matching, are also recommended (OECD 2011, pp. 30–34). In the United States, some states (for example, Columbia, Florida, New Jersey, New York and Rhode Island) have instituted dual accreditation systems for higher education graduates which constitute national work-readiness 'credentials', including both formal educational qualifications *and* testaments to graduates' generic capabilities such as punctuality, openness to supervision, decision-making, teamwork, conflict-resolution and negotiation, and responsibility for self-learning (Eisner 2010, p. 40). The latter capabilities are assessed by specific ancillary tests.

The Malaysia Education Blueprint 2013–2025 launched in September 2012, and the Australian Industry and Skills Committee (AISC) established in 2015, are good examples of the development of coherent and comprehensive governmental policy frameworks, consistent with developing employable graduates and enhancing their skills. Similarly, the Taiwanese Ministry of Labour (MOL) has been subsidising training programs in areas such as agricultural technology, business management and fashion design. The scheme requires participating institutions to bring in professionals from various industries to act as classroom mentors, and for instructors in each training program to select at least fifteen students to complete internships at companies or organisations in related fields. During 2015, 254 such programs at 80 facilities were subsidised by the MOL through this training initiative (Chung 2016). Despite such successful outcomes, however, much more will need to be done in all Asia Pacific countries and by all key stakeholders in order to effectively address the serious current and future graduate work-readiness challenges.

Education systems, at all levels, also need to be more aware of and responsive to industry labour demands; to consequently establish closer and more collaborative ongoing institutional linkages; to adapt to the dynamism of local, regional and global labour markets; and consequently, to provide education and training programs which better reflect new social, economic and technological contexts. Several observers have discussed the applications of these imperatives for vocational and higher education in particular. These include, but are not restricted to, curricula which is more balanced between theory and praxis, financial incentives to encourage and support institutional links between educational and industrial institutions, greater research on graduate destinations, enhancing skills training for innovation and strengthening the nexus between certificate-diploma-degree programs (Galagan 2010, p. 46; ILO 2014; OECD 2011). More specifically, some authors have proposed that course content will need to be revised, that new programs and pedagogies should be implemented and in particular, that there might be greater opportunities for applied work experience within existing technical and professional courses (Galagan 2010; ILO 2013, 2014; Mason et al. 2006; OECD 2015 – 'structured work experience has clear positive effects on the ability of graduates, firstly to find employment within six months of graduation, and secondly to secure employment in graduate-level jobs' (Bruni 2013, p. 24). An interesting example of how higher education institutions might approach the work-readiness challenge is provided by the National University of Malaysia (NUM). Selamat et al. (2013) explained how the NUM has developed a strategic plan to 'equip and train students with the soft skills and personality development' demanded by modern businesses (p. 22). It applies the concept of the 'learning contract' to equip students with work-ready skills, using a combination of student support, 'embedded' programs and 'campus life' experiences to achieve this goal.

With respect to *employers*, who 'tend to provide short-term remedial skill development rather than long-term development' (OECD 2011, p. 27), future imperatives might include such new initiatives as closer liaison with government education departments, secondary and vocational/higher education institutions with respect to curriculum design and the use of new pedagogical technologies; structured work experience programs, including WIL and RPL; course-funding opportunities, ongoing graduate development schemes and enhanced on-the-job and (paid) off-the-job training systems, including 'corporate university' structures where feasible. As the OECD (2011) report argued, there are significant benefits for employers who are prepared to invest in human capital development initiatives such as innovative funding strategies for firm-based training, and/or to provide greater incentives for their employees to undertake external training on their own initiative. In the case of *private training providers*, it is suggested that they might set up school-work transition programs, work to improve the input quality of school-based vocational training and participate in the development of revised skill competence and quality frameworks (ILO 2014).

As discussed earlier in relation to stakeholder theory, integrated management policies and strategies to counter these challenges necessarily involve considerable negotiation between all stakeholders, including the graduates themselves and their parents, together with long-, medium-, and shorter-term labour market planning.

Conclusion

This paper has reviewed much of the relevant scholarly, professional, government, industry and media literature on the nature, causes and effects of the reported mismatches between applicant skills and employer requirements globally and in particular in the Asia Pacific region. It highlights the challenges faced (primarily) by the key stakeholders – namely, governments, industry and educational institutions; and some of the possible ways in which they might practically address them to increase national productivity and competitiveness, improve industry effectiveness and profitability, revise vocational and higher education systems to enhance the work-readiness or employability of potential applicants and finally to provide more attractive and satisfying jobs and workplaces for present and future employees within the Asia Pacific region.

References

ABS. 2014, *Average weekly earnings, Australia*, Cat.6302.0, Australian Bureau of Statistics.

ACNielsen Research Services. 2000. *Employer satisfaction with graduate skills*. Research report by Evaluations and Investigations Program, Higher Education Division. Canberra, ACT: Department of Education, Training and Youth Affairs.

Agle, B. R., Donaldson, T., Freeman, R. E., Jensen, M. C., Mitchell, R. K. and Wood, D. J. 2008, 'Dialogue: Toward superior stakeholder theory', *Business Ethics Quarterly*, Vol. 18, no. 2, pp. 153–190.

AIM Network. 2015, *Graduate unemployment at a 20 year high*. Available at: http://theaimn.com/graduate-unemployment-at-a-20-year-high/.

Andrews, J. and Higson, H. 2008, 'Graduate employability: "soft skill" versus "hard" business knowledge: A European study', *Higher Education in Europe*, Vol. 33, no. 4, pp. 413.

AQF. 2015, *Australian qualifications framework*, Canberra: AQF.

Aspire. 2014, *Applied study in polytechnics and its review (ASPIRE)*. Report August 2014.

Boon, R. 2014, 'Graduate employment: Degrees of relevance', *The Strait Times*, October 23, 2014, 6:05 AM SGT.

Brown, P., Lauder, H. and Ashton, D. 2011, *The global action: The broken promises of education, jobs and incomes*, Oxford: Oxford University Press.

Bruni, M. 2013, *Labor market and demographic scenarios for ASEAN countries (2010–2035): Education, skill development, manpower needs, migration flows and economic growth*, DEMB Working Paper Series, No. 6, University of Modena.

Buchholz, R. A. and Rosenthal, S. B. 2005, 'Toward a contemporary contextual framework for stakeholder theory', *Journal of Business Ethics*, Vol. 58, pp. 137–148.

Burgess, J. and Connell, J. 2013, 'Asia and the Pacific region: Change and workforce adjustments post-GFC', *Asia Pacific Business Review*, Vol. 19, no. 2, pp. 162–170.

Caballero, C.L., Walker, A. and Fuller-Tyszkiewicz, M., 2011. The work readiness scale (WRS): developing a measure to assess work readiness in college graduates. Journal of teaching and learning for graduate employability, Vol. 2, no. 2, pp.41–54.

Casner-Lotto, J., Barrington, L. and Wright, M. 2006, *Are they really ready to work? Employers' perspectives on the basic knowledge and applied skills of new entrants to the 21st century U.S. workforce* (Research Report BED-06-Workforce). Washington, DC. The Conference Board, Inc., the Partnership for 21st Century Skills, Corporate Voices for Working Families, and the Society for Human Resource Management.

CBS. 2014, *Development of manufacturing industries in Nepal: Current state and future challenges*, Kathmandu: Central Bureau of Statistics [CBS].

Chatterjee, S. R., Nankervis, A. and Connell, J. 2014, 'Framing the emerging talent crisis in India and China: A human capital perspective', *South Asian Journal of HRM*, Vol. 1, no. 1, pp. 25–43.

Chung, O. 2016, 'The skills to succeed', Taiwan Today, January 1, 2016.

City & Guilds Centre for Skills Development (CSD) (2010), "Employability skills", available at: www.skillsdevelopment.org

Cheong, K. C., Hill, C., Fernandez-Chung, R. and Leong, Y. C. 2015, 'Employing the 'unemployable': Employer perceptions of Malaysian graduates', *Studies in Higher Education*, Vol. 41, no. 12, pp. 1–18.

Chew, C. S. 2013, 'Helping unemployed graduates in Malaysia', *New Straits Times*, March 14, 2013.

Chien, C. K. C., Lin, L. C. and Chen, C. F. 2013, 'The main features and the key challenges of the education system in Taiwan', *Higher Education Studies*, Vol. 3, no. 6, pp. 1.

Chung, O. 2016, 'The skills to succeed', *Taiwan Today*, January 1, 2016.

CIA. 2015, *World factbook*, Washington, DC: CIA.

Connell, J. and Burgess, J. 2006, 'The influence of precarious employment on career development: The current situation in Australia', *Education and Training*, Vol. 48, no. 7, pp. 493–507.

Cox, A. 2013, 'Human resource management in Vietnam', in Varma, A. and Budhwar, P. (eds.) *Managing human resources in Asia-Pacific*, 2nd edition, London and New York, NY, Routledge, chapter 9.

CRISIL. 2010, *Skilling India: The billion people challenge*, CRISIL Centre for Economic Research. Available at: www.crisil.com/pdf/corporate/skilling-india_nov10.pdf.

DCR Trendline, 2015. Indonesia's Slowing Economy and Workforce Challenges – Jun 01, 2015.

di Gropello, E. and Kruse, P. 2011, *Skills for the labour market in Indonesia: Trends in demand, gaps and supply*, Washington, DC, World Bank.

Dobbs, R., Madgavkar, A., Barton, D., Labaye, E., Manyika, J., Roxburgh, C., Lund, S. and Madhav, S. 2012, *The world of work: Jobs, pay, and skills for 3.5 billion people*, The McKinsey Global Institute. file:///C:/Users/ros.cameron/Downloads/MGI%20Global_labor_Full_Report_June_2012.pdf

The Economist. 2014, *High university enrolment, low graduate employment: Analysing the paradox in Afghanistan, Bangladesh, India, Nepal, Pakistan and Sri Lanka*, Economist Intelligence Unit report. Available at: www.britishcouncil.in/sites/default/files/british_council_report_2014_jan.pdf.

Eisner, S. 2010, 'Grave new world? Workplace skills for today's college graduates', *American Journal of Business Education*, Vol. 3, no. 9, pp. 22.

EIU. 2012, *Skilled labour shortfalls in Indonesia, the Philippines, Thailand and Vietnam: A custom research report*, A custom report for the British Council. Economist Intelligence Unit, London.

Ferry, T. 2015, *From studies to work and residence*, April 16, 2015, Taiwan Business Topics. Available at: http://topics.amcham.com.tw/2015/04/from-studies-to-work-and-residence/.

Fong, L.L., Sidhu, G.K. and Fook, C.Y., 2014. 'Exploring 21st century skills among postgraduates in Malaysia'. *Procedia-Social and Behavioral Sciences*, Vol. 123, pp.130–138.

Fontaine, C., Haarman, A. and Schmid, S. 2006, *The stakeholder theory*. Available at: www.edalys.fr/document/Stakeholders%20theory.pdf.

Freeman, R. E., Wicks, A. C. and Parmar, B. 2008, 'Stakeholder theory and "The corporate objective" revisited', *Organization Science*, Vol. 15, no. 3, pp. 364–369.

Galagan, P. 2010, 'Bridging the skills gap: New factors compound the growing skills shortage', *Training and Development*, February, ASTD. https://www.td.org/Publications/Magazines/TD/TD-Archive/2010/02/Bridging-the-Skills-Gap-New-Factors-Compound-the-Growing-Skills-Shortage

GCA. 2014, *GradStats: Employment and salary outcomes of recent higher education graduates*. Available at: www.graduatecareers.com.au/wp-content/uploads/2014/12/GCA_GradStats_2014.pdf.

General Statistics Office of Vietnam. 2012, *Higher education statistics*. June 4, 2016 Available at: www.gso.gov.vn/default.aspx?tabid=395&idmid=3&ItemID=11406.

Goldin, N. 2015, *Key Considerations in youth workforce development: A report of the CSIS project on prosperity and development*, Washington, DC: Center for Strategic and International Studies.

Grant Thornton. 2013, *62% Malaysian businesses find hard to hire skilled workers, highest in ASEAN*. Grant Thorton International Ltd, London.

Hariati, A. and Lee, Y. M. 2011, 'Top jobs only for those who know the language well', *The Star Online*, April 10.

Hays. 2015, *Asia at a crossroads can talent supply meet increasing demand? The 2016 Hays Asia Salary Guide*. Available at: www.hays.com.my/cs/groups/hays_com mon/@sg/@content/documents/digitalasset/hays_314680.pdf.

Heckman, J. J and Kautz, T. 2012, *Hard evidence on soft skills*, IZA Discussion Paper No. 6580, Berlin: IZA.

Ho, H. F. 2015, 'Matching university graduates' competences with employers' needs in Taiwan', *International Education Studies*, Vol. 8, no. 4, p. 122.

ILO. 2013, *Global employment trends: Recovering from a second jobs dip*, Geneva: ILO.

ILO. 2014, *Indonesia: Labour and social trends update*, Geneva: ILO.

ILO. 2015, *World employment and social outlook 2015: The changing nature of jobs*. International Labour Office, Geneva: International Labor Organisation [ILO].

ILO. 2016, *Skills and employability in Indonesia and Timor-Leste*, Geneva, International Labour Organisation [ILO].

India Skills Report. 2014, *Wheebox in association with Confederation of Indian Industry (CII) and people strong*. Available at: https://wheebox.com/wheebox/resources/IndiaSkillsReport.pdf.

India Skills Report. 2015, *Wheebox in association with Peoplestrong: Confederation of Indian Industry(CII) and LinkedIn*. Available at: https://wheebox.com/logo/India%20Skills%20Report2015.pdf.

Impetus-Private Equity Foundation (Organisation), 2014. Ready for work: the capabilities young people need to find and keep work-and the programmes proven to help develop these. http://www.impetus-pef.org.uk/wp-content/uploads/2014/09/2014_09-Ready-for-Work.pdf

Indonesia Skills Report. 2010, *Trends in skills demand, gaps, and supply in Indonesia*, Document of the World Bank, Washington, DC.

Institute of International Education (IIE). 2004, *Higher education In Vietnam update – May 2004.* Available at: http://home.vef.gov/download/Higher-Education-in-Vietnam.pdf.

Jackson, D. and Chapman, E. 2012, 'Non-technical competencies in undergraduate business degree programs: Australian and UK perspectives', *Studies in Higher Education*, Vol. 37, no. 5, pp. 541–567.

Khare, M. 2014, 'Employment, employability and higher education in India: The missing links', *Higher Education for the Future*, Vol. 1, no. 1, pp. 39–62.

Lee, P. 2015, 'University degrees: Mindset shift needed', *The Straits Times*. Monday, April 13, 2015.

Lin, E. 2015, 'Unemployment rate improves to 15-year low in June: DGBAS', *The China Post*, August 25, 2015, 12:00am, TWN.

Manpower Group. 2015, *2015 Talent shortage survey*, Milwaukee, Wisconsin: Manpower.

Mason, G., Williams, G. and Cranmer, S. 2006, *Employability skills initiatives in higher education: What effects do they have on graduate labour market outcomes?* London: NIESR, University of London.

Ministry of Manpower (MOM). 2014, *Labour force in Singapore*. Ministry of Manpower, Singapore.

Mitchell, G. W., Skinner, L. B. and White, B. J. 2010, 'Essential soft skills for success in the twenty first century workforce as perceived by business educators', *The Delta Pi Epsilon Journal*, Vol. LII, no. 1, pp. 48–49.

MoHE. 2012, *Higher education statistics*. Tracer study, Kuala Lumpur, Ministry of Higher Education.

Montague, A. 2013, 'Vietnam and skill shortages in Vietnamese manufacturing and service sectors, and some plausible solutions', *Asia Pacific Journal of Human Resources*, Vol. 51, pp. 208–227.

Mourshed, M., Farrell, D. and Barton, D. 2012, Education to Employment: Designing a system that works, McKinsey Centre for Government, National partnership for educational Access Research Brief, December 2012, NPEA, Boston, MA, USA. https://npeac.memberclicks.net/assets/education%20to%20employment_final.pdf

Nankervis, A., Cooke, F. and Chatterjee, S. 2012, *New models of HRM in China and India*, London and New York: Routledge.

Nguyen, T. I. H. 2013, *Labour market trends and vocational strategy*, Conference "Meeting Today's and Tomorrow's Skills Needs" Conference, Vietnam Chamber of Commerce and Industry (VCCI), Ministry of Labour, Invalids and Social Affairs (MOLISA) and International Labor Organisation (ILO), Ho Chi Minh City, 25 April.

Nilsson, S. 2010, 'Enhancing employability: The perspectives of engineering graduates', *Education + Training*, Vol. 52, no. 6/7, pp. 540–551.

Norton, A. 2014, *Mapping Australian higher education 2014–15*, October, 2014, Grattan Institute, Melbourne.

OECD/ADB. 2015, *Reviews of national policies for education in Indonesia: Rising to the challenge*. Paris, OECD.

OECD. 2011, *Towards an OECD skills strategy*, Paris: OECD.

Oliver, D. 2002, *The US community college model and Vietnam's higher education system*. In Texas Tech University Vietnam Center's 4th triennial symposium, Lubbock, TX, April 11–13.

O'Neil, H. F. 2014, *Workforce readiness: Competencies and assessment*, New York: Psychology Press and Taylor & Frances.

Pham, H. and Tran, T. 2013, 'Developing graduate knowledge and skills for the world of work: The case of the translation curriculum in Vietnam', *Language, Society and Culture*, Vol. 36, pp. 7–17.

Pham, T. N. 2010, 'The higher education agenda: A vision for 2020', in Harman, G., Hayden, M. and Thanh Nghi, P. (eds.) *Reforming higher education in Vietnam: Challenges and priorities*. London: Springer, pp. 51–64.

Reynolds, S. J., Schultz, F. C. and Helman, D. R. 2006, 'Stakeholder theory and management decision-making: Constraints and implications of balancing stakeholder interests', *Journal of Business Ethics*, Vol. 64, pp. 285–301.

Rosenberg, S., Heimler, R. and Morote, E.S., 2012. 'Basic employability skills: a triangular design approach'. *Education+Training*, Vol. 54, no. 1, pp.7–20.

Sanghi, S., Subbiah, M., Reddy, R., Ganguly, S., Gupta, G., Unni, J., Sarkar, S., Sarin, S., Chand, V. and Vasavada, M. 2012, *Preparing a globally competitive skilled workforce for Indian economy: Emerging trends and challenges*, Vikalpa. Available at: www.vikalpa.com/pdf/articles/2012/Vikalpa373-87-128.pdf.

Selamat, J.-H., Ismail, K.-H., Ahmad, A., Hussin, M.-H. and Seliman, S. 2013, 'Framework of soft skills infusion based on learning contract concept in Malaysian higher education', *Asian Social Science*, Vol. 9, no. 7, pp. 22–23.

Serrière, N. and Centre for Economic Development and Administration [CEDA] 2014, *Labour market transitions of young women and men in Nepal. Work4Youth Publication Series No. 12*, Geneva: International Labour Office.

Srivastava, A. and Khare, M. 2012, *Skills for employability: South Asia*, Innovative Secondary Education for Skills Enhancement (ISESE), Results for Development Institute. Available at: www.changemakers.com/sites/default/files/south_asia_skills_for_employability_21aug.pdf.

Srivastava, D. and Chatterjee, S. 2014, 'India's readiness on innovation and economic growth: A strategic analysis', *Global Journal of Human-Social Science Research*, Vol. 14, no. 3. pp.47–57.

Tran, T. T. 2010b, *Enhancing graduate employability: Challenges facing higher education in Vietnam*. Paper presented at the 14th UNESCO-APEID International Conference: Education for Human Resource Development, Bangkok, Thailand.

Truong, Q. 2013, *Vietnam: An emerging economy at a crossroads*, Working Paper No. 2013/09, Maastricht School of Management.

UNESCO. 2012, *Graduate employability in Asia*, Bangkok: UNESCO.

UNESCO. 2012, *Graduate employability in Asia*, UNESCO Bangkok Asia and Pacific Regional Bureau for Education.

Vanderklippe, N. 2016, 'Taiwan's economic woes top of mind for unemployed grads before election. AIPEI', – *The Globe and Mail*, Published Thursday, January 14, 2016 4:31PM EST.

Victorian Department of Education. 2006, *Employability skills framework*, Melbourne: VDE.

Wickramasinghe, V. and Perera, L. 2010, 'Graduates', university lecturers', and employers' perceptions towards employability skills', *Education + Training*, Vol. 52, no. 3, pp. 226–244.

World Bank. 2014, *Vietnam overview*, Washington, DC: World Bank, viewed June 4, 2016. Available at: www-wds.worldbank.org/external/default/WDSContent-Server/WDSP/IB/2013/11/26/000461832_20131126115640/Rendered/PDF/829400AR0P13040Box0379879B00PUBLIC0.pdf.

Zachau, U. and Shetty, S. 2014, *Malaysia Economic Monitor Report June2014, Boosting trade competitiveness*, World Bank, Bangkok.

Part II
Country studies

3 Labour market and work-readiness challenges

The case of Taiwan

Min-Wen Sophie Chang and Julia Connell

Introduction

Taiwan is a small island located in the heart of East Asia. It has been serially colonised by the Dutch, Portuguese, Japanese and mainland China. In the past few decades, the industrial revolution and technology advances have brought modernisation, wealth and subsequent democracy to Taiwan. In 2015, Taiwan's population was 23.5 million, while the GDP per capita was around 22,294 USD, a considerable leap from 154 USD in the 1940s, the post-colonial era (DGBAS 2016a; Ministry of Interior). In recent years, Taiwan has been going through a transition from a manufacturing to a service-driven economy after many manufacturers relocated to China. Since the late 1970s, China's relatively abundant labour and land, lower operational costs and vast domestic market have attracted many Taiwanese to relocate or run businesses there. A former Labour Minister estimated that more than 850,000 Taiwanese work or live in mainland China (Lin 2014a). That amounts to approximately 3.7 percent of the population and more than 7 percent of the workforce. Moreover, the number of people leaving Taiwan to relocate or seek jobs and business opportunities abroad is set to rise as the country is currently going through a difficult economic period. Dissatisfied with economic slowdown, low wages, corruption scandals and many other socio-political problems under the reign of the Chinese Nationalist Party (the KMT government), led the Taiwanese people to elect their first female president, Tsai Ing-wen, and her Democratic Progressive Party (DPP) in January 2016. As the celebrations following her victory wore off, it has become evident that the new government faces some tough challenges to turn the sluggish economy and deteriorating labour market around.

A key challenge is the disparity between labour demand and supply in Taiwan which has led to many problems. For employers these translate to talent deficits, labour shortages and a widening gap between the expectations of industry and education sectors – common obstacles for corporate growth and sustainability. For private sector workers, challenges relate to long work hours, low wages, and lower pensions compared to public servants, discrimination and workplace exploitation. Moreover, some of these challenges may well be some of the key contributors to early retirement and low labour participation rates.

To date, little has been published concerning the problematic state of Taiwan's labour market and the resultant challenges. This chapter attempts to bridge some of those gaps by providing a brief overview of Taiwan's labour market, followed by an analysis of the graduate work-readiness issues faced by key stakeholders and some recommendations concerning how they may be addressed.

Labour market in Taiwan: late entry and early exit become the new normal

For many years, Taiwan's labour market has been plagued by talent shortages. The overall participation rate has been rising steadily over the years to stand at 58.54 percent in 2014, but was still below the world average of 63.5 percent (DGBAS 2016b; The World Bank 2016). As can be seen in Figure 3.1, Taiwan's overall and male labour participation rates lag far behind the world average; while the female labour participation rate has outpaced the world average but is still relatively low compared to men and the average ratio.

The relatively low labour participation rates could be attributed to several key factors: (1) early retirement, (2) discrimination against female workers, (3) long working hours and low salaries and (4) young people delaying entering the workplace in order to seek further education. Each of these factors is next discussed in turn.

Early retirement

First, as shown in Figure 3.2, the labour participation rate in Taiwan is the highest among the 25- to 29-year age group. Most workers remain in work until they are 54 years old. Once they reach 55 years of age, the labour participation rate drops dramatically to 55 percent, 27 percent less than that of 25- to 29-year-olds. According to these figures, by the age of 60 to 64, only one-third of the workforce

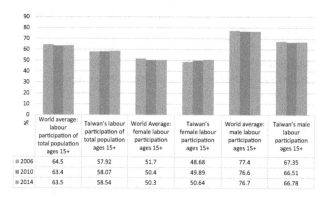

Figure 3.1 Taiwan's labour participation rate compared to world average rates

Source: DGBAS 2016b, 2014; The World Bank 2016

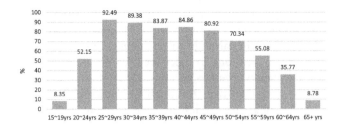

Figure 3.2 Taiwan's labour participation rate by age (2015)

Source: Ministry of labour (2016a), data bank on labour-related statistics.

remains working. In other words, the majority of workers retire after reaching 60 years of age, and this factor is likely to cause ongoing problems due to the low birth rate and ageing population in Taiwan, as discussed later in this chapter.

Even though the legal retirement age is set at 65 years, the Ministry of Labour's (2015) statistics show that the average retirement age in Taiwan is in fact 60 years of age. That said, a recent survey by Global Views Monthly 2015 (Gao 2015) found that the average retirement age is in fact even younger at 57.5 years of age. This is compared with other OECD countries where the average retirement age is 64 years (OECD 2015), and Taiwanese workers in general exit early from the workplace. One of the key contributors to the early retirement age is likely to be "the public servants' 75 system (75制) policy" (Lee 2014). According to this policy, public servants can retire with a full state pension when they reach 50 years if they have served the country for more than 25 years (50+25=75). They can then enjoy retirement with a full state pension, which can sometimes be higher than their earnings before retirement. However, this generous pension scheme is funded at great expense to the Taiwanese people. For the country as a whole, public servants' pensions constituted 7.13 percent of the government's total budget in 2012; whereas for local government, public servants' salary and pension costs represented up to 47.8 percent of their 2013 annual budget (DGBAS 2012; Zhang 2015). In an attempt to curb public-servants' early retirement, and the subsequent public finance problems, in 2010 the then ruling KMT government revised the "75 system" to the "85 system" (85制). This system allows public servants to retire at 55 if they have served the country for more than 30 years (55+30=85). Specifically, the new "85 system" makes public-servants work at least 5 more years when compared to the old "75 system". Yet, in comparison with private sector workers who can only apply for a full state pension at the age of 60, public servants still retire earlier by at least 5 years.

Public servants' generous pensions and early retirement schemes have become an increasing burden for the country as some public pension funds are already in deficit. The *Liberty Times* (Huang 2015a) reported that by 2020, pension funds for military personnel will become bankrupt, followed by bankruptcy of the teachers' pension fund in 2030 and the public servants' pension fund in 2031.

On the other side of the spectrum, most private sector workers do not have the luxury of a carefree retirement, as if they retire early their pension fund will be cut. Unlike public servants, private sector workers are fortunate to receive half of their pre-retirement earnings on retirement. This is due to caps on how private sector workers' pensions are calculated. High earners lose out the most, as the pension calculation ceiling is currently set at 45,800 NTD per month, so they will not get more than that. Although this situation is grossly unfair, the Taiwanese government argues that it helps to redistribute wealth amongst private sector retirees.

Moreover, even though private sector workers tend to work longer than public sector workers before retirement, some may be forced to leave earlier due to redundancy, ill health or work/life balance issues. Lee (2016a) suggests that older workers are at higher risk of being made redundant as they may not possess the current skills and knowledge required for their jobs. Older workers may also face difficulties in re-entering the workplace if they take a career break or retire early. Based on a recent survey by one of the major recruitment agencies in Taiwan, 70 percent of workers aged more than 45 years feel that employers are reluctant to employ them due to their age (Huang 2015a). More than 57 percent of these mature workers reported encountering age discrimination at work, while more than 80 percent of mature age workers experienced high levels of employment anxiety. On the other hand, 57.1 percent of employers reportedly hired less experienced workers to replace more experienced older workers (Huang 2015a), suggesting evidence of discriminatory practices.

Discrimination against female workers

Taiwan belongs to a group of nations – along with China, Japan, Vietnam, South Korea and Singapore – known as the Confucian Core, where Confucian-inspired beliefs are taught and practised in everyday life (Siegel et al. 2014). Li (2000) maintains that Confucianism did not invent gender bias in East Asia. However, Tatli et al. (2016) argue that the current work context in China displays entrenched gender inequalities as women's positions are subordinate to those of men in a range of life aspects within Chinese society, which has a culturally masculine orientation (p. 3). Li (2000) attributes this to the long-standing Confucian system of values and beliefs that implicitly informs interactions between men and women.

Consequently, Confucianism has resulted in restricted female roles that have been reinforced by male elites (Hall and Ames 2000). Lu (2014) suggests that, under the influence of Confucianism cultural values, it is common for Taiwanese women to encounter five types of workplace discrimination: (1) superiors disallow menstrual leave, (2) male chauvinism, (3) workplace sexual harassment, (4) employment discrimination against married or pregnant women and (5) glass ceilings. The *Epoch Times* (2014) also reported that discrimination in relation to pregnancy and sexual harassment were the most common types of gender discrimination in the workplace. For example, a total of 65 gender discrimination complaints were filed in Taipei in 2014. Of these cases 32 were pregnancy discrimination complaints and 22 cases were sexual harassment complaints.

Government statistics also reiterate these difficulties. In terms of pay, women earn 14.5 percent less compared to men and have to work 54 more days to receive the same annual pay (Ministry of Labour 2016b). Another recent government report (DGBAS 2016d) pointed out that, in 2015, 20.8 percent of employers refused to provide paternity leave, while 25.3 percent disallowed employees from taking time off for family duties. It appears that supporting work-and-family life balance may not be considered in some employers' best interests. This may also be the reason why only 31.97 percent of female workers continue working after they get married (DGBAS 2016d; Ministry of Labour 2015).

As childcare costs are high and flexible work hours are virtually non-existent in Taiwan's workplaces, new mothers are often forced to wait until their children are old enough to attend school before they re-enter the workforce. Employers can also be reluctant to hire pregnant women and new mothers for fear of the costs associated with maternity leave, maternity compensation and the costs of replacement staff as required by the labour laws.

The challenges of these unfriendly working conditions, particularly for women, can have spill-over effects on society as a whole. For example, the ratio of unmarried women rose to 32.6 percent in 2013 from 31.2 percent in 2009 (DGBAS 2015). This trend towards "staying single" means that the numbers of old people who live alone without a spouse or any children to look after them will also rise, inevitably putting more strain on the state welfare system over time. Moreover, in addition to falling marriage ratios, Taiwan also has the lowest birth rate of 1.17 when compared to most countries – thus the population is set to shrink by 2020 (DGBAS 2015), resulting in labour shortages that will inevitably worsen.

Long working hours and low salaries

Taiwanese workers have amongst some of the longest working hours in the world and the shortest paid annual leave when compared to most OECD countries (Huang 2016a). Even though Taiwan has been categorised as a newly developed economy for some time, Taiwanese workers still clocked up 2,103 to 2,134 annual work hours in 2015. This is only slightly better than Mexico's 2,246 hours, but far behind Australia's 1,665 hours. The actual working hours are probably even longer than the official figures, given that it is common for employers to exploit workers by not paying overtime or by asking them to bring work home. Frequently they then fail to record overtime on the attendance records to avoid negative labour inspections. Yet, Taiwan's labour law is skewed towards employers, where they receive only a small fine or written warning for violating labour law – practices that are highly unlikely to deter them from committing worker exploitation practises.

Moreover, in terms of paid leave/time off given to workers, Taiwanese workers are only entitled to seven days annual leave, plus twelve national days following the Ministry of Labour's plans to cut seven national holidays (Huang 2016a).

This is much less than most developed countries. For example, Australian workers are entitled to twenty days of annual leave and eight public holidays. According to the latest statistics (DGBAS 2016a), despite the long work hours and little time off, the Taiwanese workers, on average, earned 49,540 NTD per month in 2015, equivalent to approximately 1,628 USD. As living costs, inflation and house prices continue to outpace wage growth, real-wage growth has been negative for decades, leading to what has been referred to as "shrinkflation." This mixture of long work hours doesn't pay off and workplace exploitation can be frustrating and demoralising for workers, who may decide to leave the workplace for good once they feel they cannot cope with such conditions any longer.

Late entry to the labour market

It is common for young people to delay their entry to the workplace in favour of further education. Under Taiwan's 12-year compulsory educational system, children are obliged to attend state-funded education from 7 to 18 years old. The Social Services and the Household Registration Office tracks every child's compulsory education attendance to safeguard children's welfare and rights, and parents may be penalised or investigated for failing to send their children to school.

As shown in Figure 3.3, formal schooling is heavily subsidised by the state to encourage learning and lighten parents' financial burdens. Given that 12 years of compulsory education is fully funded by the state, students only pay for lunch and textbooks at heavily discounted rates. The 12 years of compulsory education is the main reason why the labour participation rate among 15- to 19-year-olds stands at 8.35 percent as most children are obliged to remain in school until the age of 18 years (Ministry of Labour 2016a). After compulsory education, teenagers can choose either to go to work or to pursue higher education. According to the latest labour statistics, approximately half of all students choose to continue higher or further education as the labour participation rate among 20- to 24-year-olds is only 52.15 percent (Ministry of labour 2016a).

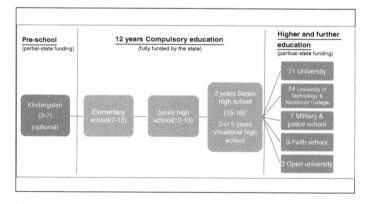

Figure 3.3 Taiwan's education system at a glance

Source: Ministry of Education (2015).

Taiwan's education system at a glance

Taiwan's education system can be largely divided into three parts: pre-school, 12 years of compulsory education, followed by higher and further education. As shown in Figure 3.3 currently there are 157 higher and further education institutes, which can be divided into 5 categories: (1) 71 universities; (2) 74 universities of technology and vocational colleges; (3) 7 military or police universities; (4) 3 faith-based schools (Christian or Taoism colleges) and (5) 2 open universities (offering a combination of classroom and distance learning). The diminishing differences between vocational and academic training, combined with problems associated with the oversupply of education providers, can have profound effects on the graduate work-readiness issues in Taiwan as explained in the following section.

Vocational training becoming more academic

After 3 years of general high schooling, students can choose to take on 4 years of vocational training (四技) to obtain a bachelor degree. Alternatively, they can undertake two years of a vocational diploma programme. For students who have graduated from 5 years of vocational senior high school, they can take either two or four years of vocational training programme to obtain a bachelor degree or a bachelor diploma. Currently, 148 schools out of Taiwan's 157 higher and further education institutes now offer vocational courses of 2 to 4 years in duration, whereas 67 schools offer 4-year vocational bachelor courses. However, vocational courses have gradually become theoretically driven and lack practical/vocational value, a result of the government's failed education reforms, unfair assessment systems and ranking methods (Lin and Ho 2015; Chang 2011).

During the government higher education system reforms between 1996 and 2014, most vocational colleges were upgraded into "universities of technologies." Chang (2011) pointed out that these education system reforms and upgrades have led to "vocational schools become universitised while university has become vocationalised". Nowadays even research-oriented top universities are offering 2- to 4-year vocational bachelor courses in attempts to recruit more students to secure survival and funding. Given that most universities and colleges are offering vocational courses, while adding vocational training elements to their academic courses, in attempts to boost ranking and government assessment credit, the distinction between vocational training and general schooling has been diminishing over the past decade.

Huang (2015c) points out that, as vocational training has become more "academicised," it has failed to equip students with the necessary vocational skills and knowledge. Although for years industry and society as whole have expressed concern over the state of vocational training in Taiwan, no drastic action has been taken by the government. As a result, a fundamental overhaul of the vocational education system is needed to eliminate underperforming schools and unsuitable teachers and to redesign curricula based on workplace requirements. That said, these measures maybe too politically sensitive and complicated to be addressed.

Oversupply of higher education institutes

Under the government's "multiple entrance program policy," there are now many entry paths to universities, such as special auditions, referrals, entry exams, transfer exams and more. For most senior high school graduates or adults who wish to take on university courses, an entry exam is probably the most common entry path. Students who sit for university entry exams are spoiled for choice as currently there are 157 higher and further education institutes which offer 4- to 6-year bachelor courses (Taiwan Ministry of Education 2015). Most university degrees take 4 years to complete, while the medicine, law and architecture disciplines often require 5 to 6 years of study.

As Mok et al. (2013, p. 264) point out, the Taiwanese people have begun to question both the quality and the 'over supply' of graduates entering the labour market. Over the years the numbers of universities and colleges continues to rise while student numbers dwindle rapidly. The oversupply of university places led to a 97.11 percent enrolment rate in 2016 (Taiwan People News 2016). This means that virtually all students sitting for university entry exams will gain a place, regardless of their grades, because there are more university places than there are students.

Consequently, Taiwan's university entry exam has lost its selective function, since many of those who are not properly qualified can now attend university. As a consequence of the oversupply of universities, even top universities are in desperate need of students and are also reluctant to expel underperforming students to avoid funding cuts or the central government's suspension orders to cease trading/operations if they fail to reach at least half of their admission targets. Overall, the lack of rigour with regard to entry selection, failure to keep up with teaching standards and reluctance to eliminate underperforming students can damage the quality of higher/further education, reputation and the perceived value of academic qualifications.

Work-readiness issues faced by Taiwanese graduates

As the distinction between vocational training and higher education has become more blurred after several failed education system reforms, Taiwan's higher and further education graduates face similar work-readiness issues: (1) a gap between education and employment, (2) inadequate career guidance and planning, and (3) struggles to enter and fit into the workplace.

Gap between education and employment

As mentioned earlier, currently there are 157 higher and further education institutes, including 147 universities, 7 military and police schools, 3 faith schools and 2 open universities. Among these institutes, military and police school graduates are probably the exception to the work-readiness problems commonly faced by Taiwanese graduates. This is because military and police schools as an extension of the military and police forces are important parts of the public sector. Their training largely focuses on the knowledge, skills, mentality, ethics and physics needed to become military and police personnel. Graduates from these schools usually have fewer problems fitting into the military or police force as they have will have undergone 4 years rigorous vocational-based training prior to graduation. As their training is mentally and physically demanding, most students are exempt from tuition fees and given a monthly bursary during their studies as a reward for staying with the military or police force. They are also given job opportunities depending on their grades and performance, which also affects their salary, their ranking and where they can work after graduation. Therefore, most students are motivated to prepare for their future jobs during their study. Work-oriented teaching, combined with guaranteed job opportunities and generous bursaries, seem to be the answer to their seamless connections between education and the workplace.

On the other hand, higher and further education graduates in general are not so fortunate to have jobs waiting for them on graduation or to receive generous bursaries while studying. As they are affected by the deteriorating quality of education and the widening gap between education and employment, young people and graduates commonly face difficulties finding work and fitting into the workplace. Although 74 vocational universities and 71 academic universities are diversifying their services in attempts to pass government assessment and enhance their ranking, teachers and school principals generally lack incentives to update their curriculum regularly to ensure that materials and methods result in graduate outcomes that match workplace demands (Ho 2013). Many higher education providers and teachers argue that universities are not vocational training institutes which produce students who are work ready prior to graduation (Lu 2009). They believe that the aim of higher education is to provide students with a general understanding of a specific discipline and independent thinking skills. However, Chang (2011) suggested that universities are also failing students in relation to developing their independent thinking and providing current discipline knowledge as the government's current education assessment and ranking systems fall short on teaching quality.

In contrast with education providers' standpoint, employers and industry have very different perceptions and expectations as to whether universities should teach workplace-related skills and knowledge. In general, industry bodies tend to believe that workplace skills and knowledge should be the backbone of higher and further education teaching contents as they help to make graduates work ready. Given Taiwan's higher education is in a state of oversupply, some universities, especially vocational universities of technology, are increasingly willing to cooperate with employers. This results in them adjusting curricula to bridge the gap between education and training and enhance the work-readiness of their students. There are also cases of universities developing customised courses commissioned by employers, in manufacturing, high tech and tourism industries. Employers are also often invited to play a role as a mentor and/or lecturer. With due diligence, such collaborative programmes can create a 'win-win' situation for all concerned. For universities, they can apply for funding from the government and earn extra credit for teaching assessment or ranking. For employers, they have access to prospective employees and ensure graduates are receiving relevant work-related information. For students, such interactions may lead to job opportunities and enhance their work-readiness after graduation as this type of programme helps them to accumulate workplace experience and subject know-how which is currently absent from most bachelor degree courses.

Inadequate career guidance and planning

Turning to career guidance, universities are also failing their students. Most schools have career advice units which students rarely use as they may not find them worthwhile, particularly as private recruitment agencies and the government's job centres can provide more up-to-date job vacancy information and more comprehensive job-seeking support (e.g., consultation, funding, free-courses, apprenticeship programs, etc.). Schools with more funding may outsource contractors to host job-fairs, but the job offers/interviews resulting from these fairs may not materialise into real jobs as they are sometimes organised for publicity or budget-consuming purposes.

Employability problems and high youth unemployment

As Taiwanese schools in general are failing to prepare students for the workplace, work-readiness problems can have a profound effect on young people's career prospects and earnings. As emphasised in a recent study by Chiu and Chuang (2016, p. 862), employability skills present consistent and significant benefits to increased earning levels. Specifically, the authors found that those people who had a comprehensive understanding of their jobs, including working environment and career plans, could earn about 5 percent more than those without. Work-readiness is, of course, related to the broader concept of employability. According to Harvey, Locke and Morey (2002), employability development has three focuses: the development of employability attributes, the acquisition of self-promotional and career-management skills, and a willingness to learn and reflect on learning. Thus, if these activities are not taking place, then work-readiness and graduate employability is not likely to be developed for much of the population.

As a result of inadequate career preparation and guidance at school, during the first few years after graduation, young people may struggle to decide what career suits them, be unable to find a job which they like, or be unsettled in the workplace. A recent study by the Ministry of Education's statistical bureau (2016b) indicates that, three years after graduation, only 79 percent of higher education graduates in Taiwan had a full-time job and steady income, while 9.6 percent had a part-time job and 11.4 percent were unaccounted for in terms of their employment status (for example, not in work, became a housewife). Of the 11.4 percent who were unaccounted for, 7.5 percent did not work at all and thus had generated no income since graduation. They may have relocated to other countries for good or become "unemployable" in the eyes of prospective employers without any work experience.

Another clear indication of Taiwanese young people's struggle with work-readiness challenges is the high youth unemployment rate. The youth unemployment rate has reached double digits since 2007 and remained stubbornly high for nearly a decade, with no signs of retreating, as shown in Figure 3.4.

Frequent/quick exits from the workplace – the flash generation

In addition to difficulties finding a job, another problem faced by young graduates is inability to fit in and settle down at work. A recent survey by one of the Taiwan's leading recruitment agencies suggested that 33.8 percent of graduates left their new jobs within a month of starting while 37.1 percent quit within 3 months (104 Manpower Agency 2015). This phenomenon of young people's frequent and quick exit from the workplace is often referred as "the flash generationz." Whereas "the strawberry generation" is another commonly used phrase to describe young people's inability to cope with pressure so they often quit after being told off or encountered unbearable pressure or frustration at work.

The underlying factors of this phenomenon are complicated. It can be a combination of failed education to prepare young people for the workplace, parents' protectionism, a mismatch between graduates' and employers' perception and expectation towards work, talent shortages, etc. For example, as talent shortages persists in Taiwan's labour market, graduates who frequently change jobs and quit within a short period of starting new career can easily find other jobs so that this would not deter them from next quick exit from the workplace. Moreover, as Taiwan's society as whole become more affluent and liberal, most parents generally don't interfere too much over their children' career choices but would provide supports when their children run into difficulties. Even though frequently changing jobs may dampen career prospects and threaten livelihood, this may not be a concern for many young people as they can always count on parents to provide shelter and a financial safety net during intervals of frequent job changes.

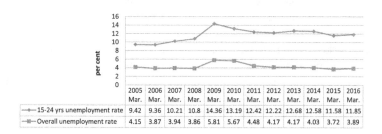

Figure 3.4 Taiwan's unemployment rate

Source: Ministry of Labour (2016a), data bank on labour related statistics.

Work-readiness issues faced by employers

Work-readiness issues do not only affect graduates. They can also have a profound impact on employers, including: (1) talent deficit and labour shortages; (2) high staff turnover among young workers; (3) can be a burden on HR and senior staff and (4) can lead to increased costs.

Talent deficit and labour shortages

Chronic talent deficits have become a major obstacle to corporate sustainability and growth in Taiwan. According to the Manpower Agency (2015) global talent shortage survey, 51 percent of Taiwanese employers experienced difficulties in finding the right talent for their companies. Oxford Economics (2014) predicts that, among the 52 countries surveyed, Taiwan will suffer from the most severe "talent deficit" by 2020. These talent shortages are likely to restrict corporate growth as well as stall the economy as a whole.

Lee (2015) suggests that the widening gap between education and employment, early retirement, women leaving work for family reasons, the low birth rate/shrinking population and young people's reluctance to join the manufacturing and agriculture sectors are key factors behind the labour/talent shortage problems. Job vacancy numbers are set to rise further as Taiwan's workforce is set to decrease by 180,000 per year while the population shrinks due to the low birth rate (Ministry of Labour 2016a). Huang (2015b) also argued that the students themselves and Taiwan's deteriorating vocational education system are both to be blamed for worsening talent deficit problems. Specifically, he suggests that the reluctance of young people to enter physically demanding manufacturing jobs and their obsession with obtaining certificates and academic degrees will not make them more successful at work. It is also likely that their parents may be keener for them to undertake university degrees than prepare for work in the manufacturing sector.

Higher staff turnover among young workers

As mentioned earlier, one-third of young graduates tend to leave their job within 1 to 3 months of starting. Government statistics and surveys also indicate that young people, especially well-educated people, have problems with job/organisation fit and with staying in their job. This can also result in employers encountering high staff turnover and talent shortage problems. According to DGBAS (2016c), workers aged under 25 years have the highest turnover rate at 8.77 percent, much higher than the 2.45 percent for 25 to 44 years old and 0.99 percent for 45 years old and above. In terms of educational level, the average turnover rate of workers with higher education qualifications is 2.97 percent – higher than their senior high school counterparts at 1.95 percent (DGBAS 2016c).

Burden on HR and senior staff

Even though employers are gradually getting used to the high turnover rates among young recruits, new recruits' work-readiness problems can still put strain on HR and senior staff. As a result of the inadequate vocation training in schools, many graduates experience steep learning curves after entering the workplace. Graduates' lack of workplace skills and proper work ethics can also put extra workload and stress on front-line managers and human resource management professionals (104 Manpower Agency 2015). For example, Chang (2016) found that, in Taiwanese franchises, first-line managers or senior staff often feel frustrated due to the considerable amount of time and energy wasted on recruitment and training new recruits, who often quit within weeks or months of joining. Managers and senior staff then have to repeat the time-consuming processes over and over again due to the high turnover among new recruits. This is because the average 3 to 7 days induction training for new recruits cannot compensate for young people's lack of communication and task-related vocational skills or address their attitude and work ethic–related problems. These include failing to turn up at work on time and being negligent and irresponsible towards work assignments. As a result, some franchises are reluctant to hire inexperienced graduates as they require more time and effort to train and are often less productive.

Increased direct and indirect costs

Taiwanese graduates' lack of workplace skills can also lead to direct and indirect cost increases. Direct cost increases can result in more money spent on training and recruitment. There are also indirect costs, such as new recruits' inability to work independently to complete tasks, senior staff time and effort spent on guiding new recruits, damage caused by new recruits' mistakes and more. Chang's (2016) study also found that high turnover among new recruits may also have a negative effect on customer satisfaction, trust and corporate reputation and brand image.

Employer responses to work-readiness issues

Even though work-readiness issues and the widening gap between employment and education are structural/macro-level problems, some employers are trying to address these deficits. The most common approach which companies adopt to tackle work-readiness issues is through mentorship systems by assigning senior colleagues to guide and train new staff. However, as mentioned earlier, this may put strain on more experienced workers who need to put in additional time and effort to guide and mentor new recruits.

In addition to mentorship, some employers are willing to collaborate with universities and vocational high schools to organise internship/apprenticeship opportunities and provide industry-focused guest lectures in order to provide insights into workplace practices and assist in the search for appropriate talent. This is a common practice between vocational schools and large companies in manufacturing, high tech, hospitality and healthcare industries which are facing severe talent/labour shortages.

Another practical approach which employers commonly adopt to cope with work-readiness issues is flexible work contracts. Tenured staff can be expensive and their contracts difficult to terminate, so new recruits are typically given a 1-to 3-month probation period with temporary employment contracts when they start working. Employers may terminate this temporary employment contract if they find new recruits are unqualified, unsuitable or uncooperative. For some years temporary work researchers have argued that such contracts can either be a 'bridge' to permanent employment or a 'trap' that workers find they cannot move out of – that is, they stay on long term temporary work contracts (see Gash 2008 for example). Recent research by Reichelt (2015) found that it was low-skilled workers that were most at risk of falling into a trap of ongoing temporary work, or even unemployment as the medium and highly skilled generally found secure, permanent work. However, employers are using temporary contracts as a legal tool to exploit both skilled and unskilled workers in Taiwan. For instance, the government employs 52,000 temporary workers. This accounts for the highest number of temporary contracts in the country, with 8.65 percent of the total 601,000 of temporary workers registered in 2015 (DGBAS 2016b). Another example is that, roughly half of all higher education teaching staff are on temporary contracts as most schools are using temporary employment contracts to cut costs (Ministry of Education's Statistical Bureau 2016a).

Even though employers are required by Taiwanese labour law to provide severance pay to new recruits who are made redundant during the probation period, most employers do not comply. Instead of redundancy and giving severance pay, they often encourage new recruits to resign voluntarily in exchange for better employment records if prospective employers seek reference checks. Moreover, once new recruits have passed assessments and/or survived the probation period, employers may offer full-time employment contracts and renegotiate pay packages and job arrangements accordingly. A recent survey of 980 job seekers by one of the leading recruitment agencies indicates that 77 percent of them have gone through a probation period, but only 70 percent passed successfully (Apple Daily 2015). Out of the 70 percent who survived the probation period, 48 percent of them were awarded a pay raise.

In a way, the probation period can function as a practical assessment tool to help both employers and job seekers determine whether it is a good match between the job and the new recruit. For employers, they can have the flexibility to terminate employment contracts and cut down costs when encountering unsuitable or unqualified new recruits. For job seekers, the "probation period" can provide graduates with an opportunity to learn how to fit in to the workplace under the guidance of superiors. They can also assess the suitability of the new job/environment and possible career prospects. Given that schools in general are currently failing to prepare students for the workplace, graduates often experience steep learning curves when they join the workplace, and many would have problems surviving the probation period. At least one-third of graduates leave their job within three months of joining (104 Manpower Agency 2015).

Government solutions to work-readiness challenges

As explained previously, Taiwan's labour market is plagued with multiple problems, including labour shortages, expensive early retirement schemes for public sector workers, workplace discrimination, work-readiness problems and more. These problems are inter-correlated and complicated, so there are no simple solutions or quick fixes. The Taiwanese government has been trying to help by rolling out multiple policies over the years, such as relaxing controls on the employment of foreign workers, establishing a system of occupational standards, raising minimum wages and more. Yet, to date, there has been little or no success – as explained when outlining some of the key strategies below.

Relaxed controls on employment of foreign workers

Low birth rates, low labour participation rates and late entry to the workplace all contribute to the talent shortages in Taiwan. As the ageing population is set to increase in the long run and talent deficits continue, the Taiwanese government has loosened controls on foreign labour. According to National Statistics (2016), more than 603,000 foreign blue-collar workers are now employed by Taiwanese manufacturers and care-related industries; while nearly 449,000 foreign white-collar workers are employed mainly in the education, art and science sectors. That amounts to more than 1 million foreign workers in total – approximately 10 percent of the island's workforce. The newly elected Democratic Progressive Party (DPP) government recently revealed plans to further relax control of 'white-collar' foreign labour to ease the current severe talent shortages. Yet, without some controls in place this strategy may not be effective as local workers may be crowded out by foreign workers, thus creating fresh turmoil in the already chaotic labour market.

Labour law revisions to tackle long work hours and low pay

In attempts to curb long-standing problems relating to long work hours and low salaries, the government has decreased work hours from 44 per week to 40 hours per week while increasing minimum wages to 21,009 New Taiwanese Dollars (NTD) per month (roughly 656 USD) and 133 NTD per hour (roughly 4.16 USD) from January 2017. Currently, some employers still pay their employees less than the set minimum wages, while many have employees working 13 days consecutively without a break or working more than 12 hours a day, resulting in considerable cases of illness or even death from overwork. Based on the analysis of government statistics, Lin (2016) pointed out that, between 2010 and 2014, 358 'overwork' cases were recorded by the government. Of these cases, 156 people died from overwork, while others suffered from illnesses related to overwork. In other words, every 5 days a Taiwanese worker suffers from illness related to overwork, while every 12 days a worker dies from overwork. The newly elected DPP government has proposed further pay rises and also plans to pressure employers who fail to provide workers with at least 1 day off after 6 consecutive days of work in order to improve working conditions and win over electorates.

Yet, the proposed revision of labour laws has led to increasing tensions and disputes between employers and workers, especially over wages, overtime payments, paid leave, paid time-off, regulations over work hours and pensions (China Times

2016). From employers' perspectives, the new labour law measures can lead to cost increases and difficulties over shift management (Apple Daily 2016; Lee 2016b). From the workers' perspective, thanks to the new government's willingness to listen and take action, workers and labour unions are now more willing to voice their concerns and fight for their rights via public campaigns, whistle blowing, demonstrations, strikes or even lawsuits, which have been relatively rare in the past for fear of losing their jobs or being marginalised as "trouble makers" (Lou 2016). The unprecedented but successful strike by China Airlines' flight attendants over issues in relation to work hours and conditions has created unforeseen ripple effects on society as a whole, as growing awareness of labour rights is on the rise. For instance, railway workers, bus drivers and energy sector workers' unions have announced their plans for strikes, forcing their employers and the government to re-negotiate pay, shift management and working conditions (Wang 2016a). Yet, as the political deadlock over labour law revisions persists, there is still a long way to go for workers to fight for labour rights as many employers will not easily give up their existing 'sweatshop practises' which they consider the key to corporate competitiveness and cost-savings (Huang 2016b). For example, a chairmen of one the leading convenience store franchises argued that the labour law revision proposal, which requires employers to give staff two days of paid-time-off per week, will lead to difficulties in shift management, cost increases in terms of hundreds of millions dollars (NTD) and drag down their net profit by at least one-quarter (Wang 2016b).

Collaborative strategies to bridge the work-readiness gap

As explained throughout this chapter, the widening gap between education and employment policies and practices has led to work-readiness problems. These have affected graduates and young people's work-readiness generally, while resulting in talent shortages for employers. In attempting to tackle these problems, the government has provided incentives such as funding, tax rebates, resources and certification for education providers, incentives for research institutes and industry to collaborate on training, job creation and the commercial application of technologies, patents and innovations. For instance, there are quite a few manufacturers in the high-tech and machinery sectors who collaborated with research institutes and schools over research projects and apprenticeship programs which have led to technical breakthroughs, patents and job creation.

Yet, the collaborative apprenticeship program operating between industry and educational institutions is often criticised as a tool to exploit young trainees, who are paid considerably less than full-time staff (Lin 2014b). The long work hours and regular overtime can also be harmful for young trainees' psychological and physical wellbeing. Even though apprenticeship or placement programs are based on good intentions to help trainees gain work experience and occupational insights, the harsh work conditions may result in deterring students from entering respective occupations. For instance, Chen and Shen (2011) have found that hospitality and tourism students who were dissatisfied with their apprenticeship experiences are less likely to work in these industries after graduation.

In addition to cross-functional cooperation, the government also proposed an "occupational standard system" which involves setting up the standards for key occupations and developing subsequent training frameworks or certification mechanisms for them. In a way, occupational standards are set up to provide critical insights into occupations and what knowledge, skills and attitudes are needed for such jobs. Such information provides important guidelines for what should be taught to prepare students for these jobs and certification examinations can be checked to evaluate training outcomes. Despite billions of dollars of funding being invested in this ambitious program, the lack of cross-functional coordination within government, slow progress, unclear utility of such complex systems and little or no incentives for industry and employers to get involved has yielded little impact so far.

In addition, different government departments do not work closely enough with each other to ascertain what occupations require talent/are needed by industry and how educational curricula should be adjusted to develop the talent needed for today and the future. Also, universities' and vocational schools' curricula are often outdated as teachers tend to teach whatever they are comfortable with. There is also a lack of external accreditation given that employers don't use occupational standards as human resource tools, arguing that these standards are too generalised and do not meet their specific operational needs (Chang et al. 2014). The only apparent positive outcome of this occupational standard policy is that some workers are keen to obtain occupational certification (e.g., professional engineering certification issued by the Ministry of Economic Affairs), which may be beneficial for job applications or career development. Even though the newly elected government seems committed to this policy for now, it will have little chance of success in the long run unless all the key stakeholders are aligned and agree to collaborate and contribute.

Discussion

It is suggested that a Triple Helix (3H) collaboration between university-industry government relations needs to be enacted to support a sustainable way forward for the various education sectors/providers in Taiwan. This type of approach requires industry, academia and government to still fulfil their core traditional functions, but collaborate at the same time, co-operating through institutional, structured and strategic approaches. Etzkowitz and Klofsten (2005) state that the focus of the triple helix model is on interaction among university, industry and government and the creation of hybrid organizations, such as the incubators, to support start-up processes. They explain that:

> Incubation is fundamentally an educational process to train organizations in adequate functioning, whether the trainees are academics or persons without

formal education. It involves an expansion of the academic educational mission from training individuals to educating organizations.

(Etzkowitz and Klofsten 2005, p. 412)

This may also mean that each party sometimes 'takes the role of the other' by adopting new, non-traditional roles; for example, companies become educators (i.e., by training students) and the university becomes more entrepreneurial (Van Winden and Carvalho 2015, p. 10) to develop long-term relationships and share knowledge, ideas and strategies towards a more effective future for all. Otherwise, the mismatch between higher education, the changing labour market and people's cultural expectations are likely to continue into the foreseeable future (Mok et al. 2013).

Conclusion

In summary, Taiwan's labour market continues to be plagued by labour shortages, discrimination and exploitation, while the imbalances in demand and supply become exacerbated. Worldwide, employers demand that the graduates they hire should 'fit' and add value to their business in both the short-term and long-term (Nankervis, Compton and Baird 2016), a situation that is far from being realised in Taiwan. Employers are having trouble filling job vacancies with the right talent as schools, vocational colleges and universities generally fail to equip students with the requisite skills and knowledge needed for the workplace. Conversely, Taiwanese young people struggle to find jobs as what they have learnt at school or university has not made them work ready, and inadequate career guidance has also failed to prepare them for their preferred career paths. As a result, both employers and young people can only use trial and error to find the right talent or jobs, but the process can be time and resource consuming and frustrating. In attempting to address some of these issues, the government has relaxed control on foreign labour and encouraged collaboration between education providers and employers. Yet, it is still failing to tackle the underlying cause of labour market imbalance as the education system is not providing the right quantity and quality of talent needed by industry, the economy and society as a whole.

Taiwan's education system requires a fundamental overhaul and restructuring. There are simply far too many universities and colleges in existence (see Mok et al. 2013). This means that many will have to be eliminated in order to safeguard the overall quality of education and resolve the oversupply of higher education for the sake of salvaging rapidly depreciating college degrees. Teaching content and training approaches also need re-examination and updating to ensure that students are workplace-ready before they graduate. Finally, government officials and education providers will also have to work with other key stakeholders, such as employers, parents and young people, to turn around the failing education system and support better-quality training that meets the contemporary real-life and workplace demands that ensure sustainability.

Table 3.1 Summary-V1

	Summary-V1
Demographics/labour market	***Shrinking population***: Taiwan's current population was 23.5 million in 2015 which is forecasted to shrink by 2020. ***Low labour participation rate***: In 2014 overall labour participation rate stood at 58.54 percent, below the world average of 63.5 percent. ***Earlier retirement***: Average retirement age is around 57.5~60, earlier than the OECD average of 64 years of age. ***Long work hours***: Taiwanese workers clocked up 2,103~2,134 annual work hours in 2015.
Economy	***Sluggish economic growth***: 2015 GDP per capita was around 22,294 USD but economic growth has remained sluggish in recent years. ***Low wages***: In 2015 the Taiwanese workers on average earned 19,540 NTD per month, equivalent to approximately 1,628 USD. Even though minimum wage and average wages have been increasing steadily over the years, inflation has outpaced wage growth and thus led to negative real wage growth.
Antecedents of the work-readiness challenges	***Over supply of university places***: In 2016, university enrolment rate stood at 97.11 percent as there are more university places than students. ***Failing University entry exam***: The university entry exam has lost it function of safeguarding the quality of students as almost all students who sit the exam can attend university regardless of their grades. ***Vocational training become academicised***- Most vocational colleges were upgraded to technology universities but the upgrades have led to vocational training becoming theoretically oriented and lacking practical value. The distinction between vocational and academic training has diminished as most academic universities now also offer theory driven vocational courses in attempts to win students and secure funding. ***Failing in teaching standards***: Education curricula has been criticised for being too theoretical, out-of-date and lacking any practical value. Even top schools can be reluctant to expel underperforming students for fear of bad review or budget cuts as funding is tide up with student numbers.

(Continued)

Table 3.1 (Continued)

	Summary-VI
	Failing Career guidance: Schools are also failing students on career guidance as students may get more help from governments' job centres and private manpower companies than school career centres.
	Apprentice become a subsite of cheap labour: Many employers use apprentices as cheap labour to cut down costs. Unpleasant apprenticeship experience may deter students from entering the profession after graduation.
Work-readiness issues:	*High youth unemployment rate*: youth unemployment has reached double digits for more than a decade and shows no signs of significant improvement. Only 79 percent graduates manage to settle down with a fulltime job after graduated 3 years.
	Talent deficit: more than half of employers experience talent shortage
	Lack of right skills and attitudes: Employers have to spend considerable time and effort training graduates as they lack the right sort of skills and attitudes needed for the workplace.
	High turnover: 1/3 graduates leave their jobs with 3 months of starting a new job as they find it difficult to fit in and settle down. Average turnover rate of 15- to 25-year-olds is much higher than worker who are more than 25 years of age.
Government policy initiatives	*Relax control on foreign labor*: Government will relax control on blue- and white-collar workers to ease talent shortages. Currently more than 1 million foreign workers are employed that makes up roughly 10 percent of the workforce.
	Incentive for collaboration: Funding for schools and research institutes to collaborate with industry to carry out research, training and co-development
	Occupational standards: Occupational standard system is meant to provide a framework of what people do and what skills knowledge they should have for this job. Schools may then use this framework to structure their curricula, but so far, no schools have done so.
Recommended strategies	• Fundamental overhaul of education system to eliminate underperforming schools
	• Teaching contents and methods need a complete update to help students become workplace ready.
	• Triple Helix (3H) collaboration between university, industry and government

References

104 Manpower Agency. 2015, *2015 human resource FBI (In Mandarin)* [Online]. Available at: www.104.com.tw/area/media/file/detail/id/167121573303174524/category/256/2015per centE4percentBAper centE8per centB3per cent87F.B.I. [Accessed August 20, 2016].

Apple Daily. 2015, 'More than half of job seekers did not get pay rise after passing probation period. (In Mandarin)', *Apple Daily*, October 29, 2015. [Online]. Available at: www.appledaily.com.tw/realtimenews/article/new/20151029/721377/.

Apple Daily. 2016, 'Apply daily comment: Two days off per week does not open employers' back doors (In Mandarin)', *Apple Daily*, June 30, 2016. [Online]. Available at: www.appledaily.com.tw/appledaily/article/headline/20160630/37289338/.

Chang, M-W. S 2016, *The use of e-learning among Taiwanese franchise: A key to franchise success (In Mandarin)*, Taipei: Commerce research development institute (Service industry research series commissioned by Ministry of Economic affair).

Chang, M-W S., Lee, S-J. and Lou, J-C. 2014, *Occupational standards of performing art professionals (In Mandarin)*, Taipei: Commerce research development institute (a study commissioned by Ministry of culture).

Chang, S-H. 2011, *Higher education liberalisation: Redefine higher education, universities are not vocational training institutes (In Mandarin)*, Lihpao Daily, December 11.

Chen, Z-L. and Shen, C-C. 2011, 'The influence of internship program on students' career choice: Case from hospitality and tourism related department in higher vocational education (In Mandarin)', *Journal of Hospitality and Tourism*, Vol. 8, no.1, pp. 22–38 Available at: http://ir.nkuht.edu.tw/bitstream/987654321/1517/1/8per centE5per cent8Dper centB71–002.pdf.

China Times. 2016, 'Don't underestimate the negative impact of dispute over workers' paid-time off on the economy as a whole (In Mandarin)', *China times*, July 29, 2016. [Online]. Available at: www.chinatimes.com/newspapers/20160729000038-260202.

Chiu, S. Y. and Chuang, H. L. 2016, 'Employability and wage compensation in an Asian economy: Evidence for female college graduates in Taiwan', *Emerging Markets Finance and Trade*, Vol. 52, no. 4, pp. 853–868.

Department of Statistics Directorate General of Budget, Accounting and Statistics (DGBAS). 2012, *Government 2012 budget (In Mandarin)*. [Online]. Available at: www.dgbas.gov.tw/public/data/accounting/government/101/總說明.doc.

Department of Statistics Directorate General of Budget, Accounting and Statistics (DGBAS). 2014, *Labor participation statistics by gender (In Mandarin)*. [Online]. Available at: http://statdb.mol.gov.tw/html/woman/103/103woanalyze01.pdf.

Department of Statistics Directorate General of Budget, Accounting and Statistics (DGBAS). 2015, *Women's marital status, child bearing and employment statistics (In Mandarin)*. [Online]. Available at: www.dgbas.gov.tw/np.asp?ctNode=2841.

Department of Statistics Directorate General of Budget, Accounting and Statistics (DGBAS). 2016a, *Latest indicators (In Mandarin)*. [Online]. Available at: http://eng.stat.gov.tw/point.asp?index=1 [Accessed August 20, 2016].

Department of Statistics Directorate General of Budget, Accounting and Statistics (DGBAS). 2016b, *Manpower survey results in June 2016 (In Mandarin)*. [Online]. Available at: http://eng.stat.gov.tw/public/Data/672275229Q5IS5JQV.pdf [Accessed August 20, 2016].

Department of Statistics Directorate General of Budget, Accounting and Statistics (DGBAS). 2016c, *2014 employment turnover survey (In Mandarin)*. [Online]. Available at: www.dgbas.gov.tw/public/Attachment/5929124445Q5IT53QV. pdf.

Department of Statistics Directorate General of Budget, Accounting and Statistics (DGBAS). 2016d, *2015 gender employment quality survey (In Mandarin)*. [Online]. Available at: http://statdb.mol.gov.tw/html/svy04/0424menu.htm.

The Epoch Times. 2014, 'Pregnancy discrimination tops employment discrimination compliant list (In Mandarin)', *Epoch Times*, May 21, 2014. [Online]. Available at: www.epochtimes.com/b5/14/5/21/n4160959.htm.

Etzkowitz, H. and Klofsten, M. 2005, 'The innovating region: Towards a theory of knowledge based regional development', *R&D Management*, Vol. 35, pp. 243–255.

Gao, Y-F. 2015, *Average retirement age 57.5, 7.5 years early than legal retirement age: Public servants are most content with retirement (In Mandarin)*, Taipei: Global Views Monthly.

Gash, V. 2008, 'Bridge or trap? Temporary workers' transitions to unemployment and to the standard employment contract', *European Sociological Review*, Vol. 24, no. 5, pp. 651–668.

Hall, D. and Ames, R. 2000, Sexism with Chinese Characteristics. In Li, C. ed. *The Sage and the Second Sex: Confucianism, Ethics and Gender*, Chicago, Open Court, 69–95.

Harvey, L., Locke, W. and Morey, A. 2002, *Enhancing employability, recognizing diversity: Making links between higher education and the world of work*, London: Universities UK and CSU.

Ho, M. S. 2013, *The political ambiguity of middle class activism in Taiwan: Chinese Middle Classes: Taiwan, Hong Kong, Macao, and China*, Vol. 112, p. 215.

Huang, C-U. 2016b, 'Never-ending strikes, row over two days off per week- why the self-proclaimed master of communication government is the culprit of most sever labour-employer standoff ever? (In Mandarin)', *Business Weekly*, July 4, 2016. [Online]. Available at: www.businessweekly.com.tw/KBlogArticle. aspx?id=17113.

Huang, G-J. 2015c, 'Vocational education academicised: Problem and solution (in Mandarin)', *Taiwan Educational Review*, Vol. 4, no. 11.

Huang, P-P. 2015a, 'Yes123'survey of mature workers: 80 per cent of mature workers experience high levels of workplace anxiety (In Mandarin)', *Liberty Times*, October 21, 2015.

Huang, W-S. 2015b, *High job vacancy rate in Taiwan: Passive students or failing vocational education to blame? News Lens (In Mandarin)*. [Online]. Available at: www. thenewslens.com/article/32797.

Huang, Y-L. 2016a, *Long work hours and short vocation time: How Taiwanese salve workers are employers favourite (In Mandarin)*. [Online]. Available at: www.the-newslens.com/article/44241 The News Lens].

Lee, C-C. 2016a, 'Taiwan's choice- don't be ignorant about declining male participation rate (In Mandarin)', *Commercial Times*, March 18.

Lee, L-S. 2015, 'Labor shortages: Taiwan is worse than Japan and Korea (In Mandarin)', *Common Wealth Magazine*, May 25, 2015, Vol. 573 [Online]. Available at: www.cw.com.tw/article/article.action?id=5067885.

Lee, U-T. 2016b, 'Deadlock on revising labour law chapter on time off (In Mandarin)', *Apply Daily*, July 22, 2016.

Lee, Y-J. 2014, *25 thousand teachers will retire with 5 years: 4 underlying reasons behind the rush to retire*. [Online]. Available at: www.thenewslens.com/article/8113.

Li, C. 2000, 'Introduction: Can Confucianism come to terms with feminism', in Li, C. (ed.) *The sage and the second sex: Confucianism, ethics, and gender*, Chicago: Open Court.

Lin and Ho 2015, 'Vocational education becomes too academic – student's work-readiness suffers as a result (In Mandarin)', *Journal of Taiwan Educational Review*, Vol. 4, no. 11.

Lin, I-T. 2016, 'Taiwan as the overworked island: 1 in 12 workers died from overwork (In Mandarin)', *Common Wealth Magazine*, March 2, 2016. [Online]. Available at: www.cw.com.tw/article/article.action?id=5074849 [Accessed August 20, 2016].

Lin, J-C. 2014b, 'Apprentices complained about being treated as cheap labour (In Mandarin)', *China Times*, May 6, 2014. [Online]. Available at: www.chinatimes.com/newspapers/20140506001433-260114.

Lin, J-L. 2014a, 'Minister pan pointed out 290 thousands are looking for overseas job vacancies (In Mandarin)', *ETtoday News*, April 21, 2014. [Online]. Available at: www.ettoday.net/news/20140421/348682.htm [Accessed August 20, 2016].

Lou, K-U. 2016, 'Labour right awareness on the rise: Don't be afraid of the economic downturn (In Mandarin)', *Common Wealth Magazine*, March 2, 2016. [Online]. Available at: www.cw.com.tw/article/article.action?id=5077200 [Accessed August 20, 2016].

Lu, H-P. 2014, 'Gender discrimination at work: 5 common discrimination encountered by female workers (In Mandarin)', *Global Views Monthly*, November 7, 2014. [Online]. Available at: www.gvm.com.tw/webonly_content_3705.html.

Lu, W-C. 2009, 'Universities are not vocational training institutes (In Mandarin)', *NPF Commentary*. [Online]. Available at: www.npf.org.tw/1/5568.

Manpower group. 2015, *10th annual talent shortage report*. [Online]. Available at: www.manpowergroup.com/wps/wcm/connect/manpowergroup-en/home/thought-leadership/research-insights/talent-shortage-2015.

Ministry of Education. 2015, *Higher and further education institutes at a glance (in Mandarin)*, 2015 October 15. [Online]. Available at: http://ulist.moe.gov.tw/Browse/UniversityList.

Ministry of Education's Statistical Bureau. 2016a, *Data bank on education related statistics (In Mandarin)* [Online]. Available at: https://stats.moe.gov.tw/ [Accessed August 20, 2016].

Ministry of Labour. 2015, *2015 workforce life and employment status survey (In Mandarin)*. [Online]. Available at: http://statdb.mol.gov.tw/html/svy04/0422analyze.pdf [Accessed August 20, 2016].

Ministry of Labour. 2016a, *Data bank on labour related statistics (In Mandarin)*. [Online]. Available at: www.mol.gov.tw/statistics/2445/ [Accessed August 20, 2016].

Ministry of Labour. 2016b, *2015 gender equal payment day is Feb 23, one day less than 2014 (In Mandarin)*. [Online]. Available at: www.mol.gov.tw/announcement/2099/24956/ [Accessed August 20, 2016].

Ministry of the Interior. 2016, *Latest population statistics:2016 June (In Mandarin)*. [Online]. Available at: www.moi.gov.tw/stat/news_content.aspx?sn=10820. [Accessed August 20, 2016].

Ministry of Education's Statistical Bureau. 2016b, *2010–2012 colleague graduate employment and salary survey (In Mandarin)*. [Online]. Available at: http://stats.moe.gov.tw/files/analysis.

Mok, K. H., Yu, K. M. and Ku, Y. W. 2013, 'After massification: The quest for entre-preneurial universities and technological advancement in Taiwan', *Journal of Higher Education Policy and Management*, Vol. 35, no. 3, pp. 264–279.

Nankervis, A., Compton, R. and Baird, M. 2016, *Human resource management* (9th ed.), Southbank, Melbourne: Thomson.

National Statistics. 2016, *Other labour statistics. (In Mandarin)*. [Online]. Available at: http://statdb.mol.gov.tw/html/mon/i0120020620.htm. [Accessed August 20, 2016].

OECD. 2015, *Ageing and employment policies – statistics on average effective age of retirement*. [Online]. Available at: www.oecd.org/els/emp/ageingandemploy-mentpolicies-statisticsonaverageeffectiveageofretirement.htm [Accessed August 20, 2016].

Oxford Economics. 2014, *Global talent 2021:How the new geography of talent will transform human resource strategies*. [Online]. Available at: www.oxfordeconomics.com/Media/Default/Thoughtper cent20Leadership/global-talent-2021.pdf.

Reichelt, M. 2015, 'Career progression from temporary employment: How bridge and trap functions differ by task complexity', *European Sociological Review*, p. jcv055.

Siegel, J. I., Pyun, L. and Cheon, B. Y. 2014, *Multinational firms, labor market discrimination, and the capture of competitive advantage by exploiting the social divide*, Harvard Business School Strategy Unit Working Paper, (11–011).

Taiwan People News. 2016, *Tiger year effect set a record: 23 universities failed to reach admission target (In Mandarin)*. [Online]. Available at: www.peoplenews.tw/news/f4aedf8d-88b1-4bfb-8c62-54cab126914a.

Tatli, A., Ozturk, M. B. and Woo, H. S. 2016, 'Individualization and marketization of responsibility for gender equality: The case of female managers in China', *Human Resource Management*, doi:10.1002/hrm.21776 accessed 20/9/2016

Van Winden, W. and Carvalho, L. 2015, *New urban economies: How can cities foster economic development and develop 'new urban economies, Urbact ii Capitalisation*, European Union Development Fund.

Wang, I-J. 2016b, 'Two days off per week will leave no flexibility over shift management: Employers will have to look after stores themselves (In Mandarin)', *Global Views Magazine*, Vol. 362, August 2016. [Online]. Available at: http://store.gvm.com.tw/article_content_31651_2.html.

Wang, U-S. 2016a, 'Ripple effects of China airline strike: Taiwan electricity and Chinese Petroleum Corporation workers also announce plans for strikes (In Mandarin)', *China Times*, June 29, 2016. [Online]. Available at: www.chinatimes.com/newspapers/20160629000034-260202.

World Bank. 2016, *Data bank: Labor force participation rate*. [Online]. Available at: http://data.worldbank.org/indicator/SL.TLF.CACT.ZS [Accessed August 20, 2016].

Zhang, 2015, 'HR related costs takes 47.84per cent of local governments' budget in 2013 (In Mandarin)', *China times*, June 20, 2015. [Online]. Available at: http://news.ltn.com.tw/news/politics/paper/890939.

4 Enhancing graduate work-readiness in Vietnam

Nguyen Danh Nguyen and Nguyen Ba Ngoc

Introduction

This chapter explores the current situation of the Vietnamese labour market with both its advantages and disadvantages. It also discusses the characteristics of the Vietnamese labour market and presents the government frameworks for the education system. The challenges of graduate work-readiness are also explained to explore how employers and educational institutions cope with such challenges. Through a series the case studies, the graduate work-readiness situations are considered in greater depth.

Overall context of Vietnam

Vietnam is a country located in Southeast Asia. In the north, it shares the long borderline with China. In the east and south, it is bordered by the Pacific Ocean and in the west by Laos and Cambodia. The country has an area of over 300,000 square kilometres and a population of 90 million, with 54 ethnic groups, of which 86.2 percent are Vietnamese and 13.8 percent are ethnic minorities. Vietnam is administratively divided into 63 provinces and cities directly under the central government (General Statistics Office 2015). Over the past 80 years, the Communist Party of Vietnam (CPV) has been in the vanguard of the struggle for national independence, liberating the country from almost a century of domination by Western colonialists. Since the country's reunification in 1975, the CPV has led the Vietnamese people in carrying out the country's renovation, modernisation and industrialisation. The CPV has established a nationwide political system which assists the party leadership and mobilises the people to realise the goals of national independence, democracy and social progress.

Since the economic and political reforms launched in 1986, the Vietnamese economy has experienced rapid economic growth and development and transformed Vietnam from one of the world's poorest to a lower middle-income country. From 1990, Vietnam's GDP per capita growth rate is above 6 to 7 percent a year. The development of the Vietnamese economy is a result of three main reform pillars: (i) promoting human resources/skills development (particularly skills for modern industry and innovation); (ii) improving market institutions, and (iii) infrastructure development (World Bank 2014).

Vietnam's economy continued to strengthen in 2015, with an estimated gross domestic product (GDP) growth rate of 6.7 percent. Vietnam's economic activity moderated in the first half of 2016, with GDP expanding by 5.5 percent, compared to 6.3 percent over the same period in 2015. This slow-down is considered a result of the severe drought affecting agricultural production and slower industrial growth. Agriculture's share of economic output has shrunk from about 25 percent in 2000 to 17 percent in 2015, while industry's share increased from 36 percent to 39 percent in the same period (General Statistics Office of Vietnam, 31 December 2015).

The pace of economic growth has slowed as a consequence of macroeconomic confusion and the low productivity of the workforce in recent years. In order to keep the pace of economic growth, Vietnam now cannot continue to rely on the size and the youth of its workforce. It needs to pay more attention to improving workforce productivity and labour employability (World Bank 2014).

The Vietnamese labour market

Vietnam had a potential labour market of over 54 million people in 2015, with an average 77 percent labour force participation rate. Employment in the agriculture, forestry and fisheries sector account for nearly 45 percent of total employment. The following table (Table 4.1) illustrates the key economic and labour market indicators for Vietnam in 2015.

Vietnam's labour productivity in 2013 was USD 5,440 higher than that of Myanmar, Cambodia and Laos but lower than the rest of the ASEAN nations (equivalent to only 55 percent of Indonesia, 54 percent of the Philippines, 37 percent of Thailand, 15 percent of Malaysia and 6 percent of Singapore). Vietnam's Global Competitive Index in 2014, Vietnam is only ranked 68th out of 144 participating countries, although this has been an improvement by two ranks in 2013 (70/148) and seven ranks in 2012 (75/144) (World Bank Report 2014).The low rates of labour productivity and competitive index ranking show that Vietnam's economy is still among the low-development countries in comparison to earlier developed countries in Southeast Asia, such as Thailand and Singapore. The low rates of productivity and development are the result of both out-of-date technology and the relatively low skills of the workforce.

In the fourth quarter of 2015, the labour force aged 15 years and over was 54.59 million people. The labour market participation rate for the same quarter was 78.84 percent, and the number of skilled workers aged over 15 years, including people who hold vocational certificates/degrees for the duration of the three months above, was 11.02 million people. The proportion of skilled workers in the workforce was only 20.20 percent of the total labour force (see Table 4.2). With only approximately one-fifth of the total labour force being skilled workers, the key challenge for the Vietnamese labour market is how to increase this proportion to meet the increased demands of today's globally competitive market, which requires a significantly higher proportion of skilled employees.

Table 4.1 Key economic and labour market indicators

Indicators	2015			
	Q1	*Q2*	*Q3*	*Q4*
1 Gross domestic product growth rate (GDP) (percent)	6.1	6.5[*]	6.9[*]	7.0
2 Labour force *(million people)*	53.64	53.71	54.32	54.59
3 Labour force participation rate *(percent)*	77.3	76.2	76.4	78.8
4 Rate of skilled labour force with certificate *(percent)*	21.24	20.06	20.22	20.20
5 Employment *(million people)*	52.43	52.53	53.17	53.50
6 Rate of paid worker in total employment *(percent)*	37.80	38.80	40.42	40.98
7 Rate of employment in agriculture, forestry and fisheries sector in total employment *(percent)*	45.00	44.69	42.54	42.30
8 Unemployment at working age *(thousand people)*	1,159.8	1,144.6	1,128.7	1,051.6
9 Unemployment rate at working age *(percent)* of which	2.43	2.42	2.35	2.18
9.1 Urban unemployment rate *(percent)*	3.43	3.53	3.38	3.15
9.2 Youth unemployment rate (aged 15–24) *(percent)*	6.60	6.68	7.30	7.21

Source: *General Statistic Offices of Vietnam statistic data and quarterly Labour – Employment survey data*, (2015)

*According to social and economic situation 2015 report of General Statistic Offices of Vietnam

Table 4.2 Quantity and rate of skilled workers

	2015			
	Q1	*Q2*	*Q3*	*Q4*
1. Quantity *(Million people)*				
Total	11.39	10.77	10.98	11.02
Primary vocational	1.98	1.77	1.66	1.68
Secondary vocational	0.91	0.81	0.76	0.71
Prof-Secondary school	2.14	2.11	2.09	2.14
Vocational college	0.24	0.20	0.22	0.18
Professional college	1.45	1.42	1.51	1.47
University and higher	4.66	4.47	4.74	4.84
2. Rate *(percent)*				
	21.24	20.06	20.22	20.20

Source: *General Statistic Offices of Vietnam (GSO) statistic data and quarterly labour – Employment survey data* (2015)

In terms of labour structure by qualification level, there were roughly 4.84 million people with a university degree (43.88 percent of total skilled workers), the highest rate of skilled workers in comparison with other tertiary education degrees. It suggests that more Vietnamese young people prefer to enter universities rather than vocational and professional institutions, though the rate of skilled workers still needs to be increased.

This is a concern, as Vietnamese authorities need to balance the percentage of skilled workers from each training institution. The International Labour Organisation (ILO) predicted that the number of jobs in Vietnam should increase by 14.4 percent by 2025 as Vietnam joined the ASEAN Economic Community (AEC) in late 2015 (Viet Nam News report), and a more skilled labour force would be required to meet international labour market demands. Currently, the number of skilled Vietnamese workers remains insufficient. However, the labour market still has several positive elements – for example, the proportion of workers continued to rise, reaching 41.4 percent, and both urban and youth unemployment rates were reduced.

Table 4.3 shows that the labour structure by industry was in constant transition: the proportion of workers in agriculture, forestry and fisheries continued dropping to 42.3 percent, the service sector climbed to 33.4 percent, and even though the industry and construction sector had a moderate decline, it remained steady at 24.3 percent. It can be seen that agriculture, forestry and fisheries still remain among the fields that employ much of the labour force in Vietnam but with unskilled and low-paid workers. In order to change this situation, more investment and industry development is necessary, especially in the construction and service sectors.

Table 4.3 Labour structure by industry and job position

	2015			Unit: percent
	Q1	Q2	Q3	Q4
Total	100.00	100.00	100.00	100.00
By 3 main industries				
Agriculture, forestry and fisheries	45.00	44.70	42.54	42.30
Industry — construction	21.50	22.13	24.46	24.30
Service	33.50	33.17	33.00	33.40
By job position				
Owner	2.98	2.84	2.75	2.87
Self-employed	42.12	40.04	39.39	40.01
Family labour	17.07	18.28	17.42	16.11
Paid worker	37.79	38.81	40.42	40.98
Cooperative members and unclassifiable	0.04	0.03	0.02	0.03

Source: *General Statistic Offices of Vietnam (GSO) statistic data and quarterly Labour – Employment survey data (2015).*

The rate of paid workers in total employment has constantly increased, and reached 40.98 percent in the fourth quarter of 2015 as shown in Table 1.3 above; unpaid family workers went down to 16.11 percent, and self-employed workers rose slightly to 40.1 percent. In the same quarter, there were 4.68 million workers with university bachelor qualifications or higher, covering 8.75 percent of total employment. On the other hand (see Figure 1.1), with the exception of the armed forces, only 76.23 percent of workers found compatible jobs, such as: "management" (7.73 percent) or jobs requiring a "higher technical profession level" (68.5 percent). Figure 4.1 also shows that more than 22 percent of those who had obtained university degrees were still working in positions that require lower-level qualifications, including "secondary technical profession level" jobs (3.57 percent), "staff" (4.27 percent), "skilled service and sales staff" (7.96 percent), "skilled worker among agriculture, forestry and fisheries" (0.58 percent), "craftsman" (1.98 percent) and "manual labour" (2.15 percent). Overall, then, a quarter of university graduates could not find a job related to their degrees, or the employers' requirements include both a university degree and also other employment capabilities, such as good attitudes and employable skills, from their potential employees.

In late 2015, Vietnam had 1,051.6 thousand unemployed people of working age, of which more than a half (559.4 thousand people) were adolescents aged

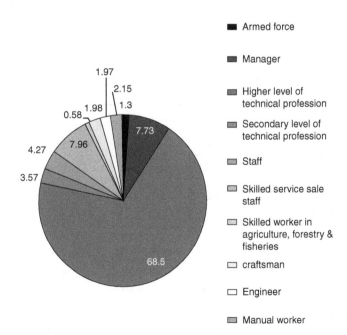

Figure 4.1 Employment structure of workers with university degree and higher qualifications in Vietnam, quarter 4/2015 (percent)

Source: General Statistic Offices of Vietnam statistic data and quarterly labour – Employment survey data (Quarter 4,2015)

15–24 (General Statistic Offices of Vietnam 2015).The unemployment rate of adolescents aged 15–24 was still high (7.21 percent) and was 3.3 times higher than the general unemployment rate. This figure shows that young Vietnamese employees who are not equipped with appropriate work skills will be unable to find suitable jobs.

According to the data in Table 4.4, people holding a professional college qualification had the highest unemployment rate (8.16 percent), followed by vocational college (3.44 percent), professional secondary vocational qualification (3.32) and university degree and above (3.30 percent). Notably, the unemployment rate of adolescents aged 20–24 with technical qualifications was very high: 19.58 percent of professional college graduates and 20.79 percent of university graduates with a bachelor degree or higher qualification. It reinforces the reality that higher education qualifications do not necessarily guarantee employment. In order to get a job in Vietnam, graduates have to master a number of other work-readiness skills and abilities in parallel with knowledge and skills from higher education institutions.

Frequent droughts, invasive mangrove growth and massive associated fish die-offs in the coastal areas have created pressure on Vietnam's 2016 economic growth target of 6.7 percent, while the motivational factors for growth from the various free trade agreements (Trans Pacific Partnership, other bilateral Free Trade Agreements) have yet to take effect or are in the inception phase (for example, ASEAN Economic Community).

Table 4.4 The unemployment rate of people in working age by gender, area, technical qualification and age group

	2015			Unit: percent
	Q1	Q2	Q3	Q4
General	**2.43**	**2.42**	**2.35**	**2.18**
No qualification	1.67	1.58	1.75	1.93
Vocational certificate under 3 months	1.31	1.45	0.97	0.98
Elementary vocational	2.05	2.71	2.11	1.69
Secondary vocational	3.10	3.90	3.45	2.25
Professional secondary vocational	3.91	4.70	3.13	3.32
Vocational college	6.69	4.76	7.95	3.44
Professional college	7.20	6.79	7.93	8.16
University/higher	3.92	4.60	4.88	3.30
4. By age group				
Adolescents (15–24)	6.60	6.68	7.30	7.21
Adult (>25)	1.48	1.44	1.19	1.22

Source: *General Statistic Offices of Vietnam statistic data and quarterly labour – employment survey data*

Government frameworks and the education system

The administration of education in Vietnam is categorised by three levels. The highest level is the Ministry of Education and Training (MOET), which is responsible for the education policy and the operation of the national system. At second level are the provincial Departments of Education and Training. This level is responsible for the oversight of district officers of education and training, upper secondary and vocational and technical colleges in each province or city. The third level of the education system are the District Officers of Education and Training. This level governs primary and lower secondary schools in their districts and reports to the provincial department.

Vietnam does not yet have a National Qualification Framework. However, there are 190 National Occupation Skill Standards (NOSS) for vocational education (VE only), administered by the Ministry of Education and Training and the Ministry of labour, Invalids and Social Affairs (MOLISA). The national government also issued a Law of Education proclaimed in 2005, which included policies related to the recognition of prior learning (RPL). In addition, the Law of Higher Education and Law of Vocational Education were proclaimed in 2012 and 2014 respectively. As indicated above, each ministry has a different role and a separate function in managing the workforce and human capital development. MOLISA and other relevant ministries are responsible for workforce development. However, the Ministry of Education and Training and other ministries are in charge of human capital development. In detail, the Ministries of Labour and Education have issued the strategies of workforce development (2011–2020), the plan for workforce development (2011–2020), the strategy of education development (2011–2020), the strategy of vocational training (2011–2020) and the strategy of science and technology (2011–2020).

In January 2013, the government issued a Prime Ministerial decision on a project referred to as "Building a Learning Society" in the period 2012–2020 — to indicate the implementation of continuous and lifelong learning. The key targets for this project are disabled people, the poor, and other disadvantaged minorities. Two particular sectors in Vietnamese society targeted for funding to improve work-readiness are programmers in army and police programmers and firefighters in their respective academies.

As observed from many industry sectors in Vietnam, the ten key sectors which are facing work-readiness challenges ranked from one to ten are as follows: (1) manufacturing, (2) information media and telecommunications, (3) professional, scientific and technical services, (4) health care and social assistance, (5) education and training, (6) finance and insurance, (7) construction, (8) transport and storage, (9) public administration and safety, (10) administrative and support services. Vietnam does not yet collect data on vocational education and training (VET) and higher education (HE) completions and graduate outcomes.

Figure 4.2 illustrates the Vietnamese education system, with seven education components, namely, kindergarten, primary, junior high school, high school, vocational education, college and university undergraduate and postgraduate education.

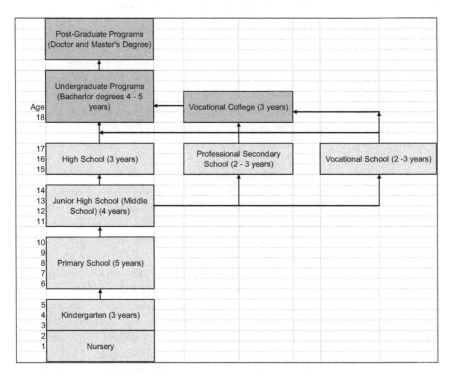

Figure 4.2 Vietnamese Education System
(Source: Ministry of Education and Training of Vietnam)

Figure 4.2 shows that the Vietnamese education system is similar to many other countries as there are multiple levels of qualifications as the graduates from different levels can enter the workforce with different kind of work-requirements. At the end of 2014, Vietnam has 204 universities and 215 vocational colleges (General Statistic Offices of Vietnam 2015). In this context, the challenges for work-readiness may not come from the structure of the Vietnamese education system but rather from the management of the system and its compatibility with employers' expectations, with respect to either the labour market generally or specific job requirements.

Graduate work-readiness challenges

As defined in chapter 2 of this book, graduate work-readiness includes the skills that students or graduates require to satisfy the needs for a job. This definition indicates that there are more than two actors who play important roles in ensuring the work-readiness of graduates. From the supply side, higher education institutions must play a significant role in equipping students with the appropriate knowledge, skills and behaviours. On the other hand, from the demand side, employers not only behave as customers but also need to partner with universities and vocational colleges to enhance the employability of students via multiple methods, from internship programs, availability of experience-sharing, job information and requirements for integration, and appropriate employment infrastructure development (Harvey 2001; Morley 2001). The government also plays a very crucial role in setting up conducive environments and policies to strengthen the deep connection and the effective partnership between the two key actors (World Bank 2014, p. 9).

In Vietnam, all the trades and sectors are currently experiencing either inadequate skills of job applicants ("skills gap") or a scarcity of workers in some occupation ("skills shortage") (World Bank 2014). Notwithstanding, the most serious industry sector cases are those industries utilising modern technologies, and sectors under pressure from competition, such as the production of goods for export (ILSSA-Manpower Group 2014). The occupational groups facing many challenges are jobs requiring specialised technical qualifications, such as machinery repair and operation, testing – analysis, and dietitians. The service sector, namely business sales, also face many challenges to recruit skilled labour, as indicated in the results of surveys conducted by the ILSSA-Manpower Group (2014).

Basically, there is no significant difference between the systems of vocational training and higher education systems as many vocational colleges are using nearly the same curriculums as universities while students have very few chances to practice at jobs because of less investment on practical tools and equipment at vocational colleges. For the university system, the requirements are set higher and the risks that graduates do not secure (or have difficulties finding) a job may be larger. For the vocational training system, similar to other countries included in this book, another key challenge is associated with the difficulty of attracting students, as discussed earlier.

Some international studies on work-readiness have been conducted in Vietnam. According to the results of a survey conducted by the World Bank in 2012 on the relevance of university graduates' skills to recruiters' requirements in seven East Asian economies, including Vietnam, work behaviour skills were considered to be in short supply (World Bank 2012). This was especially true with soft skills, including creative thinking, information technology, leadership and problem-solving. As stated in the Vietnam Development Report of World Bank in 2014, 'most employers said that recruitment is hard as candidates do not have appropriate skills (shortage of skills), or due to a shortage of available candidates in a number of industries and occupations (shortage of skilled employees)' (World Bank 2014, p. 7). Similarly, a survey conducted by the Institute of Labour Science and Social Affairs (ILSSA)-Manpower in 2013 showed similar circumstances, with nearly 30 percent of foreign direct investment (FDI) enterprises facing difficulties in recruiting direct workers and office staff. Foremost among the qualities found lacking in potential workers/office staff was an awareness of quality and punctuality/reliability, as reported by approximately 30 percent of the group of direct workers and factory foremen; followed by the ability to adapt to changes, such as working in teams, an ability to learn and apply new technologies, and a lack of fundamental computer skills (ILSSA 2014).

Causes of these graduate work-readiness challenges

There are many causes of the above challenges. First, there is a lack of mechanisms, policies and appropriate orientation programs for encouraging competition and improving quality. Human resource planning is vague and lacks specificity, implementation systems are often inadequate, employment conditions and wages are unreasonable, placing direct impact on workers. Second, planning for the overall education and training systems is ineffective, with too many institutions being established, and training sectors are not in line with market demand (Chau et al. 2008; Lam 2013). In 2001, the number of higher education institutions in Vietnam was about 178. However, there were 419 universities and colleges in 2015. A lack of long-term strategies for the orientation of trades training according to the needs of the economy has led to an imbalance in trades training. There are about nearly 40 percent of Vietnamese students enrolled in the business-economic field while only about 25 percent of them are enrolled in science-technology fields (Thang and Lan 2013). Furthermore, forecasts of the labour market in the short term and long term are weak; information about jobs and careers has not been fully updated in an accurate and timely manner; and the activities of vocational orientation, consulting and job recommendation are limited.

Third, training in many vocational colleges and universities is of relatively low quality. Most colleges carry out training based on what they have, rather than on labour market requirements. Even when capturing market requirements, many colleges still do not have enough capacity (teachers, facilities, training programs) for the necessary changes. The education system lacks interaction with employers and industry, and many programs are not practical, limited in both skills and knowledge, making it immensely difficult for labourers to find jobs (Chau et al. 2008; Lam 2013; Thang and Lan 2013). Fourth, employers do not have close collaborations with the training institutions for them to offer appropriate training programs. Employers also do not take full social responsibility, as they require quality from the educational institutions but often do not collaborate with them on joint programs to encourage students to do apprenticeships or share information with teachers. State-owned enterprises evaluate employees based primarily on their qualifications, thus reinforcing the social trend to merely possess a university degree (Lam 2013; Tran 2013). Counting on the government, rather than engaging students and their families in the learning process as well as during job-seeking activities, together with parents' preferences of not wishing their children to attend vocational colleges, aggravate these challenges.

Strategies to address graduate work-readiness

The government and the relevant ministries in Vietnam have set some goals and developed and issued some strategies to address the above challenges to improve the quality of human resources in order to increase the readiness to meet the requirements of the labour market. For example, the government has a strategy for human resources development until 2020 which includes the law on vocational education and the prime minister's decision on building high-quality schools to approach regional and international levels. In addition, the government has issued some policies on the development of the business sector through creating more jobs. The Ministry of Labour, Invalids and Social Affairs has actively implemented activities and measures including the Labour Code of 2012 and the Employment Law of 2013, as well as approving the National Target Program of employment and vocational training between 2012 and 2015.

MOLISA in 2012 has proposed policies to support job creation and the national fund for employment, which stipulates policies to support youngsters in making a career, starting a business, boosting labor market forecasts and the dissemination of employment information and workplace availability to help youth and students to obtain suitable jobs after graduation. Employment service centres should strengthen collaboration with training institutions, especially colleges and universities, in activities of consultation, job recommendations and career orientation for students. They might also coordinate with the Association of Universities and Colleges of Vietnam to organise activities to support jobs for students, and coordinate with the Ministry of Education and Training to implement the participation of students after graduation in the labour market.

The education system has also implemented many new policies, from changing the organisation of entrance exams at all education levels to the input recruitment exam. Before 2014, universities and colleges were delegated to set up their own entrance exams under the requirement of MOET. However, since 2014, MOET built up a new entrance exam system with only one national test, and all the higher education institutions are using the same test results database to select their students. Furthermore, universities and colleges have made many attempts to innovate, change textbooks and alter the learning techniques for students so as to enhance teaching and the transmission of knowledge and experiences as well. Vocational training has reviewed its standards and organised contests for checking practical skills in order to recognise and assist workers to find jobs not only in the country but also overseas. Other strategies include connecting with and facilitating enterprises to recruit students from schools, or create mechanisms to help students after school to work as a trainee, thus directly obtaining relevant work experience.

Industries and businesses have expanded and upgraded the training colleges which they are associated with to provide more practical industry training, and co-designing more appropriate training programs. They join together to sign many cooperation agreements that companies may allow students to stay more time at work stations during internship programs or business officers can come to have a class at universities. Other techniques include better human resource management plans, such as staff exchanges and getting to know the candidates thoroughly to make the best recruitment choice. Many companies have also recruited newly graduated students with corresponding specialisations for extra training in order to acquire further work-related expertise.

As the economy continues to grow and the unemployment rate is kept stable, training has shifted towards the directions associated with the market. Some universities and vocational colleges have made great efforts to innovate the curriculum, programs and training methods, and to strengthen the capacities of teaching staff and facilities, to improve the training quality and provide better preparation for students in terms of knowledge and skills, especially the skills for readiness to participate in the labor market, thus better meeting the requirements of employers. Nevertheless, the effectiveness of those strategies is limited due to a lack of strong and comprehensive solutions and particularly the changes in the national entrance examination. The Law on Career Education took effect from July 1, 2015, but to date has not been effectively implemented. Thus there still appear to be many qualifications which do not meet actual industry requirements, and many gaps in training methods and practice modes.

Summary and conclusion

Vietnam faced many challenges in its labour market, in which the unbalanced labour workforce lacks skilled workers is the main concern of Vietnamese authorities. Many Vietnamese firms and large FDI enterprises report that the current graduates do not meet their requirements and that there is always a shortage of the right skills of workers in labour market. The target of Vietnam authorities is to improve the quality of labour force to meet the higher requirements of the employers. From now to 2020, the Vietnamese labour market needs to build up an adequate labour force to meet the needs of industrialisation and international competition in the context of globalisation.

Overall, there are many consequences of these work-readiness challenges. The imbalance between supply and demand, and the status of both shortage and surplus of labor is increasingly serious. In addition, work productivity is low and the competitiveness of enterprises as well as of the nation is weak, increasing the risk of losses for Vietnam in the process of regional and global integration. This has impacts on the development of effective competition between countries, creating opportunities for foreign workers to enter Vietnam, thus making it difficult for Vietnam's internal resources to be promoted, and having long-term influences on the quality of human resources and economic development. Furthermore, the waste of human resources and increases in unemployment (actual unemployment, and 'disguised' unemployment due to doing jobs which are not associated with their trained specialisation) lead to other social consequences, such as poverty, inequality, crime and social evils. Vocational student graduates find it hard to get a job while enterprises are short of appropriately qualified, skilled employees. In addition, a costly re-training process often has to be undertaken by enterprises after recruitment.

Table 4.5 Summary of key findings

	Summary
Demographics/labour market	***Population:*** Vietnam's current population was 94.3 million in 2015 which is among top 15 in the World. The size of population increase currently 0.95 percent annually. ***Demographics:*** young population with more than 75 percent of labour participation rate, higher than world average of 63.5 percent. ***Demographic Challenge:*** total rate of labour who have participated in training institutions before work is still comparatively low (one-fifth of workforce). There are seemingly not enough higher education institutions to satisfy the need of market while the quality of their training is still inconsistent.
Economy	Growth rate was slowed down to 6.5 percent in the last 5 years due to macroeconomic turmoil and low labour productivity. Equitization programs and banking system restructuring are among the top priority of government efforts to drive the economy out of the middle-income trap.
Educational Structure/ Work-readiness challenges Work-readiness issues:	***Regulatory Framework:*** Several frameworks to boost up employability of Vietnamese workforce; however, the effectiveness of these policies is still uncertain. Both the Ministry of Education and Training and Mistry of Labour, Invalid and Social Affairs are involved in setting up a lot of strategies and policies to reduce work-readiness challenges, but there is a lack of coordination and consistency. ***VET Sector:*** the training quality has not met the businesses' requirements with regard to perception, social behavior, technical expertise, soft skills, foreign language, job skills and work attitude. Training programs mainly focus on theory, with a lack of practical knowledge. Teachers are not of corresponding quality. ***HE Sector:*** training curriculums are not appropriated to the skills required by industries. The unemployment rate of university graduates is highest in comparing with other workforce groups. ***Summary of Skill Mismatches/Shortages:*** The labour market in Vietnam is characterised by both candidates do not have appropriate skills (shortage of skills), and shortage of available candidates in a number of industries and occupations (shortage of skilled employees).

(*Continued*)

Table 4.5 (Continued)

	Summary
	Industry Links: Higher institutions were not welcome and initiative to cooperate with industries while employers tend to use low-skilled employees as cheap labour.
	Shortage of skills: Vietnamese young employees usually lack soft skills, including creative thinking, information technology, leadership and problem-solving
	Shortage of skilled employees: industries utilising modern technologies, and sectors under pressure from competition, such as the production of goods for export.
Policy Initiatives and recommended strategies for improved graduate work-readiness	*Government policy initiatives:* Setting up strategy for human resources development until 2020, law on vocational education, the prime minister's decision on building high-quality schools to approach regional and international level.
	Higher education institutions: innovate the contents, programs, training methods, strengthening teaching staff, facilities, to improve the training quality, better preparation for students in terms of knowledge, skills, especially the skills for readiness to participate in the labor market, better meeting the requirements of employers.
	Employers: more open to universities and colleges. Initiation of cooperation with HE and VET, open business environment for students and teachers to work with

References

General Statistics Office. 2014, *New letter Vietnam's labour market*, Vol. 25, quarter 4 of 2014.

General Statistics Office. 2015, *New letter Vietnam's labour market*, Vol. 24, quarter 4 of 2015.

General Statistics Office. 2016, *New letter Vietnam's labour market*, Vol. 9, quarter 1 of 2016.

Harvey, L. 2001, 'Defining and measuring employability', *Quality in Higher Education*, Vol. 7, no. 2, pp. 97–109.

ILSSA-Manpower. 2014, *Demand for work skills in the foreign invested sector*, Hanoi, ILSSA

Lam, N. B. 2013, *Solution to solve the problem of quality and quantity in Vietnamese Higher Education system*, Higher Education in Vietnam: Quality and Management, Vietnamese: Vietnamese Education Publishing House.

Morley, L. 2001, 'Producing new workers: Quality, equality and employability in higher education', *Quality in Higher Education*, Vol. 7, no. 2, pp. 131–138.

Thang, N. D. and Lan, N. H. 2013, 'Labour demand of enterprises and students' employabilities', *Journal of Economics and Development*, Vol. 197, no. 2, pp. 90–96.

Tran, T. T. 2013, 'The perception of employability and the subsequent role of higher education in Vietnam', *The Journal of the World University Forum*, Vol. 6, pp.1–11.

World Bank. 2012, *Putting higher education to work, skill and research for growth in East Asia, Regional Report*, Washington, DC, World Bank.

World Bank. 2014, *Vietnam development report – skilling up Vietnam: Preparing the workforce for a modern market economy*, Hanoi. Available at: http://vietnamnews.vn/society/275276/labour-market-set-for-stiff-competition.html.

5 Work-readiness in Malaysia

*Noorziah Mohd Salleh, Jude Emelifeonwu,
Jonathan Winterton and Kwok Mow Chan*

Introduction

This chapter discusses graduate work-readiness challenges in Malaysia in the light of government efforts to achieve developed nation status by 2020. The low level of work-readiness among Malaysian graduates, despite continued government initiatives to facilitate human resource development, is one of the major challenges. The key contributions to the Malaysian economy are from services, manufacturing, mining and quarrying, which in total accounted for more than 80 percent of the gross domestic product (GDP) of US$296.3 billion in 2015 and which is growing at an average annual rate of 5 percent (Department of Statistics Malaysia 2017; World Bank 2016). These sectors are also the main sources of employment for more than 83 percent of the labour force. It is more challenging that the current proportion of skilled human capital in Malaysia is at 28 percent, whereas 40 percent is required to achieve developed nation status. Malaysia enjoys political and economic stability, which has contributed to it becoming one of the top fifty economies in the world. The country appears to have adequate labour market conditions, economic infrastructure and educational systems to achieve developed nation status, so the problem of work-readiness is even more vexing.

Methodology

The methodology adopted in this study is investigative and qualitative underpinned by an interpretivist approach using content analysis on existing literature on employability (Piekkari et al. 2009). The researchers consequently interviewed and administered questionnaires to both management and employees of government agencies and educational institutions, as well as to officials of both service and manufacturing enterprises in Sabah, Penang, Sarawak and Kuala Lumpur (see table 5.1 Confidentiality guarantees preclude the possibility of naming specific companies and government ministries). The research also made use of documentary evidence, such as government reports to complement data obtained from interviews and questionnaires (Easterby-Smith et al. 2008; Scott 2006).

Table 5.1 Interview and Questionnaire distribution

	Sector	Number of respondents	
		Interviewed	*Questionnaires*
Date			
2016			
14th March	Government 1	5	5
12th April	Government 2	2	2
6th-19th April	Industry	4	4
6th-19th April	Higher and Vocational Institute	4	4
25th-29th June	Manufacturing	3	3
25th-29th June	Service	12	5

Sources: Compiled by authors

Furthermore, to validate information, the interviews and questionnaires used similar questions: some of these questions are listed below.

- Could you please describe the work-readiness challenges with Malaysian graduates?
- How do you help graduates solve work-readiness challenges?
- Do you have programmes to augment when there is a shortfall in some candidates who have technical skills but are not eloquent enough to express themselves in English?

The concluding section summarises the findings, which align with similar studies conducted by the World Bank (see the work-readiness and skills mismatch section).

The Malaysian labour market

Although Malaysia gained its independence from the United Kingdom 1957, the British influence on the country's form of parliamentary democracy is particularly evident (Singh and Singh 2008). The Malaysian economy has grown steadily since independence and remains resilient to external and internal business cycles. During the colonial era, there was a substantial influx of Chinese and Indian workers to augment the labour force, thus establishing two ethnic groups in the country in addition to the dominant *Bumiputera*, a collective term for the Malay descendants of Arab traders and the diverse indigenous peoples of the archipelago (World Bank 2016). With a population of 31 million (see table 5.2), an unemployment rate of 3.4 percent (see table 1.3) and a labour force participation

Table 5.2 Population of Malaysia (2015–2017)

Year	2017	2016	2015
Population	31,164,177	30,751,602	30,331,007
Median Age	28.9	28.9	29
Fertility	1.96	1.96	1.97
Urban Population	23,981,117	23,444,458	22,898,099

Source: www.worldometers.info/world-population/malaysia-population

rate of 67.6 percent (in 2016), Malaysia has the potential to grow further, albeit in a context of global economic uncertainties (Department of Statistics 2017).

According to the Malaysia Economic Monitor (World Bank 2017), the country's economic development has been founded on openness to trade, which is seen as an instrument for facilitating economic and social growth. Second, an export diversification plan increased the total exports of the country in 2014 through a new trade agreement, opening up market access for the export of goods and services. These efforts, particularly through Malaysia's involvement in the Trans-Pacific Partnership (TPP), were important for employment creation in the country. The World Bank (2016) predicted that TPP implementation could boost manufacturing output, requiring high skilled labour intensity, particularly in the machinery and electrical equipment sectors.

Average annual labour productivity growth between 2011 and 2015 was reported to be 1.8 percent (see table 1.4), whilst the 11th Malaysia Plan set an annual target of 3.7 percent. Thus, the country needs to double its productivity, and this requires an increase in skilled workers. Since the proportion of skilled workers remains relatively low, the workforce skills challenge facing government is quite overwhelming. According to the Malaysian Employers Federation, the government's actions to remedy the situation have shown a mixed result, with a gap between the plan and the actual results. A shortage of skilled workers has undoubtedly contributed to slow productivity growth and an over-reliance on documented unskilled foreign workers, reported to be of the order of 1.9 million workers, which is another major problem that the government must review (*Business News* 26 Nov 2016). The pressing need for more unskilled workers to meet industrial demand has led the government to allow increased numbers of foreign workers to enter from Bangladesh (*Nikkei Asian Review* 10 March 2016).

Previous studies of the Malaysian workforce have reported that graduates were lacking a range of key skills and attributes, including communication skills, problem solving, creativity, and an ability to take up challenges (Ooi 2017), which have possibly contributed to the highest unemployment rate of youth aged from 20 to 24 years. The main issue contributing to high unemployment among Malaysian youth was a lack of communication skills, particularly communicating in English language. Language skills are important to the main sectors but implementation plans to improve English proficiency among graduates have not been successful (*Business News*, 26 Nov 2016). Nevertheless, the government explicitly recognises the challenges of transforming Malaysia's labour force into employable or work-ready human capital: according to the same evidence, businesses in Malaysia need an increased proportion of highly skilled workers for automation processes in the manufacturing sector.

According to the Department of Statistic Malaysia (2017), the labour force participation rate (LFPR) was 67.9 percent and 67.7 percent in 2015 and 2016 respectively. Although the male LFPR dropped 0.4 percent, the percentage of men in the labour market exceeds the average national LFPR. The overall participation in the labour market was highest for age group 25 to 34 years old, for men, and exceeded 90 percent for those between 25 and 54 years old, while for women the LFPR was more than 55 percent for those aged between 25 and 54 years. The main sectors employing women were health, education and agriculture. Over fifteen years, male and female participation rates narrowed from an initial difference of 10 percentage points because of more women working (see table 5.4) (Cheong et al. 2015). A survey undertaken by the Malaysian Ministry of Women, Family and Community Development, in 50 corporate sectors listed under Kuala Lumpur Stock Exchange between 2001 and 2003, found that 22.4 percent of decision makers were female (Ministry of Women, Family and Community Development Malaysia 2001–2003).

Due to the effects of globalisation, the Malaysian labour market requires a more flexible workforce (Yet-Mee et al. 2016) with advanced technical skills as well as well-developed generic skills of creative thinking, problem solving and

Table 5.3 Comparative data of Malaysia and youth unemployment rate

Years	Malaysia unemployment %	Youth unemployment %
2000	2.8	8.5
2001	3.7	10.5
2002	3.8	10.6
2003	3.6	1
2004	3	10.8
2005	3.6	10.9
2006	3.5	10.3
2007	3.2	10.7
2008	3.3	10.6
2009	3.7	11.6
2010	3.5	11
2011	3.1	10
2012	3	10.2
2013	3.1	10.6
2014	2.85	6.7
2015	3.2	
April 2016	3.4	

Sources: CIA World Factbook and Department of Statistics Malaysia and http://data.world bank.org/indicator/SL.UEM.1524.ZS?locations=MY.

Table 5.4 Comparative data of Malaysia male and female labour force participation
ratio

Year	Male	Female
	%	%
2000	57.4	44.6
2001	57.3	44.5
2002	54.3	44.4
2003	53.3	44.4
2004	53.3	44.4
2005	52.2	44.3
2006	51.1	44.3
2007	50	44.3
2008	48.9	44.3
2009	47.7	44.2
2010	47.4	44.1
2011	47.4	44.3
2012	47.6	44.3
2013	47.7	44.4
2014	47.8	44.5

Sources: Http://www.theglobaleconomy.com/Malaysia/Female_labor_force_participation/

Sources: CIA World Factbook and Department of Statistics Malaysia and http://data.world
bank.org/indicator/SL.UEM.1524.ZS?locations=MY.

analytical skills (Singh and Singh 2008) to support economic growth. The Malaysian 11th Plan (2016–2020) provides the necessary infrastructure to attract trade investment and further improve industrial growth. Although Malaysia is politically and economically stable to achieve its main aim to be a developed country, youth work-readiness is a limiting factor. As already noted, Malaysia requires 40 percent of skilled workers, whereas currently the proportion is only 28 percent. As such, there is an urgent need for strategies to increase the level of work-readiness in Malaysia.

Work-readiness and skill mismatch

The World Bank (2016) argued that in order to improve the work-readiness of Malaysian youth, it was necessary to explore the matrix of skill mismatches and to survey the gaps between industry expectations and the outcomes of tertiary education institutions. Working with Talent Corp, a Malaysian government initiative aimed at addressing skill mismatches, the World Bank undertook a graduate work-readiness assessment in 2014. The purpose of the survey was to examine employers' perceptions of the quality of Malaysian graduates, as well as to evaluate the effectiveness of job/vocational services in universities and government-financed graduate work-readiness initiatives. The World Bank had conducted a similar survey in 2011, which concluded that one of the reasons for the high graduate unemployment rate in Malaysia was the employers' reluctance to offer remuneration meeting the expectations of fresh graduates to attract the requisite talent. The World Bank reported that employers felt graduates were demanding unrealistic wages, particularly given the high level of mismatch between the skills graduates possessed and those that employers expected. Increasingly, and possibly because *Bahasa Melayu* replaced English as the language of instruction in schools in 1978, a staggering 81 percent of respondents claimed that fresh graduates in Malaysia lack the ability to communicate effectively, think critically or have problem-solving abilities (World Bank 2016). The situation is further compounded by the cultural challenge of a high power-distance index (Hofstede 1991) associated with an imbalance of power between the providers of knowledge, in this case a conservative educational system, especially in government schools, and students, who must not question the teachers. This cultural challenge also hinders critical thinking and other attributes necessary for developing soft skills among Malaysia graduates in the service industry, especially when graduates need to interface with their counterparts and consumers from other parts of the world (Franck 2012; Nikitina and Furouko 2012).

Yet-Mee et al. (2016) similarly argued that poor communication skills amongst accounting graduates in Malaysia is one of the major causes of graduate unemployment. Employers are looking for three sets of attributes: values; personality; and competencies, which are reportedly grossly deficient in Malaysian graduates (Cheong et al. 2015; Franck 2012). The World Bank asserts such skills mismatches are the primary cause of unemployment, a lacuna that post-secondary educational institutions, and especially those under government control, have failed to fill to keep pace with industry demands (Ismail et al. 2011). Nikitina and Furouko (2012) commented that teaching methods in some public universities were too conservative and rigid, and in extreme cases, universities were enrolling students in courses with no job prospects. In such a context, it is not surprising that Malaysian employers overwhelmingly concur that the curricula and quality of local university education, supplied with intake by a feeble primary and secondary education system, fails to prepare students sufficiently for the labour market and does not produce graduates with the requisite soft skills (Hanapi and Nordin 2014). It is perhaps for this reason that Malaysia is heavily dependent on foreign workers in the oil and gas, manufacturing and service sectors, which employed an estimated 3.6 million foreign workers in 2008. Of course, these foreigners include contingent workers in the so-called '3D' (dirty, difficult and dangerous) jobs. According to Deputy Prime Minister Ahmad Zahid Hamidi, the Malaysian Government would bring in 1.5 million foreign workers from Bangladesh to work in Malaysia over a period of three years (Nikitina and Furouko 2012) because they are willing to fill 3D vacancies in construction, automotive maintenance, cleaning services and other similar occupations (see table 5.5).

Malaysian economic growth dropped from 5 percent in 2015 to 4.2 percent in 2016, resulting in reduced job opportunities in the labour market. The demand for professional jobs only represented 10 percent, and a higher percentage of demand was from elementary jobs (see table 1.5). As result, the government

Table 5.5 Vacancies and Placements in Malaysia

No of vacancies by Year	2011 2,259548	2012 1,619473	2013 1,402,690	2014 1,074018	2015 763,883 occupational category	Percent
Managers	23,225	28,777	8,228	6,515	19,687	0.6
Professionals	228,046	44,900	32,830	30,233	22,694	2.8
*Technicians	41,167	34,831	23,948	21,844	10,198	2.0
Clerical support workers	31,758	18,919	15,767	14,152	45,064	1.5
Service and sales workers	115,892	112,793	97,827	83,825	200,839	9.1
*Skilled agricultural	166,757	134,880	228,923	12,355	8,308	1.2
*Craft	82,253	46,850	41,659	25,343	18,632	2.4
Plant and machine	164,036	140,827	124,826	121,260	67,849	1.3
Elementary occupation	1,309,161	1,040,758	1,016,564	742,874	518,538	69.2

Source: Malaysia Ministry of Human Resources (2015)

*Technician and associated professionals
Skilled agricultural, forestry and fishery workers
Plant and machine operators and assemblers
Craft and related trade workers

announced the intention to bring in 1.5 million unskilled Bangladeshi workers to work in elementary occupations (*Asian Review*, 10 March 2016). According to the Malaysian Standard Classification of Occupations (MASCO 2008), these elementary occupations consist of dirty, difficult and dangerous jobs, and most Malaysian graduates are not inclined to do such jobs. Graduates are over-qualified for filling available jobs, so there is increased demand for unskilled foreign workers (*Asian Review*, 10 March 2016). To illustrate, table 1.5 shows that the highest number of available vacancies were in the elementary category in 2015. Jobs were available, but there was a qualitative mismatch between available jobs and job seekers, with no less than 43,215 vacancies reported in elementary occupations in 2015 (Malaysia: vacancies by state and occupational category 2015).

Malaysian government efforts at minimizing mismatch in the labour market

The government has been implementing various plans to address skill mismatches in the labour market, establishing between 2011 and 2015 during the implementation of the 10th Malaysian Plan, a committee known as the Industry Skills Committee (ISC) to monitor the needs of industry and provide insights to Higher Education Institutions (HEIs) and other training institutions. Major companies were encouraged to participate, with some benefits in the form of tax deductions. Other bodies with similar functions also established include the Industry Centres of Excellence (ICoEs) and Academia Industry Graduate Development Centres (AIGDCs). The sectors mainly targeted were automotive, biotechnology and health services. The government also planned to create a Critical Skills Committee (CSC) led by Talent Corporation and the Institute of Labour Market Information and Analysis (ILMIA), with the main role of identifying specific relevant skills needed and developing measures to improve graduate employability, especially in science-related programmes.

In 2009, the government established a Graduate Employability Management Scheme (GEMS) to prepare unemployed graduates with marketable skills that would increase their chances of obtaining employment. Talent Corp has successfully articulated its agenda to enhance 'graduate employability', promote 'talent diversity' and attract talented Malaysians working overseas to return home and help actualise the 2020 vision. Talent Corp's Structured Internship Programme, which offers tax credits to employers to recruit Malaysian university students as part-time interns, has apparently been well received (Talent Corporation Malaysia Berhad 2015). Other industry-linked programmes include the MyProCert programme involving companies such as Huawei and Oracle to offer discounted certification programmes to companies wanting to increase the skill level of their employees. Most recently, MDeC announced the Knowledge Workers Development Centre, a RM27.4 million ($8.8 million) facility in Cyberjaya that will host training facilities for companies including Huawei IBM, and Agilent Technologies. Increasingly, universities are offering '2+2' courses, whereby students study for two years followed by two years of practical training, in an effort to bridge

the gap between education and the workplace. The government has also introduced the CEO Faculty Programme, inviting senior executives from the private
sector to speak at public universities. Companies participating in this programme
include 22 companies such as Samsung, Shell and Air Asia (Jusoh 2016).

As mentioned earlier, it is pertinent to note an increased female LMPR from
47.2 percent in 2000 to 55.0 percent in 2016 (Department of Statistics Malaysia 2017). This suggests that government initiatives to increase the LMPR of
women has had a positive effect through strengthening the platform for up-
skilling women, increasing their access to entrepreneurial activities and providing childcare facilities in the workplace. The government also encouraged the
involvement of private companies since 2011, so more than 19,000 graduates
received training and were placed in companies, including Malaysia Airlines
(MAS), Permodalan Nasional Berhad (PNB), Gamuda Group Bhd, Sime Darby
Bhd (Sime Darby), Celcom Axiata Bhd (Celcom) and Malaysia Airports Hold-
ings Bhd (*Malaymailonline* 2015).

Minister in the Prime Minister's Department Datuk Seri Abdul Wahid Omar
reported that the government had launched several programmes to increase jobs
such as Jobs Malaysia and the 1Malaysia Training Scheme (*Malaymailonline*
2015). Other innovative programmes initiated by the government to enhance
graduates' skills include Development Skill Training Centre (DSTC), E-Jobseek-
ers Portal, SL1M (Training scheme 1 Malaysia), ICT Skills, Human Development camp, Mind transformation Boot camp, National Talent Enhancement
Programme (NTEP), Sabah Skills Technology Centre (SSTC) and Soft Skill
Training Centre.

Malaysian education system

The Malaysian education system reflects the three major constituencies of the
population: *Bumiputera* (67.4 percent); Chinese (24.4 percent); Indian (7.3 percent); and others (0.7 percent) (Musa 2003). The language of instruction in
primary schools is either Malay (*Bahasa Melayu*), Chinese or Indian, whilst the
lingua franca in HEIs and tertiary education is English, Malay or both in some
cases (Musa 2003). The Department of Education is responsible for monitoring
the progress of higher and primary education and the academic year runs from
January to November (Minghat and Yasin 2010).

General primary and secondary education

Only primary school education is compulsory in Malaysia, where multi-lingual
public schools, private schools and home educators co-exist (Musa 2003). Following unregulated pre-school education, a child enters primary school at age 7
for a period of 6 years, and after schooling in the community language of their
choice, students must sit the primary school achievement test to qualify for further study. The test results determine the next schooling choice, which includes
boarding schools, religious schools or regular secondary schools. Students with

good grades have better potential to be accepted in a good school, which mainly specialise in the science stream (Musa 2003).

Secondary education entails two phases (see table 5.6). The first phase takes three years to complete and at the end of the third year, students have to sit for *Pentaksiran Tingkatan 3 (PT3)* or Lower Secondary Evaluation. Depending on PT3 results, students must then choose from three streams: Academic Stream (Science/Art); Technical and Vocational Stream; and Religious Stream (Musa 2003). The Malaysian education system follows 6–3–2 structure, six years in primary school, three years in lower secondary level and two years in upper secondary level. Thereafter, they enter either arts or the science stream according to personal choice and teacher advice for another 2 years. The advice given based on the students' upper level public examination known as *Sijil Pelajaran Malaysia (SPM)* [Malaysia Certificate of Education] in the eleventh year of school. The results determine whether the students enter post-secondary education, matriculation or Sixth Form. Once in a particular stream, switching opportunities are limited. For Sixth Form students, they will sit an examination called Sijil Tinggi Pelajaran Malaysia (STPM) [Malaysian Higher School Certificate] at the end of the second year. This certificate is usually required for entry to local public universities for undergraduate courses.

The Malaysian Government recognises the necessity of a workforce with qualifications in science, technology, engineering and mathematics (STEM) as well as

Table 5.6 The Major Group of the MASCO 08 can be categorised according to the following four common skill levels

Skill Level	Educational Level	Major Groups
4th	Tertiary education leading to a university or postgraduate university degree; Malaysian Skills Advance Diploma (DLKM) Level 5–8	Professionals
3rd	Tertiary education leading to a University postgraduate university degree; Malaysian Skills Advanced Diploma (DLKM) Level 4	*Tech & Assoc Professionals
2nd	Secondary or post-secondary education; Malaysian Skills Certificate (SKM) Level 1–3	Clerical Support Workers Service and sales workers Skilled agricultural, forestry and fishery workers Craft and related trade workers Plant and machine operators.
1st	Primary Education	Elementary occupation

Source: Jobsmalaysia.gov.my Resources (2008)

*Technician and associated professionals

arts and commerce fields. At secondary school, STEM students represented only 90,000 of the 500,000 students sitting for SPM in 2015, well below the targeted 270,000. Although educational attainment has improved, the workforce qualified in STEM fields was only 3 percent, which is still very low compared to other industrialised countries like Japan, the United States, Germany and Singapore that have about 30 percent of their workforce with STEM qualifications (Zulaikha 2016). Government-directed efforts at encouraging secondary students to enrol in STEM fields to respond to the needs of higher demand for skilled workers in these fields. The stereotypical Malaysian students' thinking that art and teaching are fields suitable for women and that science and technology are suitable for men consequently led to female students choosing art and educational courses (Kamogawa 2003), which also explains higher female participation in the sectors mentioned above. *Bahasa Melayu* was the language of instruction in public schools and is a compulsory subject for primary and secondary school since independence in 1957. Eventually the Malay language became the main language, and English became a second language. The Malaysian Education Department changed the language used for mathematics and science to Malay in 2003 but reverted to English as the language of instruction in STEM subjects in 2009. This flip-flop possibly explains both the low proportion of skilled workers in STEM fields and the low level of English language proficiency. Controversy continues to surround heavily subsidised Malaysian tertiary education because of tight quotas that protect the majority ethnic group. Nevertheless, there has been some progress in the direction of greater meritocracy, and disadvantaged students have the opportunity of enrolling at private or foreign branch universities.

Vocational education and training

Until the study by Loose et al. (2008), vocational education and training (VET) in Malaysia was not well documented. In the 1890s, trade skills training began in Malaysia with the establishment of vocational schools to prepare Malaysian youth to work as mechanics and fitters in the railway sector (Francis Wong and Ee 1975). In 1902, the then British colonial government established a teacher technical school to train technicians for the railways (Maznah 2001). In 1926, a federal trade school was opened in Kuala Lumpur, whilst in 1945 the former technical school was renamed a Technical College, then elevated to university status in 1972 as 'Universiti Teknologi Malaysia' (UTM). Prior to that development, in 1956, the government published a report directed at improving work-readiness in Malaysia, usually referred to as the Rasaq Report.

The Rasaq Report advocated a tripartite approach through which Malaysian youth could become employable, comprising technical colleges; technical institutes; and trade schools. In 1960, the Rahman Talib Report endorsed more alterations, such as the integration of the prescribed secondary school structure into academic and vocational streams (Ministry of Education 2007). The report recommended that trade schools change to secondary trade schools, and these were subsequently converted to secondary vocational schools (SVSs). The cabinet report of 1979 established that the secondary school scheme should comprise both academic and vocational streams (MOE 2007).

The Cabinet Report established the following:

- **Technical Colleges**: Establishments of post-secondary education to deliver full time courses for those who had finished a full 5 years of secondary schooling.
- **Technical Institutes**: Institutes of post-junior secondary education to offer courses of 3 years' duration for persons who had finished 3 years of secondary education and who pursue technician occupations.
- **Trade Schools**: Colleges, particularly those in rural areas, to offer course of 2 years' duration to persons who have completed primary schooling: courses should be associated to the environment of the school and the requirements of service, and generally conducted in the Malay language.

The Malaysia VET system was designed along the lines of higher education; technical and vocational education; and skills training (Minghat and Yasin 2010). Furthermore, Blumenstein et al. (1999) identified three sub-systems in the Malaysian educational system. The first sub-system related to technical and vocational training undertaken by the Ministry of Education. The second subsystem is the training undertaken by other Federal Ministries besides the Ministry of Education as well as private training centres. The third subsystem culminates in the award of a certificate of occupational skills extrapolated from the National Occupational Skill Standards and Certification System. It began with a 3-tier expertise accreditation classification (elementary, intermediate and advanced) and later on expanded into a 5-tier skill criterion in 1992.

In evaluating the locus of Technical Education and Skills Training (TEST) in Malaysia, research undertaken by Australian experts through the Asian Development Bank technical support venture, established that vocational education under the supervision of Ministry of Education Malaysia was one key factor in the Malaysian public sector VET system.

The Department of Skills Development oversees the establishment and operation of all public and private vocational education and training (VET) institutions. Almost 1,000 standards for certificate, diploma and advanced diploma training were developed, and the department is rolling more out in some 20 identified key areas (Minghat and Yasin 2010).

Graduates' work-readiness challenges

This section discusses the challenges of work-readiness faced by the Malaysian government, employers and educational institutions. As discussed in the previous section of this chapter, the main challenges faced are that graduates lack the required skills that match the requirements of employers; and educational institutions produce graduates who lack practical capabilities and merely possess theoretical skills. Based on common themes of work-readiness identified by Nankervis et al. (2017), our research found that the skills employers say as lacking are mostly personal characteristics (attitude, communication skills, critical thinking skills and problem solving skills); technology (technical skills); and other attributes, particularly the capability of multi-tasking ability and having a 'strong-willed' character.

Stakeholders also face work-readiness challenges due to graduates' behaviours according to respondents from participating manufacturing companies. The manufacturing employers specifically mentioned that engineering graduates emphasised the salary being offered and did not take up challenges to gain experience. Many engineering graduates were apparently unable to perform technical-related jobs, so the companies provided on-the-job training. Trained engineers, however, also tend to move to other employers that offer a better remuneration package. A Japanese-owned manufacturing company reported a similar situation. Companies are losing workers after initial training to other, usually larger, companies. Employers complain of being the ones who develop workers' new skills, only to see them poached by other companies, who succeed in attracting them with a minimal increment in salary. Therefore, with high turnover among local graduates, companies resort to employing either low-skilled workers or foreign workers (or those who fall in both categories).

For tourism industries, participating employers gave similar responses; employers reported that graduates' behaviour was the main problem to achieving a high level of work-readiness. They similarly reported that graduates were not keen to receive salary below their expectations, despite being unable to take up challenges of learning skills or cope with hardship at workplaces.

Educational institutions appear to have implemented plans to meet employers' requirements through regularly revising syllabi and curricula. The educational institutions mentioned that students focused on their academic studies and made insufficient effort to undertake practical training. HEIs report that collaboration with industry is still weak, leaving students without the opportunity to develop the skills employers say they want. Educational institutions struggle to find sufficient internships, noting that companies only tend to approach them when they need workers, so the focus is on short-term needs rather than long-term human capital development. In Sabah especially, limitations in both the quality and quantity of internship placements for industrial training has further disadvantaged graduates. Socio-economic factors also appear to play a part, with graduates preferring unemployment to accepting a low salary, and reluctant to leave their comfort zone. Graduates' attitudes, knowledge application skills and communication skills are still major challenges with which the key stakeholders need to contend.

Vocational institutions, by contrast, typically focus on hands-on training, which involves trainees having internships or serving an apprenticeship with a company. The vocational institutions that participated in this research reported industrial linkages with multinational corporations such as BMW, Samsung and an electrical supply provider company. Trainees, however, when sent for practical training overseas, experienced culture shock and problems in adjusting and so often returned home before their training period had ended. A high-ranking officer in a government human resource department commented on Malaysian graduates' qualifications, saying he would look at the graduates' personalities rather than their grades, emphasizing that relevant survival skills were the most important area to look at when they enter employment. Other respondents from government agencies made similar comments in interviews, mentioning that graduates were lacking good communication skills, which hinders their ability to perform at workplaces, leading to low self-confidence and an inability to obtain employment. Government respondents all mentioned up-skilling opportunities given to graduates, including communication, technical and personal development programmes.

In terms of career prospects and remuneration, employers generally offer unattractive remuneration and benefits packages, especially during the early stages of career in the manufacturing sector. Moreover, in the current context, budgetary constraints mean that companies are often less willing to invest in training, and this makes it more difficult to train graduates effectively. On the other hand, fresh graduates usually demand unrealistic remuneration, so employers prefer to hire unskilled workers, who are willing to accept a less-generous compensation package. With limited job availability, some graduates are willing to accept any job openings, accepting positions that do not match their qualifications, which mean either they need more training or that they are overqualified for their jobs (or both). Table 6.6 shows that many of the available jobs are categorised as 3D jobs. Graduates are not willing to take up these 3D jobs, a situation exacerbated by parental expectations concerning the potential careers of their children. The dissatisfaction of parents having children in 3D jobs is one of the reasons graduates prefer to be unemployed than to demonstrate they are failing to fulfil their parents' aspirations. Graduates from rural areas are also quite unwilling to move from their hometowns, and most jobs are in urban conurbations.

Based on the cases presented above, graduates' behaviour is the main work-readiness challenge faced by the stakeholders. Employers usually provide further training for graduates lacking the requisite skills. The graduates need to be strong-willed and have a positive attitude to obtain employment and prepare to be work ready. Workplaces are continuing to evolve, and this too will affect work-readiness, employment prospects and future working lives. Government and educational institutions have taken many different approaches to overcome the problems faced by graduates and industry.

This section recommends some practical steps to respond to the work-readiness challenges discussed in this study. Key skills gaps identified amongst Malaysian graduates include the lack of communication skills, problem solving skills, creativity and good personality traits.

A key focus to respond to work-readiness challenges is on strengthening the country's educational institutions, recognising that education is a key component in the future growth of Malaysia's human capital. The education sector should continue its aim to develop the entire value chain, from early childcare and education (ECCE), through basic primary and secondary education, technical education and vocational training (TEVT). The sector could organise more programs that would directly improve graduates' work-readiness and employability, making them more 'marketable' and ready to face the labour market. A few educational institutions have been organising various programmes, such as the career expo placement seminar mentioned above and clinics to prepare graduates to be more work ready. High priority should be given to elements such as interpersonal skills, communication skills, leadership and team building in developing graduates' work-readiness.

Programmes need to be managed to ensure that graduates get the benefits from such training. One HEI officer mentioned that programmes to develop students' capabilities are limited due to tight class schedules, resulting in students often being unable to participate in the programmes. The aims of the programmes should be on employability skills and not merely academic knowledge. Institutions need to be flexible when organising any programmes or activities, taking into account students' already busy timetables to maximise their availability to participate. Organizing such programmes during semester break or weekends would resolve such difficulties. Clearly, institutions should organise programmes to help graduates access job opportunities before they finish their course of study. Motivational sessions with alumni and encouraging them to draw on alumni networks should be emphasised. Academic curricula should include creative and innovative elements to build those skills that employers demand. Educational institutions should consider providing graduates with a period of practical training in a particular industry to expose them to the working environment; such collaboration with industries would also help students get jobs. Although collaboration with industry is not always easy, the government should create awareness of the positive outcome resulting from their participation. Continuous collaboration with industry enables adequate training placements for students. This would not only improve graduates' work-readiness but could also give students preferential access to job openings.

There is a need for continuous monitoring of the 'employability skills' demanded by employers. The government could create a strategic industrial board for each state in Malaysia, enabling parents and students to have comprehensive information about industry needs, the types and numbers of vacancies, types of employers and the working environment, which would improve the acceptance level among parents. Similarly, Toast Masters clubs involve members from industry who actively encourage students at schools to participate, enabling them to develop competence in speaking skills and building their confidence.

Conclusion

The success of multinational corporations (MNCs) in the service industry (hotels, global business centres and accounting firms) hinges on their ability to attract and retain high-quality human capital (Philips and Phillips 2015). The World Bank (2015) argued that it was necessary to explore the matrix of skills mismatches and to survey the gaps between industry expectations and the outcomes of tertiary educational organizations. Our research suggests that Malaysian graduates are not adequately equipped with 'soft skills', especially in the service industry. This notion was further asserted by Lim et al. (2016), who also argued that the lack of communication skills amongst accounting graduates in Malaysia is one of the major reasons Malaysian graduates are not work ready for the service industry. Employers are looking for three sets of attributes: values, personality and competencies, which are reportedly grossly deficient in Malaysian graduates (Cheong et al. 2015). The World Bank asserts that such skills mismatches are the primary cause of unemployment. Shah (2008) makes the important point that teaching methods in some public universities were too conservative and rigid.

Findings

The overwhelming results emanating from the interviews conducted and questionnaires distributed indicate that Malaysian employers believe that a large proportion of Malaysian graduates lack the soft skills necessary to compete, particularly in the service industry. This skills gap includes critical thinking, interpersonal skills accentuated by lack of expression evident also in lack of self-confidence. The power distance syndrome in Asia (Hofstede 1991) further compounds this as it affects the personality of Malaysian graduates. Graduates intending to work in the service industry should be capable of engaging and interacting with customers of diverse racial backgrounds or colleagues around the world. The Malaysian graduates' inability to articulate their thoughts has hindered them from securing middle management positions in the service industry. Employers further argued that when you find a Malaysian graduate who has the necessary soft skills mentioned above they most likely studied abroad and are demanding for unrealistic wages.

A summary of the findings as are follows:

- Language, where competency in spoken English was especially poor amongst most, although not all, local university graduates.
- Spoon feeding and not taking initiatives (inflexible and lacking adaptability).
- Strong parental protection, breeding over-dependence for instruction.
- Negative perceptions from parents on the hospitality industry, especially amongst the Chinese.
- High salary expectations.

Table 5.7 Summary of findings, Malaysia

	Summary – Malaysia
Demographics/labour market	**Population:** 31.7 million citizens and permanent residents. Labour force of 14.2 million of which 3.6 million foreigners are mainly involved in the 3D jobs of dirty, dangerous and difficult. These foreign workers are mainly involved in the oil and gas industry as well as service industries Unemployment rate 3.5 percent. *Demographics:* Malaysia has a median age of 28.9 years old, which reflects a workforce that is young, if trained can sustain its economic growth adequately. Its total Fertility Rate is 1.96. *Demographic Challenge:* Malaysia is still relatively dependent on foreign workers. It employs foreign workers in the oil and gas industry as well as both service and manufacturing sectors. *Economic Growth:* Malaysia's economy has an average growth rate of 4.73 percent from 2000 to 2016, with its highest rate of 10.30 percent in 2010. Malaysia's per capita income was USD $26,300 in 2015.
Economy	*Labour Market Challenge.* Malaysian real wage growth improved from MYR 2231 per month in 2014 to MYR2312 per month in 2015, but recorded a low of 1814.00 MYR/Monthly in 2011.
Educational Structure/ Work-readiness frameworks	The Malaysian educational system has resulted in low levels of educational attainment (World Bank, 2013). For example, 37.2 percent completed upper secondary school, and 15.3 percent of 25- to 29-year-olds in 2012 completed a bachelor's degree. Malaysia between 1990 and 1995 sponsored and sent 20 percent (100,000) of all Malaysian students abroad, mainly to the US and the UK, to study and this cost an estimated US$800 million annually. After the Asian financial crisis 1997, the number of students sponsored by the Malaysian government dropped by 20 percent, thus in 2010 about 80,000 Malaysians studied internationally (World Bank, 2013). The educational system in Malaysia replicates the major ethnic groupings which are distributed as follows: Malays also known as Bumiputera (67.4 percent); Chinese (24.4 percent); Indians (7.3 percent); and others (0.7 percent). Bahasa Malay, Chinese and Indian languages are the mediums used in schools depending on the location. On the other hand, English or Malay (or both) are the languages of instruction at secondary and tertiary educational levels.

Primary school education is compulsory in Malaysia, and the medium for teaching could be in Malay, Chinese or Indian, dependent on the choice of the parent. Primary schools in Malaysia are either private or publicly owned and children enter primary school at the age of 7 for a period of 6 years. Worthy of mention is that home learning is also available, and if a child wants to progress into secondary school, they must sit for a qualifying test to advance to secondary school.

Post-primary education is divided into two stages. The lower level takes 3 years to complete, after which the student sits for an exam called *Pentaksiran Tingkatan 3 (PT3)*. Based on PT3 results, 3 strands are available for the student to choose from, namely Academic Strand (Science/Art), Technical and Vocational Strand and last, the Religious Strand. Fundamentally, education in Malaysia takes on the 6–3–2 arrangement; primary school runs for 6 years, lower secondary level runs for 3 years, and 2 years are spent in the upper level. Subsequently, the student can enter either the arts or the science strand, allowing them to make a personal choice or taking on board the tutor's advice, to spend an extra 2 years before taking the public examination known as *SijilPelajaran Malaysia (SPM)*/ Malaysia Certificate of Education in the 11th year of school. The results obtained determine whether the candidates will progress to tertiary education or 6th form education. For the 6th-form students, they sit an examination called Sijil Tinggi Pelajaran Malaysia (STPM)/Malaysian Higher School Certificate at the end of the second year. These certificates (SPM and STPM) are typically the criteria to gain admission into public local universities or for undergraduate courses.

The VET system is broken down as follows

Technical Colleges: Setting up of post-secondary education to deliver full-time courses for those who have finished a full 5 years of secondary schooling.

Technical Institutes: Three-year courses are offered to students who have finished lower secondary education and when the student want to pursue technician jobs.

Trade Schools: Colleges especially in the rural areas provide courses for a 2-year period to students who have finished primary education: Usually these courses are taught in the Malay language.

The World bank identified that there are 5 strands of the VET system

• Communal advanced education system, which frequently educates students who do not participate in pre-university scholarships.

• Malaysian Skills Qualifications framework, 5 structured expertise qualifications centred on the National Occupational Skills Standards (NOSS) which was introduced by the National Vocational Training Council in 1993.

(Continued)

Table 5.7 (Continued)

	Summary – Malaysia
	• Company-based training conducted through the company's training school. • Private higher education, mainly under the supervision of the Private Higher Education Institutions Act 1996, and recognised by the National Accreditation Board. • Continuing education and training which addresses the demands of businesses and the public at large for additional teaching, proficiency progression, re-skilling and professional development.
Government initiatives and reforms	The Malaysian government has declared its intention to put in place a new strategy in order to manage skills gap in the labour market with the institution of the Critical Skills Committee (CSC) jointly led by the Institute of Labour Market information (ILMIA) and Talent Corporation and Analysis. CSC will help the Industry Skill Committee (ISC) and the National Human Capital Development Council (NHCDC) in recognising where skills gaps exist and important strategies are necessary to correct skill lacunas and thus to improve work-readiness in Malaysia. Nevertheless, the government encourages companies to provide up-skilling and multi-skilling programmes for their existing employees in order to meet demands for advanced skills as identified by industry leaders.

References

Blumenstein, G., Borgel, H., Greinert, W., Grunwald, E., Jarck, K., and Kaloo, U. 1999, *Basic study on the design of a dual vocational training scheme in Malaysia.* GTZ, Kuala Lumpur.

Cheong, K., Hill, C., Fernandez-Chung, R. and Leong, Y. 2015, 'Employing the "unemployable": Employer perceptions of Malaysian graduates', *Studies in Higher Education*, Vol. 41, no. 12, pp. 2253–2270.

Department of Statistics Malaysia Official Portal. 2017, *Key indicators*, viewed March 27, 2017. Available at: www.dosm.gov.my/v1/.

Easterby-Smith, M., Thorpe, R. and Jackson, P. 2008, *Management research*, 3rd edition, London: Sage.

Franck, A. K. 2012, Factors motivating women's informal micro-entrepreneurship: Experiences from Penang, Malaysia. *International Journal of Gender and Entrepreneurship*, Vol. 4, no. 1, pp. 65–78.

Hanapi, Z. and Nordin, M. 2014, 'Unemployment among Malaysia graduates: Graduates' attributes, lecturers' competency and quality of education', *Procedia – Social and Behavioral Sciences*, Vol. 112, pp. 1056–1063.

Hofstede, G. 1991, *Cultures and organizations: Software of the mind*, London: McGraw-Hill.

Ismail, R., Yussof, I. and Sieng, L. W. 2011, Employers' perceptions on graduates in Malaysian services sector. *International Business Management*, Vol. 5, no. 3, pp. 184–193.

Jusoh, I. 2016, *A vision to succeed*, viewed October 24, 2016. Available at: www.the-businessyear.com/malaysia-2016/the-vision-to-succeed/vip-interview.

Kamogawa, A. 2003, 'Higher education reform: Challenges towards a knowledge society in Malaysia', *African and Asian Studies*, Vol. 2, no. 4, pp. 545–563.

Lim, Y.M., Lee, T.H., Yap, C.S. and Ling, C.C. 2016, Employability skills, personal qualities, and early employment problems of entry-level auditors: perspectives from employers, lecturers, auditors, and students, *Journal of Education for Business*, Vol. 91, no. 4, pp. 185–192.

Loose, G., Spöttl, G. and Sahir, Y. Md. (eds.) (2008), *'Re-engineering' dual training – the Malaysian experience*, Frankfurt: BIBB.

Malay Mail Online. 2015, *Graduates among 400,000 currently unemployed in Malaysia, says minister*, viewed March 27, 2017. Available at: www.themalaymailonline.com/malaysia/article/graduates-among-400000-currently-unemployed-in-malaysia-says-minister.

MASCO 2008, Malaysia Standard Classification of Occupation (MASCO). Ministry of Human Resources, Putrajaya, viewed Septemeber 18, 2017. Available at: http://static.jobsmalaysia.gov.my/html/jobsm/masco/en/MASCO_BI_master.pdf.

Maznah M. 2001, *Adult and continuing education in Malaysia*, UNESCO Institute for Education /Universiti Putra Malaysia Press, Kuala Lumpur.

Minghat, A. D. & Yasin, R. M. 2010, Sustainable framework for technical and vocational education in Malaysia. *Procedia – Social and Behavioral Sciences*, Vol. 9, pp. 1233–1237.

Ministry of Education (MoE). 2008, Malaysia Education for All Mid-Decade Assessment Report 2000–2007. Ministry of Education, Kuala Lumpur.

Ministry of Human Resources. 2015, *Malaysia: Vacancies by state and occupational category 1st edition*, view 2017 March 27. Available at: www.mohr.gov.my/pdf/LMR2016/lab_feb2016/tab09_dec2015.pdf.

Musa, B. 2003, *An education system worthy of Malaysia*, New York, NY: Universe.

Nankervis, A., Verma, P., and Cameron, R. 2017, 'Literature analysis of job readiness: Challenges and solutions', in Cameron, R., Dhakal, S. and Burgess, J. (eds.) *Transitions from education to work: Workforce ready challenges in the Asia Pacific*, Chapter 2, London: Routledge.

Nikitina, L. and Furuoka, F. 2012, Sharp focus on soft skills: a case study of Malaysian university students' educational expectations. *Educational Research for Policy and Practice*, Vol. 11, no. 3, pp. 207–224.

Ooi, K. B. and Ting, S. H. 2015, Work experience and polytechnic students' expectations of working life. *Advanced Journal of Technical and Vocational Education*, Vol. 1, no. 2, pp. 1–8.

Phillips, J. and Phillips, P. 2015, *High-impact human capital strategy: Addressing the 12 major challenges todays organizations face*, New York, NY, American Management Association.

Piekkari, R., Welch, C. and Paavilainen, E. 2009, 'The case study as disciplinary convention: Evidence from International Business Journals', *Organization Research Methods*, Vol. 12, no. 3, pp. 567–589.

Podsakoff, P. M., MacKenzie, S. B. and Podsakoff, N. P. 2016, 'Recommendations for creating better concept definitions in the organizational, behavioural and social sciences', *Organizational Research Methods*, pp. 1–45.

Scott, J. 2006, *Documentary research*, London: Sage.

Shah, N. Z. 2008, 'Are graduates to be blamed? Unemployment of computer science graduates in Malaysia', *Computer Science*, Vol. 3, pp. 19–15.

Singh, G. G. and Singh, S. 2008, *Malaysian graduates' employability skills*, viewed March 18, 2017. Available at: http://ejournal.unitar.edu.my/articles/Gurvindermalaysian.

Spielhofer, T., Golden, S. and Evans, K. 2011, *Young people's aspirations in rural areas*, Slough: National Foundation for Educational Research.

Talent Corporation Malaysia Berhad. 2015, viewed October 24, 2016. Available at: www.talentcorp.com.my/.

Wong, F.II.K. and Hong, E.T. 1975, *Education in Malaysia*. Heinemann Educational Books (Asia) Ltd, Kuala Lumpur.

World Bank. 2016, *Malaysia overview*, viewed March 18, 2017. Available at: www.worldbank.org/en/country/malaysia/overview.

World Bank. 2017, *Data for Development*, viewed September 18, 2017. Available at: http://documents.worldbank.org/curated/en/993771497248234713/Malaysia-economic-monitor-data-for-development.

Yet-Mee, L., Teck, L., Yap, C. S. and Chui, L. 2016, 'Employability skills, personal qualities, and early employment problems of entry-level auditors: Perspectives from employers, lecturers, auditors, and students', *Journal of Education for Business*, Vol. 91, no. 4, pp. 185–192.

Zulaikha, I. 2016, 'Declining number of Malaysian students taking science and math in school', *Malaysian Digest*, viewed March 27, 2017. Available at: www.malaysiandigest.com/news/614553-declining-number-of-malaysian-students-taking-science-and-math-in-school-here-s-why.html.

6 "The perfect storm"

Constraints on Indonesian economic growth posed by graduate work-readiness challenges

Soegeng Priyono and Alan Nankervis

Introduction

This chapter explores the dilemmas facing Indonesia as it strives to become a competitive Southeast Asian economy, with the advantages of a stable political system and the demographic dividend of a large and relatively young potential workforce; but significant disadvantages with respect to the levels of work-readiness of its vocational and higher education graduates. The chapter discusses the nature and characteristics of the Indonesian labour market; government policies, and the structure of the education system; the particular graduate work-readiness challenges faced by employers and educational institutions, and their causes; and a range of practical strategies which have been developed to address these challenges. Two company cases are also included which illustrate these dilemmas.

Geography, politics and religion in brief

The Indonesia archipelago consists of five major islands: Sumatra, Java, Kalimantan, Sulawesi and Papua – and 17,000 smaller islands. The total population now is around 250 million with almost 60 percent of them inhabitants of Java. The country consists of 34 provinces, 511 municipalities, 30 metropolitan areas and large cities. Gross domestic product per capita in 2015 was USD 3,500.

Indonesia is now the third-largest democracy on the planet after the USA and India and has involved a major political and social transformation program since the nation decided to modernise in the latter half of 1998. Today, after eighteen years the people in general are still wondering whether democracy is really the way to go for Indonesia, knowing that there are more than two dozen political parties registered to participate in elections. Political parties are seldom perceived as a useful tool to voice genuine people's aspirations. As in many other developed and developing countries, they seem to have become elitist groups who think more about their self-interest rather than the common interest, busy arguing among themselves, and do not exhibit transparent financial management. Many political party members, bureaucrats or legislators have been convicted by the KPK (Committee for Eradication of Corruption), with potentially many more to come.

Any good initiative or transformation program, especially technical and vocational education (TVET), will have to go through a very long process and many times disappear without a trace. Making changes for improvement takes courage and good leadership, with strong understanding of the subject matter, which is often lacking in Indonesia.

In general Indonesians are religious. In fact, Indonesia is one of the few countries in the world which has a Ministry of Religious Affairs within the government. The majority of the population (estimated to be eighty percent) are Muslim, mostly moderates, and the majority are of the Sunni denomination. Other minor religions include Christianity, Hinduism, and Buddhism. Amongst the Muslims there is only a very small percentage (estimated to be less than five percent) are *Wahabis*, or fundamentalists. However, they are very militant and often use force to intimidate others including their fellow Muslims. During the *Orde Baru* (New Order – President Suharto) administration (1966–1998), this sect was effectively suppressed by the government, but since the collapse of this regime in 1998, they have become more active, in the guise of democracy, freedom of expression, and human rights.

The Indonesian labour market

Indonesia is currently the sixteenth-largest economy in the world and the largest economy in Southeast Asia, with an estimated 122 million skilled workers spread throughout rural and urban areas, and across three key sectors – agriculture and fisheries, industry and services (Oberman et al. 2012, pp. 4–8; CIA 2016; UK Trade and Investment 2016). Future projections suggest that it will become the seventh-largest global economy, with a demand for more than 113 million new workers by 2030, the majority of whom (71 percent) will be employed in urban areas, primarily in the industrial and services sectors (Allen 2016, p. 2). As evidence of the latter, it is reported that while agriculture employs 39 percent of the workforce in largely semi- or unskilled jobs and industry has 13 percent; the growing primarily urban services sector employs 48 percent, with fourteen million new jobs created between 2006 and 2016 (Allen 2016, p. 2). The median age of the population is estimated to be between 28 and 29 years – often referred to as Indonesia's 'demographic dividend' – with nearly 67 percent of working age (CIA 2016). Of considerable concern, the current youth unemployment rate hovers around 19 percent (CIA 2016). Real Gross Domestic Product (GDP) is estimated at approximately 5 percent (CIA 2016; UK Trade and Investment 2016).

According to Asian Development Bank (ADB) analyses, 'slow jobs growth and high levels of labour under-utilisation' (Allen 2016) threaten both Indonesia's future economic development and its ability to match labour demand and supply. Particular characteristics of these issues include the need for greater productivity; fluctuating annual labour market performance; uneven employment outcomes across regions and industries (especially in manufacturing); and disappointing labour force participation rates estimated at less than 70 percent (Allen 2016, pp. 4–6).

Key challenges for Indonesia's government into the future include improving its overall productivity, stabilising its uneven growth distribution and effectively addressing its significant infrastructure and resource constraints (Oberman et al. 2012, p. 13). As Allen (2016, p. 2) suggests,

> increased investment in education has expanded the pool of educated workers, although these investments have not translated into substantial gains in labour productivity. Underqualified workers still fill many positions, with skills shortages a continuing challenge. Access to up-skilling and re-skilling opportunities is limited . . . without involvement in better quality education and training, access to quality jobs and career mobility is extremely limited.
> (Allen 2016, p. 2).

Other significant concerns include the persistent use of short-term job contracts rather than continuing employment, particularly in the services and industry sectors; a lack of compliance with employment legislation; high youth unemployment and ever-growing skills shortages and mismatches with business requirements.

The variable quality of secondary, vocational and higher education systems and their graduate capabilities is of major importance following the establishment of the ASEAN Economic Community, as the competitiveness of the Indonesian labour market, and its capacity to attract and to service regional and multinational corporations, are potentially threatened. As an example of external perceptions of these issues, the World Competitiveness Rankings (ASEAN Countries) 2014 placed Indonesia in the thirty-fourth position, in contrast to Thailand (31), Malaysia (20) and Singapore (2) (Kurniawan 2015). Similarly, a recent OECD comparative study of thirty-three economies reported that Indonesia was one of the lowest-scoring countries in relation to literacy and numeracy (in both cases below the OECD average), and that nearly 60 percent of the population have not completed upper secondary school compared to less than 40 percent in Singapore (OECD 2016, p. 22). More broadly, the latest Human Capital Index report ranked Indonesia overall as number 72 of 130 countries assessed, averaging between 63rd and 77th respectively in each of the age categories (World Economic Forum 2016, p. 5). The report assessed the quality of Indonesia's business schools as 4.6, its capacity to attract talent at 4.3 and to retain talent at 4.1 out of 7, concluding that '(some) educational systems are disconnected from the skills required to function in today's [fourth industrial revolution] labour markets' (World Economic Forum 2016, p. 28).

Government frameworks and the education system

Since the ascension of the Joko Widodo government on 20 October 2014, infrastructure development, especially in relation to 'the construction of highways, ports, railways, irrigation and power generation', has understandably been a key imperative (Kurniawan 2015 blog). However, recognising the current and future labour market challenges the country faces, the government has also begun to turn its attention to the reform of secondary schools, vocational and higher education infrastructure, course content, pedagogies and graduate outcomes. Relevant legislation includes the National Education System Law 2003, which prescribes the levels of education and their structures; the Manpower Act 2003, which regulates the national training system and qualifications framework (*Kerangka Kualifikasi Nasional Indonesia*); the Teacher Law Act 2005, which dictates the organisation of the teaching profession and quality assurance processes (Directorate of Technical and Vocational Education 2016, p. 11); and the Labour Law Act 2003, which administers a national vocational training system (Danasasmith 2015, p. 54). The overall coordinating department is the Ministry of Education and Culture (MEC), under which sit a General Secretariat, National Institute for Educational Research and Development, General Inspectorate and four General Directorates (basic and secondary education, higher education, non-formal and formal education, quality improvement of teachers and educational personnel, Directorate of Technical and Vocational Education 2016, p. 10). As indicated above, there is also a national qualifications framework, with more specific vocational skills criteria in the automotive, heavy industry, culinary and geomatics sectors; and an overarching recognition of prior learning (RPL) process administered by the Ministry of Education and Culture.

Figure 6.1 illustrates the structure of secondary, vocational and higher education in Indonesia. It should be noted that Islamic education is formally included in the structure, as are 'non-formal' and private education providers.

Observers of the Indonesian labour market have noted a range of related factors, which provide serious challenges for the government, employers and all levels of the education system, in their efforts to achieve universally agreed goals of 'producing and accumulating human capital; generating, disseminating and applying knowledge; innovating and inventing new information and technology' (UNESCO 2012, p. 3) in order to assure the country's ongoing productivity and competitiveness within the ASEAN Economic Community (AEC) and globally. To address these challenges, secondary, vocational and higher education systems bear significant responsibilities in concert with the government and all employers.

Broadly, these challenges are associated with the growing skills gaps and mismatches between employer requirements and perceived graduate capabilities. Whilst there has been significant government investment in many levels of education, the outcomes of increased funding have often been disappointing. As examples, OECD, UNESCO and the World Bank (as discussed above) routinely report that Indonesian secondary school leavers lack high-level competencies in math, science and literacy compared to their regional counterparts; youth unemployment is high and appears to be an intractable problem; there are persistent skills shortages in many occupations, and it is reported that only 40 percent of new employees are 'well-matched' to industry needs (Allen 2016, p. 11); TVET graduate demand continually exceeds supply; and the quality of both vocational and higher education graduates' technical and work-readiness skills is frequently criticised by employers (Allen 2016; ICEF Monitor 2016; OECD 2015, 2016;

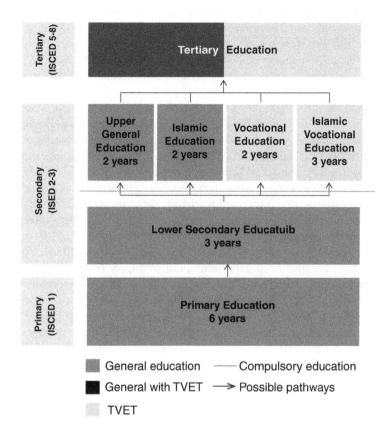

Figure 6.1 Indonesia's education system

(Source: Directorate of Technical and Vocational Education 2016, *Strengthening TVET Competence and International Partnerships*, Jakarta: Ministry of Education & Culture, p. 8)

UNESCO 2012; WEF 2016; World Bank 2010). Employers appear unwilling or unable to provide new graduates with opportunities for complement educational outcomes with appropriate induction, up-skilling, re-skilling or ongoing human resource development programs – 'only short-term remedial skill development' (World Bank 2010, p. 24), in spite of their own self-interest, and these deficits are exacerbated by the preference for short-term employment contracts and the flouting of the relevant labour legislation (Allen 2016; OECD 2015, 2016; UNESCO 2012).

Indonesia's dual system of senior general secondary schools (SMAs) and senior technical and vocational (TVET) secondary schools (SMKs) – see Diagram 1 above – is designed to appeal to students who are attracted to either an academic or a technical career. SMKs offer forty-seven skills-focused three-year programs in occupations such as technology, engineering, health, arts and crafts, information and communication technologies, tourism, agro-business, agro-technology and business management (Directorate of Technical and Vocational Education 2016, p. 8). The TVET system is a key focus of the government's Master Plan for the Acceleration and Expansion of Economic Development in Indonesia (MP3EI), which aims to provide the economy with 113 million additional skilled workers by 2030.

However, the ability of the TVET system, at both secondary school and polytechnic levels, to contribute to this desirable outcome has been seriously questioned on several grounds. A discernible 'lack of sufficient correspondence between the practical training and skills taught in TVET and the implications and demands of the labour market' (UK Trade and Investment 2016, p. 5) is attributed to a lack of strong linkages between the training institutions and their industry counterparts; the appointment of teachers without technical expertise and/or relevant work experience; and inadequate (or an absence of) student internships, work placements (*pemagangan*) or quality apprenticeships (Allen 2016; ICEF Monitor 2016; OECD/ADB 2015; UK Trade and Investment 2016). Concerns about TVET have also been expressed about its supply (rather than demand) driven strategy; its fragmented and inconsistent quality across provinces and between public and private providers; and importantly, its low status as perceived by employers, students and their parents (OECD/ADB 2015, pp. 34–35).

Similar concerns have also been expressed about Indonesia's higher education system, in particular with respect to its curriculum, which is overly focused on theory rather than industry skills and an associated lack of industry links and lecturer work experience, its outdated pedagogies and its relatively weak graduate outcomes – 'the majority of higher education graduates can only be classified as "fair"' (World Bank 2010, p. 21). Apart from these institutional and systemic issues, the socially determined choices of graduates and their families appear to contribute to these problems. For example, the overall majority of Indonesian public university students enrol in teacher training programs, encouraged by the Teacher Law of 2005, which raised teachers' salaries considerably, but only 20 percent undertake economically important programs such as law, economics and social sciences (ICEF Monitor 2016). Further, two-thirds of university graduates are employed in the public rather than the private sector.

The key challenges for governments, employers and both vocational and higher education systems appear to be the inability of all levels of the education system to produce an appropriately skilled modern workforce; an unwillingness of many employers to continue updating these skills over time; and an absence of government support for these endeavours through effective and integrated national strategies, policies, funding and evaluation mechanisms (World Bank 2010, p. 21). There are, however, two encouraging recent policy developments in addressing these issues. First, a new National Higher Learning Institutions Coordination Body was formed to 'coordinate a national response to the persistent issues of linking graduate skills to labour market requirements, driving innovation and creating links between academic research and industry' (ICEF Monitor 2016 blog). Second, a new Ministry of Research, Technology and Higher Education was established, with the specific responsibility of 'improving the higher education system, including the employment prospects of graduates and improving innovation' (ICEF Monitor 2016 blog).

Reflecting the observations of some international agencies that 'improved access to all levels of education and better alignment of graduate skills to labour market requirements' (ICEF Monitor 2016 blog) is the key to increased productivity and regional competitiveness, the Indonesian government has formulated a number of imperatives to address these issues. Some of them are discussed later in this chapter.

One particular government initiative, known as Curriculum 2013, has an ambitious objective – namely, 'to create productivity, creativity and innovation through strengthening affective attitudes, skills and integrated knowledge' in Indonesian vocational education (Ramadhan and Randari 2013, p. 125). It remains to be seen how effective the program's implementation and outcomes will be.

The following section of the chapter focuses on the challenges faced by the Indonesian government, employers and educational institutions with respect to the lack of work-readiness of many of its graduates. Subsequent sections discuss the causes of these challenges, and present a multiple stakeholder strategy towards resolving them.

Graduate work-readiness challenges

There are many definitions and analytical frameworks which attempt to encapsulate the specific components of graduate work-readiness. Chapter 2 explores these concepts in detail based on the various research studies which have been undertaken globally and in the Asia Pacific region. These studies reveal considerably more similarities than differences in the nature, extent and implications of graduate work-readiness challenges. Thus, an OECD report (2016) categorised them as basic foundation skills (literacy and numeracy), higher-level cognitive capabilities (problem-solving and analytical), interpersonal skills (communication), teamwork and negotiation, technological flexibility, learning skills, creativity and entrepreneurship (pp. 14–15). Wickramasinghe and Perera (2010) suggested that there are three key purposes of work-readiness – namely, the ability to gain employment, the ability to maintain employment, and importantly, the ability to 'make transitions between jobs and roles' (p. 226). In pursuit of these goals, they divide the pertinent skills requirements into two categories – subject skills and transferable skills, thus associating the latter with graduate career paths.

With specific application to Indonesia, a World Bank report (2010) observed that while unskilled positions are relatively easy to staff, finding the right profile for director and professional jobs is perceived to be difficult by over 80 percent and 60 percent of respondents respectively. The most severe skills gaps in Indonesia (both quantity and quality) appear to be found in the agriculture, forestry, hunting and fishing, transport and storage industries, together with those service sectors which have experienced recent rapid growth – namely, finance, insurance, real estate and business services (APEC 2015, p. 32). Our own research in Indonesia suggests, in addition, that tourism, construction, electricity and gas and water utilities also suffer from a lack of suitable vocational and higher education graduates. Executive managers, scientists, engineers, environmental and aerospace engineers are particularly hard to attract and retain. Inadequate linkages between employers and training organisations, skills mismatches, an absence of ongoing training and job creation opportunities for young people are some of the key skill issues in the Indonesian workforce (ILO 2016). A recent APEC report reinforced these findings, suggesting that 'Indonesia does not suffer from a lack of graduates, but it does suffer from a *lack of appropriately skilled workers*' (APEC 2015, p. 32).

The latter skills deficit has been segmented into three discrete but inherently inter-connected domains – namely, a qualifications mismatch, a skills mismatch, and a field of study mismatch (OECD 2016, p. 132). The qualifications mismatch refers to the failure of Indonesian vocational and higher education systems to develop programs which include content and workplace-related experiences relevant to the contemporary business and industry environments, and thus to equip graduates with both the technical and the 'soft' competencies necessary to effectively undertake the positions to which they aspire and for which they have attempted to prepare themselves. The skills mismatch encompasses both this perceived failure of education systems and the unwillingness or inability of employers to bridge the gap between education and employment by providing graduates with appropriate ongoing skills development opportunities. Finally, the 'field of study' mismatch concerns the government's lack of comprehensive labour market analysis and planning, which might more accurately predict the current and future jobs and skills trends, and develop national education and labour market strategies to ensure a congruence between industry demand and education system supply. It may also include the responsibilities of the graduates themselves to choose vocational or university programs which best equip them to more effectively compete in the job market. As the OECD report concludes,

> ensuring a good match between the skills acquired in education and on the job and those required in the labour market is essential if countries want to make the most of their investments in human capital, and to promote strong and inclusive growth. It affects job satisfaction and wages, increases the rate of turnover and may reduce productivity and GDP growth.
>
> (OECD 2016, p. 129)

So, which particular graduate work-readiness challenges are most evident in the Indonesian economy? UNESCO (2012) identified personal integrity, intellectual capacity, teamwork, analysis and problem-solving skills as key issues; with communication, writing and communication skills, a lack of self-confidence and 'character' of secondary importance (p. 19). The OECD report (discussed earlier in this chapter) revealed more basic skills gaps, including the lowest regional scores on literacy and numeracy tests, especially in the 25 to 34 age group (OECD 2016, p. 63). In addition, it suggested that practical workplace competencies such as job flexibility, work sequencing, time management, cooperation with co-workers and willingness and ability to train others are deficient qualities in many vocational and higher education graduates. The World Bank (2010), on the other hand, identified deficiencies in critical thinking, communication and independent working competencies, together with leadership, team orientation, creativity, English language fluency and information technology skills (p. 13).

Our research confirms these findings and further suggests that in general, Indonesian employers face medium- to high-level challenges in recruiting graduates who are ready to perform the job at a competitive salary level. For information technology and accounting graduates, caregivers and medical operators, the difficulties are high. For nurses, there are stages of 'apprenticeship' that help to ensure work-readiness. The key problem is that demand far outweighs supply in many such occupations, and the qualities of graduates are less than adequate to bridge that gap. However, despite the above-mentioned challenges, employers' expectations may also be somewhat unrealistic in the sense that they expect graduates to be ready to perform the job at a competitive salary level and demand high and long-term loyalty from them, but in many cases are only willing to offer them positions as temporary or contract workers without accordant commitments to re-skill or up-skill them.

The Indonesian government faces challenges to set curricula and regulations that are relevant to industry and are updated periodically to anticipate current and future needs; to reduce the conflicts between different government departments (e.g., Ministry of Education and Culture, Ministry of Manpower, Ministry of Industry); to have smooth and open communication with industry or its associations so that synergy can be achieved; to create consistent competency standards across the country for the same job skills, and to have unified national certification standards. The latter problem is exacerbated by the numerous disconnected and geographically isolated provincial governments whose policies and practices are difficult to coordinate from Jakarta; and the lack of effective communication systems between different departments and between government institutions and industry, which are either currently non-existent or at best ineffective.

The TVET and higher education institutions that we researched expressed concerns about the denseness of the government curriculum and its lack of relevance to current industry needs, and reported that they have had to develop additional in-house/local programs to strengthen the curriculum as an effort to make the graduates more ready and more competitive, without adding too much workload if possible. To do this, such schools require additional funding sources for the enhancement of laboratory facilities and additional instructors. These are either limited or difficult to find.

At senior secondary school level, altering government curriculum for vocational education is not an option. At the polytechnic level, there is a guideline from the Ministry of Education and Culture (MEC) for basic skills and general subjects, but the polytechnics may also develop their own complementary programs dependent on the provision of adequate funding and resources.

The polytechnics emphasise skills-building, and consequently the operational cost is high. Skills such as English language, Mandarin, creative thinking, interpersonal communication, work administration and teamwork are not in the standard curriculum, and appropriate training modules and instructors may not be available in-house. Consequently, many employers are proactively seeking mutually beneficial partnerships with selected TVET and higher education institutions to fulfill their own needs.

For the students, to get admitted into a good TVET or higher education institution is not easy because of the competition and sometimes the option is to leave the hometown/regency/province to go to a good school. In addition, whilst secondary schools, polytechnics and universities in Java are popular, institutions in other regions of Indonesia have to build their reputations and credentials in order to attract students.

Strategies to address graduate work-readiness

From the above discussion, a broad range of practical strategies to address these graduate work-readiness challenges is proposed, involving the key stakeholders – namely, the government, industry, vocational and higher education institutions, as well as the graduates themselves. This section of the chapter canvasses the significant issues and the key responsibilities of each of these stakeholders within a national 'multi-faceted approach to accelerating labour productivity . . . across education, infrastructure, economic sectors and social sectors, in order to promote quality employment and support' (Allen 2016, p. 2).

The primary imperatives are to create more and better-quality jobs within an expanding economy; to develop a more integrated national education and training system and national qualifications framework which more closely reflect the requirements of Indonesia's industry structural transition, and which approaches world's 'best practice'; to strengthen multiple graduate pathways within high-quality secondary, vocational and higher education systems; to encourage, and provide incentives for, employers to engage more directly with educational institutions, and to value and develop their human capital more deliberately; and to continuously improve skills assessment and accreditation processes.

Government

For the government, these imperatives will require policies and strategies which strengthen labour market skills analysis and planning; facilitate the review of education curricula and pedagogical techniques in order to better meet present and future industry skills requirements; and review the remuneration of lecturers/teachers to attract higher quality applicants. They might also encourage employers to become more closely involved in course design, presentation, work-based learning and program evaluation; tighten the accreditation criteria and processes for public and private education and training providers whilst also providing them with greater internal autonomy. Such initiatives will inevitably be heavily reliant on maintaining consistency across Indonesia's multiple provincial administrations, as well ensuring that the multiple government agencies which are responsible for labour market policies and for graduate outcomes are effectively aligned towards a common purpose. It also seems timely for both the national and provincial governments to redress the negative perceptions of vocational education through national promotional campaigns. Table 6.1 illustrates some of the present government's initiatives in these areas, but the evidence of their effectiveness will inevitably lie in the long-term evaluation of their implementation.

Table 6.1 Government education and employment imperatives, Indonesia

1	**Standardisation of competencies**	Strengthening productivity through the standardisation of competencies for technical and entrepreneurship training programs and through promoting the independent operation of certification authorities.
2	**Standard of trainers**	Improving training and instruction through setting standards for the skills and competencies of trainers in public and private training institutions.
3	**Training facilities**	Developing and improving technical vocational education and training facilities through investing in training infrastructure.
4	**Apprenticeship programs**	Supporting access to employment for young people through apprenticeship programs that provide a combination of classroom learning and on-the-job training.
5	**Entrepreneurship training**	Promoting entrepreneurship through providing support for improving productivity in enterprises, identifying best practices interventions, and through provision of entrepreneurship training.
6	**Employment agencies**	Provision of public and private employment services to provide job matching and employment counselling services, including job fairs and online job matching websites.
7	**Labour market information systems (LMIS)**	Promoting access to employment through the development of labour market information systems, including collecting and analysing data on job seekers and job vacancies.
8	**Public employment programs**	Expanding employment through public employment programs that provide short-term work opportunities for informal economy development for vulnerable groups – particularly the unemployed, underemployed, and the poor.
9	**Expanding employment**	Expanding employment through supporting Indonesian migrant worker placements, including provision of pre-departure training, placement abroad, improvement of the procedures and protections for Indonesian migrant workers, international cooperation.

(Source: Allen 2016, Analysis of the trends and challenges in the Indonesian labour market, *ADB Papers on Indonesia*, Manila: ADB, pp. 30–31)

Vocational and higher education providers

For secondary, vocational and higher education service providers, the implications include serious reviews of the practical skills outcomes of their programs, involving curriculum redesign, revised lecturer/trainer selection criteria and development opportunities. The use of more modern learning technologies and activities, such as inquiry-based and project-based student techniques, need consideration, as well as greater internationalisation of the curriculum. It may also be useful to provide students with complementary work-readiness courses which focus on the specific workplace skills required by employers in particular industries, occupations or disciplines. Active engagement between these institutions and employers including cross-institutional placements, greater employer representation on course advisory and curriculum development committees, and the development of appropriate student work placements, internships and work-related assignments, would also represent positive approaches to resolving the graduate work-readiness challenges.

Employers

As well as the above issues, employers are also pivotal to the effective resolution of these issues. Their willingness to become more involved with vocational and higher education institutions, and subsequently to hire and develop local graduates, is in many ways the key to success. Employers also need to ensure that their work-readiness skill expectations are more clearly defined and demonstrably relevant in their dynamic workplaces. In summary, 'education institutions at all levels share the same responsibility in developing current and future generations of young people as do governments, employers, non-governmental organisations and civil society organisations' (UNESCO 2012, p. 4). The following section provides an illustration of a state-owned company's graduate work-readiness challenges and its effective approach to resolving them, together with a less successful private company.

Industry graduate work-readiness cases

Company A: addressing GWR challenges through an integrated cultural transformation strategy

Background

The company provides manpower supply, security guards, event organising, training and oil and gas, advisory services. It is a large, state-owned company. Its employees number around one hundred permanent and another hundred contract employees. The company also manages and supplies around 8,000 people to their clients on a contract basis (1–2 years), 90–95 percent of which consist of security guards and medium- to low-skilled workers (for example, truck drivers, aircraft re-fuelling/de-fuelling operators).

The size of potential business from the company's 'captive' market – the subsidiaries of its parent company – alone is impressive. For example, the company's revenue last year was a little over AUD 100 million, with around 20 percent average growth annually. The revenue target for subsequent years is approximately AUD 120 million. With the significant recent decrease in world oil prices, unavoidable efficiency measures have had to be taken by the Indonesian parent company which has directly impacted all subsidiaries, including this company. To sustain the expected annual growth of 20 percent, the company has had to start looking for business opportunities outside of the captive market, which poses different challenges, together with its drive towards captive market intensification.

Business challenges

Given the company context, the major business challenges facing the company include:

1 The profit margin they can generate is very limited because more than 95 percent of their customers are its own holding company and a few subsidiaries. The corporate policy is that the pricing model is cost plus a maximum 8 percent margin, based on the assumption that projects are 'given' and not 'won'. Despite this policy, customers still attempt to negotiate lower margins by comparing its margin with that of competitors. In general the average margin can be as low as 5 percent. Below this, the company potentially may lose money.
2 The company is also suffering from an 'inferiority complex' because the major customers are the shareholders themselves and the subsidiary companies. Business contract negotiation skills are undeveloped, especially within the Indonesian business culture, whereby management styles are very hierarchical. As such, the chances to satisfy, let alone 'delight', the customers are minimal.

HRM and graduate work-readiness challenges

Historically, the employees have not been accustomed to pursuing business proactively because projects have always come from the holding company and other subsidiaries. Recruitment is still heavily influenced by a 'who knows whom' mentality, despite efforts by the current management to make it more professional.

Organisational culture

Given the business challenges discussed above, the HRM implications affect business process and the quality of recruits, amongst other issues, which eventually lead to the attraction and retention of low-quality employees. Obedience is a key employee criterion, reflecting both Indonesian traditional influences and the organisational culture inherent in a state-owned enterprise. However, in 2014 the board of directors realised the urgent need to transform the organisation to be more professional and outward-looking. The average age of the current employees is forty years or older, and they generally share the values of the older paradigm, whilst most of the managers also come from an 'old school' mentality.

Management capabilities

Managers' capabilities are often seriously lacking with respect to such aspects as diligence, consistency and flexibility in good business practices, such as proposal preparation, deal negotiation, contract management and project management. These deficits have sometimes created serious cash flow problems for the company, which in turn has led to problems in taxation, industrial relations, speed of service, billing and collection administration. Consequently, it is a big challenge for the company to be able to penetrate and compete on the open market successfully, which is becoming imperative given the significant drop in world oil prices that affect the spending budgets of existing customers. Information technology skills are in a serious shortage despite the growing need for internal automation. These skills are becoming increasingly urgent, not only to streamline internal business systems but also to provide the ability to create new products for the market. Without it, the company's future essentially is in jeopardy. Corporate culture transformation needs to be continued, improved and nurtured, and exemplary leadership is a major prerequisite for effectiveness.

Current GWR strategies

In the past 18 months, the company engaged with an external management consulting firm to assist it in the transformation process. The consultant conducted a diagnostic assessment to acquire the overall picture of the situation, define the problem and recommended stages of implementation with target outcomes and dates. The assessment included aspects from strategy and planning, people and organisation, finance and administration and last but not least the technology. His cultural transformation strategy included:

1   Providing input on strategic matters to the board of directors, such as organisational restructuring and development, talent management and strategic alliances with potential partners.
2   Delivering one-on-one coaching to all divisional managers to make them aware of the proper business process management, people development and business development processes.
3   Engaging with vocational schools for the future supply of information technology programmers on a project basis. The process started with a small project to build an Executive Dashboard to monitor all projects, starting from proposal preparation, deal follow up and negotiation, contract signing, billing and collection. A phone app was made accessible by the board of directors from their Android and IOSX gadgets.

4   Proposing improved recruitment strategies and processes for new young talent, to be developed early on through a professional on-boarding/induction program, including appropriate behaviours and understanding of the company values, and an ongoing graduate development program.
5   Suggesting the employment of a professional hire firm for assistant manager–level employees and above.

Outcomes

The company for the time being is in the right direction for its transformation to a more professional organisation. However, it needs to be accompanied by external consultant to ensure objectivity, that targets are met and interim evaluation is regularly conducted; and to propose adjustments or improvements in time, as necessary.

New graduate work-readiness programs need to be prepared and built up over time. Hiring professionals in the short-term and leveraging alliances with partners in order to enhance the readiness and quality of the work team is imperative in order to capture immediate opportunities. For the longer-term, the need to build young professionals' capabilities from within is mandatory, especially to support its training and consulting line of business, and to maximise project profitability. The company must transform itself to become a learning organisation, so that, when the work-ready employees leave the company for any reason at any time, it will survive and prosper. This is a very sensitive period for the company, as if the incumbent management does not make the right decisions, the company will miss the opportunity to break through the current challenges.

Company B: top-down management restricts innovation and talent attraction

Company context

The company is a space frame manufacturer based in Jakarta, Indonesia, and established in 1983. A space frame is a steel structural network that consists of three kinds of elements, namely nodes, pipes and connector sets. The structure can be designed to any architectural shape that has the capability for extraordinary cantilevers that span up to 100 metres. It is suitable for canopies, exhibition halls, stations, stadiums, skylights, towers, hangars and auditoriums.

The company has a track record of delivering space-frame projects to more than twenty-four countries across the world and has intellectual patent rights from three different economies – PRC, Chinese Taipei and Indonesia. Under the founder's leadership, the company has weathered many ups and downs, having grown from a garage machining shop in the downtown area to a modern manufacturing company situated in a large industrial complex.

The company is a medium-size space frame manufacturer with forty employees working on the manufacturing floor led by a German-trained local engineer, seven sales and marketing professionals and thirteen people in back-office administration. Its production capacity is 10,000 square metres of space frame per month worth US$11.5 million or so per year from its first shift operation. Extra capacity could be readily achieved by adding shifts. Like many other small and medium enterprises in Indonesia, it is still run by the owner/founder, who controls company operations and has his own vision for the company. The financial structure roughly consists of 60 percent materials, 25 percent labour and 15 percent overhead costs.

Management style

Whilst the founder is still active and productive, the need for skilled workers is not a serious issue as he feels that he knows exactly what to do and where to source the appropriate employees and their necessary training and direction. His management style is top-down, especially concerning strategic planning and decision-making. In his absence, the company would not function well, and employees are only expected to fulfill their production responsibilities. Business processes are not documented.

All sensitive information, such as past sales performance and the business plan, are mostly held by the founder, partly because of his fear that such information might fall into unfriendly hands, like the tax authority or competitors. Currently, the owner feels uncertain about the company's sustainability in the future, as he has been the driving force behind the company since its establishment. Now in his early seventies, he wonders how effective the engineering team will be in his absence. Whilst he hopes that at least one of his three children will someday take over the company, this is unlikely to happen as they are more interested in working in the Indonesian financial sector.

Business challenges

An important strength of the company is its long-term relationships with customers, business partners and suppliers. Its functions are always a subset of a construction project, and as such, selling has always been done through the main contractors, with space frame tendering never operating as a stand-alone activity. Relationship management then is extremely sensitive and complicated, and so having enough skilled relationship officers is crucial to boost sales.

The strongest competitors in the international market are manufacturers from China, Turkey, Korea, Spain, England, Mexico and the USA. The fast progress of manufacturing technology coupled with pervasive Internet technology has made the competition fiercer. Buyers have more options than ever before at their convenience. In the domestic market, although the company's fiercest competitors are still two levels below it, they can offer lower prices coupled with stronger sales forces. The company local price in general is around 20 to 30 percent higher than that of competitors although product quality is better. Unfortunately, the customers don't always need those high-level specifications.

HRM and graduate work-readiness challenges

This company should have been an ideal place for VE and HE graduates to do their apprenticeships and to work subsequently. But due to the unwillingness of the founder to share key knowledge and experience, the company faces difficulties in attracting and retaining the needed talents. To date, the company has not successfully devised good people and organisation development programs to help ensure its sustainability for the longer term.

The owner is trying to open up bigger and better manufacturing facilities in mainland China to tap the huge local market and skilled workers and to springboard them to a broader international market. However, the company has experienced considerable difficulties in finding appropriate investors, due in part to the lack of transparency in its financial reporting, which in associated with the owner's managerial style.

It is difficult to predict whether the company will thrive after the founder is no longer in control, due to both the financial and HRM issues discussed above. The founder, if time still permits and if it all possible, must allow professional assistance to help the company transform into a more modern, professional organisation that is not dependent upon an individual to operate, profit and grow.

Summary and conclusion

Only a relatively small percentage of vocational and higher education graduates in Indonesia are recruited by top-tier multinational and large local companies. The remainder have to settle for jobs in smaller- and medium-size companies, or become self-employed. With the current economic situation in Indonesia, many companies have simply ceased recruiting new employees, and some have even begun to reduce their workforces.

The most significant job opportunities actually lie with the small and medium enterprise (SME) sector, which is the real driver of the country's economy. In 2013 there were only five thousand large companies (0.01 percent) as compared with almost 58 million micro, small and medium enterprises (99.99 percent) operating in Indonesia (Ministry of Cooperatives and SMEs August 2015). In order to thrive, the SMEs will require skilled resources at an affordable cost.

Some stakeholders believe that vocational education should be the domain of industry associations in terms of defining the curriculum, rules, competencies and certifications because they are the practitioners who are supposed to know their needs better. However, the Ministry of Education and Culture does not share this view, preferring the German system of state control as their model.

The mainstream paradigm in Indonesia, amongst the government, industry, educational institutions and even graduates and their families, is that formal university qualifications are more important than vocational degrees, although this is shifting to some extent. This explains why a significant number of young people still prefer higher to vocational education. But ironically, companies find it increasingly difficult to recruit the right people with the right talent at the right price. Young workers with in-demand skills (e.g., information technology) tend to be over-priced, and many of them prefer to work as freelancers, thus contracting to rather than being employed by either large or SME companies. The main reason is that they can earn more money by working on simultaneous parallel projects.

Consequently, serious skills gaps (in both quantity and quality) exist and are likely to continue to grow in many areas of the Indonesian public and private sectors and are exacerbated by the nature of government policies and strategies and the mismatched expectations of employers, vocational and higher education systems; and the preferences and work-readiness deficits of graduates and their families. Only an integrated strategic approach by the multiple stakeholders is likely to be effective in addressing these intransigent labour market challenges.

Table 6.2 Summary of key findings Indonesia

	Summary
Demographics / labour market	The population of Indonesia in 2015 was around 250 million, 60 percent of them inhabiting one island: Java. The labour force is close to 50 percent of the population. There are currently estimated to be 122 million skilled workers spread throughout urban and rural across three key sectors: agriculture and fisheries, industry and services. It is projected that by 2030, more than 113 million new workers will be in demand, with 71 percent of them in urban areas working in the industrial and services sectors. Indonesia is enjoying a demographic dividend with nearly 67 percent of the population at working age for at least the next 15 years or so. The unemployment rate is hovering around 19 percent.
Economy	The 2008 global financial crisis still has an impact on the Indonesian economy, and it has been aggravated by the political situation which tends to be democratically liberal, with more than twenty political parties involved. Massive public sector corruption (executive, legislative and judicative) has become inevitable. Slow jobs growth and high levels of labour under-utilisation have become apparent. The president ordered a significant budget cut in 2017 to all government offices and focused on capital expenditure to complete the infrastructure projects already started, such as mass rail and light rail transport systems, toll roads, air/ sea ports and so on.

	Summary
Educational Structure/Work-readiness challenges	With more than 250 million people, Indonesia faces very complex challenges in managing its education and facilitating better work-readiness for its TVET and HE graduates, in both quality and quantity vis-a-vis the demand. There are multiple regulators involved within the government (Ministry of Education, Ministry of Manpower, Ministry of Industry, BNSP), with no clear separation of roles and responsibilities; and there are associated challenges in communication, coordination and collaboration between them, let alone other key stakeholders such as industry associations, students, and parents. The good thing is that TVET has caught the attention of the president as one of the priority areas to be focused on. This opens up opportunities for any party to propose, proof of concept, do pilot project related to TVET and improve work-readiness. Could be government-to-government, business-to-business and/or business-to-government projects.
Work-readiness issues	As the main government body overseeing education and training, the Ministry of Education (MoE) should improve their capacity to communicate with all stakeholders. MoE is of course not an industry player, and so for TVET, they must work together well with industry and its associations. All education institutions must follow strictly the MoE curriculum although it may be too heavy, obsolete, and/or not addressing the demand of the current and future times. Adding local content (language, soft-skills) to the curriculum would generate an extra burden to the students, and additional resources beyond budget capabilities. Another problem area is that companies in general (especially SMEs), which do not undertake effective human resource planning. They tend to recruit employee resources from the labour market as the need arises, rather than developing them more proactively.
Policy Initiatives and recommended strategies for improved graduate work-readiness	Greater collaboration between the government regulators, industry and education institutions. MoE should only dictate basic curriculum and give the education institutions more freedom to come up with local content based on their own observation of industry needs. They should also encourage more companies to collaborate with education institutions, including implementing Work Based Learning.
	A Recognition of Prior Learning (RPL) mechanism is also urgent to be put in place. Certification is becoming more and more important to ensure consistent and standard competencies of the graduates.

References

Allen, E. R. 2016, 'Analysis of trends and challenges in the Indonesian labour market', *ADB Papers on Indonesia*, Manila: ADB.

APEC. 2015, *A report on the APEC region labour markets: Evidence of skills shortages and general trends in employment – the value of better labour market information systems*, Singapore: APEC HRD Working Group.

CIA. 2016, *World factbook*, Virginia: CIA. Available at: www.cia.gov [Accessed October 7, 2016].

Danasasmith, E. K. 2015, 'Continuing professional development for the personnel of vocational schools in Indonesia', *Third UPI International Conference on TVET*, Amsterdam: Atlantis Press.

Directorate of Technical and Vocational Education. 2016, *TVET mission, legislation and national policy or strategy*, Jakarta: DTVE.

ICEF. 2016, *Indonesia looks to education to help drive growth*, Bonn: ICEF Monitor. Available at: www.monitor.icef. com [Accessed January 8, 2016].

ILO. 2016, *Skills and employability in Indonesia and timor-leste*, Geneva: ILO.

Kurniawan, H. 2015, 'AEC 2015 – benefits and challenges for Indonesia', *Thomson Reuters Tax and Accounting*, October 6 blog. Available at: www.tax.thomsonreuters.com.

Ministry of Cooperatives and SMEs. 2015, Available at: www.icsb.org [Accessed September 18, 2016].

Oberman, R., Dobbs, R., Budiman, A., Thompson, F. and Rossi, M. 2012, *The archipelago: Unleashing Indonesia's potential*, Shanghai: McKinsey Global Institute.

OECD/ADB. 2015, *Education in Indonesia: Rising to the challenge*, Paris: OECD.

OECD. 2016, 'Skills matter: Further results from the survey of adult skills', *OECD Skills Studies*, Paris: OECD.

Ramadhan, M. A. and Randari, S. D. 2013, *Vocational education perspectives on curriculum 2013 and its role in Indonesian economic development*, Yogyakarta State University, Yogyakarta.

UK Trade and Investment. 2016, *Vocational education for work-readiness: Challenges and Strategies*, London: UK Trade and Investment.

UNESCO. 2012, *Graduate employability in Asia*, Bangkok: UNESCO.

Wickramasinghe, V. and Perera, L. 2010, 'Graduates', university lecturers' and employers' perspectives towards employability skills', *Education and Training*, Vol. 52, no. 3, pp. 226–244.

World Bank. 2010, *Indonesian skills report: Trends in skills development, gaps and supply in Indonesia*, Human Development Department (East Asia and Pacific region), Washington, DC: World Bank.

World Economic Forum. 2016, *The human capital report 2016*, Cologny, Switzerland: WEF.

7 Work-readiness in Singapore

Peter Waring, Christopher Vas
and Azad Singh Bali

Introduction

Of all the countries considered in this text, none is perhaps so obviously dependent upon the skills, talents and knowledge of its people than Singapore. The small island nation of just 700 square kilometers and 5.4 million people – often endearingly described by its citizenry as 'our little red dot' – was unceremoniously ejected from the Federation of Malaya in 1965 and left to forge for survival in the absence of significant resource endowments (including no permanent water source) or a hinterland.

The fledgling republic did enjoy a strategic location at the end of the Malayan peninsular and was more developed than many of its Asian neighbours (see Ghesquire 2006; Lee 2015) — one of the more positive legacies of years of British colonial rule. In spite or perhaps because of the natural limitations of its land, the country's economic history and the prosperity it has enjoyed since the 1960s is remarkable and underpinned by a strong focus on the development of first-class education and training systems. Indeed, the state's focus on education can be seen on one side of the Singapore $2 note, which features a classroom setting with the single word 'Education'. Singapore now has an economy worth $402 billion and a per capita national income of $69,283 (up from US$511 in 1965), which places the republic within the top ten wealthiest countries in the world.

The history of Singapore's early years as a new republic have been well documented and the strategic choices of the ruling People's Action Party (PAP) led by the irrepressible Lee Kuan Yew closely examined. The reluctant republic's very survival was at stake, and this called for heavy state intervention of a scale and type normally found within centrally planned economies. Rapid industrialization was the key to a sustainable future, and for this plan to succeed, Singapore would need to attract foreign capital in large volume. This occurred through a mixture of tax incentives, subsidies and the prospect of accessing a large pool of skilled, compliant and comparatively low-wage workers. The moderate wing of the trade union movement was cultivated while more radical elements were suppressed. The ruling party invested heavily in education and the development of a skilled workforce. Vocational and technical institutes were set up in the 1960s to produce technicians and skilled workers for manufacturing. Bilingualism was introduced as an official education policy with English the common language designed to unify and again make Singapore an attractive destination for foreign investment. At the same time government linked corporations were established and nurtured according to the state's long-term industrial policy. Over the course of the 1980s and 1990s, manufacturing as a share of the economy declined while services grew rapidly (Bali et al. 2016). Manufacturing now contributes around 20 percent of Singapore's GDP (Singapore Department of Statistics 2016b). Despite significant economic success, Singapore has experienced low productivity growth. As Figure 7.1 illustrates, most of Singapore's growth stems from changes in labour and capital inputs rather than advances in productivity.

To address Singapore's anemic productivity growth, the government initiated a series of structural economic reforms beginning in 2011. The reforms most relevant to this volume are reforms targeted at improving the productivity of businesses and reforms targeted at improving the skills and work-readiness of the resident labour force. The resident labour force is defined as members of the labour force who are citizens and permanent residents. The productivity reforms are largely targeted at small to medium enterprises (SMEs), which account for about 70 percent of total employment in Singapore. Through a series of policy initiatives, the government has made available large grants and generous subsidies to SMEs to automate and incorporate technology solutions in their business processes. For example, in 2015, the government paid out S$1.1 billion to defray information technology and related expenditure under the Productivity and Innovation Credit (PIC) Scheme (Channel News Asia 2016).

The second set of reforms are targeted at 'upskilling' the resident labour force in the context of acute global competition, disruptive shifts in technology and business models and improving their work-readiness. 'Skills Future', a national movement that represents a whole of government approach, is the primary vehicle of achieving this vision. These reforms also sit neatly with recent changes to education policy and reflect the aspirations of citizens to participate in tertiary education (Waring 2014). For instance, Singapore's higher education participation rate now sits at 30 percent with plans to raise this to 40 percent by 2020 (MOE 2015).

Figure 7.1 Contribution of Multifactor Productivity to Real GDP in Singapore 1975–2015

Source: Singapore Department of Statistics (2016a)
Source: Bali et al. (2016)

This chapter engages with the issues surrounding work-readiness and employability in Singapore. It focuses on the efficacy of recent efforts of the government under the novel Skills Future program, and the changes made in Singapore's education policy which give Singaporeans increased access to tertiary education at publicly funded universities. These efforts represent a renewed emphasis and commitment across government agencies to foster productivity growth and offer the resident labour force opportunities to improve their skills.

The rest of the chapter is organised as follows. Section 2 describes Singapore's contemporary labour market conditions and the composition of its labour force. This is followed by a brief review of Singapore's education and training system in Section 3. Section 4 focuses on recent efforts to improve work-readiness, particularly the Skills Future program and changes to Singapore's education policy. The final section offers concluding observations of the potential impact and limitations of the government's recent efforts.

Singapore's labour market

This section presents a broad overview of the defining features of Singapore's labour market.[1] They are (i) high dependence on foreign labour; (ii) a rapidly ageing labour force; (iii) low unemployment rates; (iv) low productivity growth.

(i) High Dependence on Foreign Labour

Singapore has historically relied on foreign labour to meet its manpower needs. Its economy at the time of independence was a thriving epicenter for trade and commerce in region, and the continual flow of migrant workers advanced the interests of the then colonial authorities. Since independence, the government has actively managed the flow of foreign labour through an orchestrated use of quotas, levies and 'dependency ratios' that vary across industrial sectors and the sectors of the economy in which foreign workers can be employed in. For example, the list of 'source countries' whose citizens can work in the manufacturing sector differs from other sectors such as construction or services. These instruments essentially increase the cost of hiring foreign workers in Singapore. The government continues to make parametric and frequent changes in the settings of these instruments, largely in response to the overall business climate in Singapore. However, fueled by robust economic growth and sustained downward pressures on wages, businesses have continued to rely on foreign labour to meet their manpower needs.

By the 1990s, the foreign workforce in Singapore had grown to 248,000 and to 670,000 by 2006 (Yeoh 2007), doubling again by 2014 in less than 7 years. This contributed to a steep rise in Singapore's total population from about 2.0 million in the 1970s to about 5.3 million in recent years. Singapore's total population grew by about 33 percent between 1990–00, and 38 percent between 2000–15, while the corresponding growth in the resident population during across both periods was about 20 percent (Table 7.1).

Table 7.1 Demographic and labour market trends, 1970–2015, Singapore

Population	1970	1990	2000	2015
Total Population ('000)	2,074.5	3,047.1	4,027.9	5,535.0
Resident Population ('000)	2,013.6	2,735.9	3,273.4	3,902.7
Singapore Citizens ('000)	1,874.8	2,623.7	2,985.9	3,375.0
Permanent Residents ('000)	138.8	112.1	287.5	527.7
Population Density (Per sq km)	3,538	4,814	5,900	7,697
Median Age (Years)	19.5	29.8	34.0	39.6
Total Fertility Rate	3.1	1.9	1.6	1.2
Old-Age Support Ratio				
Persons aged 15–64 years	17.0	11.8	9.9	6.2
Persons aged 20–64 years	13.5	10.5	9.0	5.7

Source: World Development Indicators (2016); Singapore Department of Statistics (2016a); Ministry of Manpower (2016)

As at the end of 2015, the total resident labour force stood at just over 2.32 million people (62 percent of the total labour force) while foreigners made up the balance (38 percent) or just under 1.4 million people (Ministry of Manpower 2015). As Table 1.2 highlights, the single largest employer of foreign labour is the construction industry, which in 2014, employed nearly 28 percent of the total foreign labour pool of 1.41 million workers. Other work permit holders (visa for unskilled or semi-skilled foreign workers) work as cleaners, in marine and offshore engineering, road maintenance, manufacturing and in other industries where local workers are typically not to be found. A significant number (227,500) of foreign workers are female domestic workers from countries such as India, Philippines, Indonesia and Myanmar.

The increased growth in the non-resident labour force intersected with observations by policymakers that industrial sectors which relied most heavily on foreign workers also experienced lower productivity growth. As part of the economic reforms to encourage businesses to improve their productivity, the government gave businesses generous grants to automate and mechanise, while increasing the cost of hiring foreign workers by reducing the quotas, recalibrating dependency ratios and increasing monthly levies. The government also implemented the Fair Consideration Framework in 2015, requiring all jobs filled by foreigners to be advertised for a 14-day period on a national jobs portal. Because of these measures, Singapore's growth in non-resident labour force reduced from 11.2 percent per annum between 2004 and 2009 to 5.2 percent per annum from 2009 to 2014.

Table 7.2 Foreign labour force by work visas

Pass Type	Workforce Numbers	Explanation/comments
Employment Pass	180,800	For professionals and executives with wages in excess of $3300 per month. The threshold salary required to qualify for the visa increases with age. The exact thresholds are not explicitly stated
S Pass	173,800	Largely for diploma holders and those with a technical skill base with wages more than $2200 per month
Work Permit (Total)	993,900	Work permits for unskilled/ semi-skilled foreign guest workers
Work Permit (Foreign Domestic Workers)	227,100	Mostly female domestic workers
Work Permit (Construction)	322,400	22 percent of the foreign workforce
Other Work Passes	19,700	Includes holders of Training Work Permits and Letters of Consent
Total Foreign Workforce	1.368 million	

Source: Ministry of Manpower (2016)

(ii) Ageing Labour Force

While Singapore's dependence on foreign labour was a key pillar of its growth strategy (see Asher et al. 2015), it is also increasingly a consequence of an ageing population. Singapore had a high total fertility rate (TFR) in the 1960s, about 5.4 children per woman, but this rapidly declined to a replacement rate fertility of 2.1 by 1975. While this was partly attributed to increasing incomes and female labour force participation, the government implemented a range of policy measures to incentivise families to have fewer children. These included legalizing abortion, encouraging voluntary sterilization, increased hospital fees to deliver any subsequent baby after the second child, only two paid maternity leaves and lower priority in preferred choice of schools for a family's third, fourth and subsequent children (Wong and Yeoh 2003, p. 7). Declining fertility rates coupled with advances in longevity resulted in a rapidly ageing population and resident labour force as evidenced by rising median age and declining old-age support ratios. The ageing challenge still exists today: in the next 10 years, Singapore will see a doubling of the share of those aged above 65 and tripling of those aged above 80 in their population (UNDESA 2015). Singapore has been more open in addressing this challenge through foreign labour than other economies in East Asia such as Japan and the Republic of Korea.

(iii) Low Unemployment Rates

Despite a series of economic and financial crises over the past decade, Singapore's unemployment rates have remained low compared to other economies at similar levels of income (Table 1.3; Hui and Toh 2014). The average unemployment rate through the 1990s was around 2.0 percent, peaking at 5.2 percent in 2003. Except during short recessions 1973–74; 85–86; 1997–98; 2008–09, Singapore has enjoyed full employment (Pang and Lim 2015). Until the mid-1990s, stemming from robust economic growth and stability, job vacancy rates in Singapore were always higher than unemployment rates. This, however, changed after the 1997 economic crisis, after which the job vacancies rate has always lagged the unemployment rate (Hui and Toh 2014). Even during the global economic crisis in 2008, the seasonally adjusted unemployment rate did not exceed 5 percent. Singapore's low unemployment rate is often attributed to government efforts to increase the employability of workers through using subsidised training and grants to employers to retain their workers (Hui and Toh 2014).

(iv) Low Productivity Growth, Low Wage Share, and Low Real Wage Growth

Another defining feature of Singapore's labour market is the low labour productivity growth, low wage share, and low growth in real wages, especially in the lower part of the income distribution. In the short run, low productivity growth may not matter as returns on labour and capital can still drive growth. However, in the long run productivity growth is imperative to sustain economic dynamism. Labour productivity growth in Singapore has also not matched growth in real wages. For example, between 2005 and 2015, the real average monthly earnings grew at a compounded annual rate of 1.5 percent while labour productivity at 0.5 percent (Foo 2016, p. 89). If labour productivity does not keep abreast of advances in real wages, it portends many challenges for businesses as

Table 7.3 Employment in Singapore (2004–14)

Year	Labour Force ('000)		Employed ('000)		Unemployed ('000)		Unemployment Rate (%)	
	Total	Residents	Total	Residents	Total	Residents	Total	Residents
2004	2341.9	1733.4	2238.1	1632.1	103.8	101.3	3.6	4.7
2009	3030.3	1985.7	2905.9	1869.4	124.1	116.3	3.2	4.5
2012	3361.8	2119.6	3149.7	1998.9	87.4	81.2	2.1	2.9
2014	3530.8	2185.2	3440.2	2103.5	90.7	81.8	1.9	2.8
2015	3610.6	2232.3	3516.0	2147.8	94.6	84.5	1.9	2.8

Source: Ministry of Manpower (2016)

it is financially unsustainable in the long-run. This is particularly worrying when productivity and wage growth across industrial sub-sectors are compared. The real average wage growth has outpaced productivity growth in large sectors, such as Food and Beverage, Real Estate, Transportation, and Education. However, in some sectors such as biomedical manufacturing, precision engineering and wholesale trade, real wage growth lagged productivity growth (Foo 2016). This suggests that labour productivity is stronger in export-oriented-sectors than in domestically-oriented sectors (Foo 2016). This underscores the need for programs such as the Skills Future that aim to bring incremental changes to skill-set of the resident labour force.

Low productivity growth has also contributed to low real wage growth for the lowest three deciles of the income distribution (Figure 7.2). Singapore has a relatively low wage share in its national income among high-income countries. It would be a reasonable assumption to make that this stems from Singapore's growth strategy which focused on it remaining an attractive destination for businesses, investments and a conduit for wealth (Asher et al. 2015). The government focused its efforts on developing extremely flexible labour market arrangements, including cheaply available foreign workers, the absence of minimum wages, social security benefits and allowing large sections of the workforce (i.e., foreign workers) or employees earning more than $4500 per month (including manager and executive positions) to remain outside the purview of the statutory Employment Act. For example, the Employment Act of 1968 set limits on 'fringe benefits'; the Industrial Relations Act prevented collective bargaining on issues such as retrenchment and dismissal. This in turn placed downward pressures on wages, and consequently impacted decisions on the use of manpower in a firm's business model.

Singapore's education and training system

Singapore's education and training system is sophisticated by most international standards and has been shaped by the state to support the country's national developmental and economic goals. As such policy makers have actively borrowed best practice policies from around the world and tailored these for the

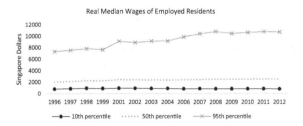

Figure 7.2 Real wage growth across income groups, Singapore

Source: Graph based on data presented in Hui and Toh (2014)

local context. Changes in the system over time have tended to reflect the pragmatism of the ruling PAP government and the evolving needs of the Singapore economy.

Singaporeans commence their learning journey from an early age – typically around 3.5 to 4 years of age. Towards the end of their primary school years, all students are required to sit for the Primary School Leaving Examination (PLSE), which influences their secondary school admission and usually their post-secondary education options. Those students who achieve strong results in the PLSE tend to proceed to studying for A Levels at junior colleges before moving on to higher education opportunities – whether in the public universities in Singapore, the private education sector or at institutions outside of Singapore. There are now five public universities in Singapore. National University of Singapore (founded in 1905); Nanyang Technological University (1981); Singapore Management University (2000), Singapore University of Technology and Design (2009), Singapore Institute of Technology (2009) and one private university which attracts public funding UniSim (2005). Singapore Institute of Technology and UniSim until recently did not offer their own degrees and offered courses in partnership with overseas institutions. However, it was announced recently that these institutions will now offer their own degrees (Straits Times 2015).

There are also a variety of foreign universities with branch campuses or partnerships in Singapore that offer their programs in the private education sector. Some of these institutions were attracted to Singapore under the now-abandoned 'global school house initiative', which was designed to attract world class universities to Singapore (see Waring 2014).

Those of medium academic ability tend to complete four years of secondary before taking Diploma level studies at one of five Polytechnics. Polytechnic education in Singapore is geared to producing diploma graduates with industry-relevant skills, and as a result, there is a close connection between the curricula and industry needs. The diplomas that Polytechnics offer tend to incorporate aspects of vocational and pre-university level education and a large proportion of the diploma graduates go on to tertiary education opportunities.

In addition to the Polytechnics, there are three colleges of the Institute of Technical Education (ITE). The ITE offers vocationally focused courses and traineeships designed to prepare graduates for immediate job opportunities and the prospect of diploma-level education at the Polytechnics.

As can be observed from Table 7.4, Singapore's education system has resulted in high levels of educational attainment. Some 32 percent of the resident labour force are degree qualified, with a further 19 percent holding a diploma-level qualification. Only 12 percent of the resident labour force have just a primary education.

Similar to the mainstream education system, Singapore's Continuing Education and Training (CET) system has been purposefully designed to ensure that there is an adequate supply of skilled labour to meet industry needs. A key institution in the CET system is the Singapore Workforce Development Agency (WDA),[2] established in 2003 to advance national workforce development through adult

Table 7.4 Educational attainment of Singapore's resident labour force, 2014 (thousands)

Highest Qualification	Total	%	Males	%	Females	%
Primary & Below	250.8	12	143.1	57	107.7	43
Lower Secondary	168.9	8	101.5	60	67.4	40
Secondary	390.1	18	197.7	46	192.4	44
Post-Secondary (Non-Tertiary)	250.4	11	153.8	61	96.5	39
Diploma & Professional Qualification	426.1	19	230.5	54	195.6	46
Degree	699	32	375.9	54	323	46
Total	2,185.2	100	1,202.6	55	982.6	45

Source: Ministry of Manpower (2016)

continuing education and training, and to facilitate employment and re-employment through skills development. The WDA coordinates and regulates training providers and administers the Workforce Skills and Qualifications (WSQ) qualifications system and associated training funds, 49 Continuing Education and Training (CET) centres and over 400 Approved Training Organizations. As Sung et al. (2013) explain, these training providers are able to compete with one another on price for WSQ training courses and other training courses they may wish to offer. Both WSQ and non-WSQ courses attract significant subsidies from the government, which can cover up to 90 percent of course fees.

Singapore's WSQ Framework is said to be designed on principles of 'open access, competency-based training and assessment' (Bound and Lin 2011). There are 34 WSQ frameworks covering industry sectors as diverse as Aerospace, Floristry and Tourism through to generic occupations and skills areas such as Leadership and People Management, Service Excellence and Human Resources. Willmott and Karmel (2011, p. 1) has observed that Singapore's WSQ system was heavily influenced by the vocational and continuing education system of Australia, especially the Australian Quality Training Framework (AQTF) and the National Vocational Qualifications. Perhaps the only key difference is that the apprenticeship system which has long been a feature of Australia's system of vocational training is not present in Singapore's system (Willmott and Karmel 2011, p. 9).

For each framework, there is an 'Industry Skills and Training Council' with representation from employers, unions, industry associations and training organizations. Each Industry Skills and Training Council has responsibility for developing an 'industry competency map' designed to chart the employability skills, occupational skills and industry knowledge required for that industry. In addition to the industry-specific skills and knowledge mapped within each framework, there are also common 'Foundational Skills' which are described as 'skills, knowledge and attributes' designed to assist individuals to improve their 'employability' and which are portable across industries.

These Employability skills are offered at three occupational levels – PME (Professional, Manager, Engineer) and Operations and Supervisory Levels. And cover five broad categories which include:

(a) Analytical, Conceptual & Evaluative Skills
(b) Informational & Communication Technologies Skill
(c) Interpersonal Skills
(d) Personal Management and Development Skills
(e) Manage Job Safety Skills

Additionally, these foundational skills also include workplace numeracy and literacy competencies.

The strong demand for skilled labour combined with the comprehensive and first-class education and training system has resulted in high levels of graduate employability in Singapore. However, as the trend data in Table 7.5 above shows, the proportion of graduates has declined over the last decade for the three key

Table 7.5 Employability of graduates, Singapore: 2007–15

Institutions	2007	2011	2015
Universities			
Proportion of Graduates Employed (%)	94.5	91.4	88.9
Full-Time Permanent	89.8	86.4	82.4
Part-Time/Temporary	4.7	5.0	6.6
Median Gross Monthly Starting Salary	2,750	3,000	3,300
Polytechnics			
Fresh Graduates			
Proportion of Graduates Employed (%)	93.0	92.1	88.9
Full-Time Permanent	75.3	67.0	57.9
Part-Time/Temporary	17.7	25.1	31.0
Median Gross Monthly Starting Salary	1,700	1,850	2,100
Post-NS Graduates			
Proportion of Graduates Employed (%)	92.7	94.7	91.5
Full-Time Permanent	82.3	80.1	70.8
Part-Time/Temporary	10.4	14.6	20.7
Median Gross Monthly Starting Salary	2,000	2,100	2,500
Institute of Technical Education (ITE)			
Fresh Graduates			
Proportion of Graduates Employed (%)	92.9	84.1	83.2
Full-Time Permanent	71.1	63.5	48.4
Part-Time/Temporary	21.8	20.6	34.7
Median Gross Monthly Starting Salary	1,217	1,300	1,700

Institutions	2007	2011	2015
Post-NS Graduates			
Proportion of Graduates Employed (%)	93.9	89.6	86.8
Full-Time Permanent	79.8	79.7	63.0
Part-Time/Temporary	14.2	10.0	23.8
Median Gross Monthly Starting Salary	1,400	1,600	1,950

Source: Ministry of Manpower (2016)

categories of ITE, Polytechnic and university graduates. This is of some concern for policy makers, who have responded with several new initiatives to improve employability and work-readiness, which are outlined in the next section.

Future proofing and being job-ready

Building on the success of its 2010 Economic Strategies Committee (ESC), Singapore has set up its Committee on the Future Economy (CFE) as a key policy-generating mechanism to help steer the country into the future. This 30-member committee drawn from government and industry – national and international – focuses on five key pillars to future proof the economy – corporate capabilities and innovation; growth industries and markets; connectivity; city; jobs and skills (Gov.sg 2016). These five pillars that emphasise innovative capacities in organizations, creating value through partnerships and international business models, building a smart and connected city, are all linked through one key element – a future-ready workforce. Accordingly, the Singapore Government's Research, Innovation and Enterprise (RIE) plan 2016–2020 set aside S$19B to support key research and research commercialization initiatives (NRF.gov.sg 2016). It is no surprise then why the RIE plan has set aside over 40 percent of the S$19B funding allocation to develop manpower, further academic research and support the development of innovative enterprise to remain competitive.

The RIE plan not only tackles low productivity growth in specific industry sectors but also acts as a catalyst to spurring innovation in new areas. For instance, 21 percent of the funding has been set aside for the health and biomedical sectors and 13 percent apportioned for 'white space' research, e.g., emerging areas such as cyber security. At the same time, the government has set aside about 17 percent of the allocation to the advanced manufacturing and engineering sector – a sector which has been plagued with low productivity levels and inaction in the light of age-old traditional manufacturing approaches. This evidence became clear in a recent productivity and innovation benchmarking study of 2015 undertaken for the SMEs in Singapore's manufacturing sector (Murdoch University 2015) wherein it was identified that poor Technology and Capital Utilization practices was a drag on productivity in the sector. Eighty percent of SME leaders interviewed acknowledged that the preference was to adopt industry standard tools and techniques as opposed to embracing innovation and making use of state-of-the-art technologies. This research also made clear that the sector was reluctant to invest in R&D activities, collaborate with the education sector and undertake benchmarking or regular technology assessments. One outcome of such less-than-optimum practices was that firms were investing less in training and education – about 16 hours on average per employee per annum. It may be reasonable to assume that the experience of the manufacturing sector is not unique, and other workforce-heavy sectors such as retail, tourism and hotel sector encounter similar issues.

By making such significant investments in research and innovation activities now, Singapore is not only following rhetoric with action but also more importantly preparing its workforce for the future. Creating a flexible lifelong system of education with a focus on skills, knowhow and job performance is where the government hopes to take the economy. There is an explicit policy disposition in Singapore, which favors developing occupations such as data scientists, software engineers and healthcare professionals. To prepare for this future, Singapore has created, under its Adapt and Grow strategy, a Professional Conversion Program (PCP) for the ICT sector whereby mid-career Professionals, Managers, Executives and Technicians (PMETs) from across the economy are being encouraged to re-skill with necessary competencies and where possible switch careers. Not only is the government providing course subsidies of 70 to 90 percent but also salary support, which extends up to 90 percent for PMETs to those who are aged over 40 (WDA 2016). Singapore clearly sees the need for collaboration between humans and robots or "cobot" in the decades to come (Sin 2016).

In both recessionary and non-recessionary periods, the government has actively encouraged skills upgrading and improved employee competency to enhance employability. To improve work-readiness a 'new CET 2020 masterplan' was introduced in 2014 with a focus on building expertise within the workforce and increasing training provided during employment; to provide career guidance and high-quality learning opportunities (WDA 2016). Specific initiatives under the CET 2020 include sectoral manpower strategies that identify the manpower needs of each industrial sub-sector every five years and charts out measures to achieve them; competency frameworks; online education and training, piloting an 'individual learning portfolio'; blended learning and financial support for structured workplace-based learning (TODAY online 2014).

Over the past five years (2011–2015), there have been over one million WSQ training events completed at different levels. A survey conducted by the WDA in 2015 found that 91 percent of businesses interviewed reported that the employees who had completed WSQ certifications performed 'more efficiently' or 'more effectively' and around 50 percent indicated that it positively impacted productivity. About 8 percent of employees who completed the training reported to receiving a promotion, and 11 percent a pay increment in the same survey (SSG-WSG. gov.sg 2016).

To enhance the efficacy in the system at the macro level of policy-making and direction setting, the Singapore government in 2016 announced the formation of two new statutory boards – Workforce Singapore (WSG) and Skills Future

Singapore (SSG). WSG subsumes the WDA under the oversight of the Ministry of Manpower and SSG under the purview of the Ministry of Education. It is the intention for the two boards to coordinate and implement Skills Future – a key platform that has been created for Singaporeans to prepare for the future. In May 2016, the government also established a tripartite Council on Skills, Innovation and Productivity (CSIP) drawing on expertise from the government, industry, unions and educational institutions to further the work related to Skills Future and develop Industry Transformation Maps (Skills Future 2016a). We discuss Skills Future in further detail later in the chapter.

At the level of institutional capacity building, the government in 2011 announced that it would make available 2000 additional university places between 2011 and 2015 at Singapore's four universities: National University of Singapore (NUS), Nanyang Technological University (NTU), Singapore Management University (SMU) and Singapore University of Technology and Design (SUTD). This would increase higher education participation from 26 to 30 percent by 2015. It also announced a Committee on University Education Pathways Beyond 2015, to explore avenues for increasing higher education participation beyond 30 percent. The CUEP's recommendations were accepted in 2012, and the government announced that two educational institutes, the Singapore Institute of Technology (SIT), a public institution which partners with foreign universities to deliver their courses in Singapore; and UniSIM, a private institution, would be given university status. They would now admit full-time students and be tasked with awarding their own degrees. This would enable the government to increase university seats by 3000 students a year by 2020 (Waring 2014), and target a higher education participation rate of 40 percent by 2020.

Skills future

In recognizing the need for enhanced training, the government launched Skills Future in 2014, a skill-upgrading program. The program is budgeted to spend S$1 billion annually until 2020 on improving skills of the domestic workforce through a range of training, development and certification programs. Singapore citizens, of all age groups, can apply for a range of programs and receive partial funding. In most cases the funding covers up to 90 percent of cost of the training programs. Singapore's Deputy Prime Minister, Mr. Tharman Shanmugaratnam, said:

> we will create a new environment for lifelong learning. It is critical to our future. It will develop the skills and mastery needed to take our economy to the next level. More fundamentally, it aims to empower each Singaporean to chart their own journey in life, and gain fulfilment at work and even in their senior years. We have called this development effort 'Skills Future'. It marks a major new phase of investment in our people, throughout life.
>
> (Skills Future 2015, p. Part C)

The aim of the program is to improve competitiveness by increasing skills and productivity of the workforce; to develop a strong Singapore-core workforce; to incentivise businesses to 'go lean'; get more done with less by relying on automation, mechanization and relying on technological solutions. There are four broad programs under Skills Future, each targeting a specific part of the population.

Students in school

To target students in tertiary institutes, Skills Future aims to provide early career guidance and counselling for students in ITEs, Polytechnics, and publicly funded universities; local internship opportunities for second- and third-year students of polytechnics; and funding for polytechnic and ITE students if they get selected for overseas internship programs.

Early career employees

In addition to the career guidance and counselling, early career workers now can participate in 'Place-and-Train' programs that aim to 'place' at least 3000 trained professionals, managers and executives in SMEs by December 2017. The training fee is subsidised by 90 percent, and grants of $5000 are provided to SMEs if the employee is retained beyond six months. A credit of S$500 is available to all Singaporeans above the age of 25, which they can use to defray the cost of any training program. The government aims to make ad-hoc top-ups to this scheme annually.

Mid-career employees

In addition to the schemes available for early career workers, Skills Future aims to provide specific modular courses focused on the requirements of specific industrial sub-sectors. All Singaporean's aged above 40 will receive a 90 percent subsidy for these courses in publicly funded institutions.

Employers

Under the Skills Future program, employers receive financial subsidies for encouraging training and retention of their employees post training. Under the Place-and-Train program, SMEs receive $5000 for retaining newly hired employees for 6 months training programs in identified sectors (hotel, retail, food services, built environment and public buses); and grants up to $15,000 to offset on-the-job training for polytechnic graduate hires.

Since the launch of Skills Future, many initiatives have taken shape – Skills Future Credit, the Skills Future Earn and Learn Program and the Skills Future Study Award for specific industries. Republic Polytechnic launched one such program for the hotels and operations management sector enrolling the largest cohort of Skills Future diploma graduates in an Earn-and-Learn Program. The program was launched in partnership with the Singapore Tourism Board backed by 54 hotel partners that will see 48 trainee placements, thereby creating an integrated system of education, training and career development. As part of the program, participants will complete in-company projects, thereby integrating theory and practice (Skills Future 2016b).

In addition to skill and competency building, the Skills Future program is also linked to industry transformation. This is evidenced in the retail sector manpower plan (SMP) that was developed by the Singapore government. Acknowledging the sector-based developments with the spread of ecommerce platforms and digitization of processes and ongoing workforce challenges, the government has focused one of the key pillars for this sector on business remodeling and job redesign. The objective of this effort is to help retail employers create higher value-adding jobs while adopting leaner operating models (Skills Future 2016c). Finally, the government has also set aside S$45m over three years for a Skills Future Mentors program targeted at SMEs to help them become employers-of-choice. This program is expected to reach at least 2000 SMEs with the support from 400 mentors who will work with SMEs to enhance their systems, processes, define job scopes and implement better training mechanisms for employees (Ibid.).

Singapore, as a pragmatic nation, understands that building workforce capabilities, particularly in SMEs that employ over 70 percent of the labor force, underpins organizational innovative capacities, which in turn contributes to the broader economic growth agenda. Emulating Germany's success with how its SMEs play an important role in economic development, Singapore is keen to move from a multi-national centric to a SME-led economy. To do so, Singapore needs to leverage its industry-based trade associations to support SMEs become growth-focused, global and competitive. As a result, the Singapore government has set aside S$30m over the next five years to build capacity in the 150 active trade associations and chambers (TAC). In addition, the government is also looking to place its officers in these TACs to forge new partnerships that can help support firm level growth (Lim 2016).

Conclusions

This chapter provides an overview of recent measures to improve work-readiness and employability of Singapore's domestic labour force. These measures stem from a series of recent reforms underway that aim to foster productivity-led growth in Singapore. Businesses are actively incentivised to automate, adopt technology solutions in their business models and reduce the reliance on foreign labour. Programs such as the Skills Future, increased vocational training and alternate pathways to tertiary education are aimed at improving job-readiness in Singapore.

The Singapore government has always actively intervened in the labour market during economic recessions by providing temporary subsidies or training programs for retrenched workers (Hui and Toh 2014). The current initiatives, however, are a departure from usual policy responses of the government in as much as they represent a concerted effort to address the structural constraints of Singapore's labour force: (i) heavy reliance on foreign labour; (ii) inadequate work-readiness in the resident labour force.

Programs such as the Skills Future are aimed at addressing short-term training needs of those already employed in the labour force, while increased opportunity to access tertiary education through Singapore Institute of Technology and Uni-Sim, will in the long-term, help meet the demand by local businesses for skilled workers from within the resident labour force.

Table 7.6 Summary of key findings, Singapore

	Summary – Singapore
Demographics/ labour market	***Population:*** 5.35 million of which 3.90 million are citizens and permanent residents. Labour force of 3.6 million, and foreigners constitute about 38 percent of the labour force.
	Unemployment rate: 1.9 percent. Singapore has historically enjoyed full employment (except during short periods of recession in 73–74; 85–86; 97–98; 08–09).
	Demographics: Singapore is ageing rapidly and relies to a large extent on foreign workers (at both ends of the skill spectrum) to support its economy. Its Total Fertility Rate has been below replacement rate since 1975. In the next 10 years Singapore, will see a doubling of the share of those aged above 65 and tripling of those aged above 80 in their population.
	Demographic Challenge: Singapore has been relatively open to relying on foreign workers (and accepts skilled migrants) to meet its labour market needs and overcome the challenges of an ageing population. In recent years, however, congestion externalities and increasing demand for positional goods by the citizenry have placed political constraints on the number of foreign workers that Singapore can admit.
	Economic Growth: Singapore has witnessed spectacular economic growth as evidenced by its per capita income of S$70,000 (current $) in 2015, up from S$1309 in 1960. Manufacturing accounts for 19 percent, and Services about 75 percent of Singapore S$402 billion economy in 2015.
Economy	***Labour Market Challenge:*** Singapore has experienced low productivity, low real wage growth and low share of wages in national income. Between 2005 and 2015, the real average monthly earnings grew at a compounded annual rate of 1.5 percent while labour productivity at 0.5 percent.

Educational Structure/ Work-readiness frameworks	Singapore's education system has resulted in high levels of educational attainment. Some 32 percent of the resident labour force are degree qualified with a further 19 percent holding a diploma-level qualification. Only 12 percent of the resident labour force have just a primary education.
Reforms Underway	Singapore's Continuing Education and Training (CET) system oversees the supply of skilled labour to meet industry needs. A key institution in the CET system is the Singapore Workforce Development Agency (WDA)[1], established in 2003 to advance national workforce development through adult continuing education and training, and to facilitate employment and re-employment through skills development.
	The WDA coordinates and regulates training providers and administers the Workforce Skills and Qualifications (WSQ) qualifications. There are 34 WSQ frameworks covering industry sectors as diverse as Aerospace, Floristry and Tourism through to generic occupations and skills areas such as Leadership and People Management, Service Excellence and Human Resources. For each framework, there is an 'Industry Skills and Training Council' with representation from employers, unions, industry associations and training organizations. Each Industry Skills and Training Council has responsibility for developing an 'industry competency map' designed to chart the employability skills, occupational skills and industry knowledge required for that industry.
	The government aims to increase tertiary education participation to 40 percent by 2020. To accomplish this, the government has increased the number of seats at public universities, as well as given 'university' status to erstwhile private providers.
	To improve work-readiness, the government launched Skills Future in 2014, The program is budgeted to spend S$1 billion annually until 2020 on improving skills of the domestic workforce through a range of training, development and certification programs. Singapore citizens, of all age groups, can apply for a range of programs and receive partial funding. In most cases the funding covers up to 90 percent of cost of the training programs.

[1] It was announced at the time of writing that the Workforce Development Agency would be renamed 'Workforce Singapore' while a new Statutory agency called 'Skills Future Singapore' would be created by 2017 that would take over some of the skills and training functions of the former WDA.

Notes

1 For more detailed overview see Pang and Lim (2015) and Hui and Toh (2014). Au Yong (2014) provides a detailed historical overview of Singapore's productivity (including labour productivity) issues and the overall policy context.
2 It was announced at the time of writing that the Workforce Development Agency would be renamed 'Workforce Singapore' while a new Statutory agency called 'Skills Future Singapore' would be created by 2017 that would take over some of the skills and training functions of the former WDA.

References

Asher, M. G., Bali, A. S. and Kwan, C. Y. 2015, 'Public financial management in Singapore: Key characteristics and prospects', *Singapore Economic Review*, Vol. 60, no. 3, pp. 1–18.

Auyong, H. 2014, *Singapore's productivity challenge*, LKY School of Public Policy, National University of Singapore, accessed October 16, 2017. Available at http://lkyspp2.nus.edu.sg/wp-content/uploads/2014/05/Productivity-challenges-in-Singapore-Part-1.pdf (Accessed on Oct 16, 2017).

Bali, A., McKiernan, P., Vas, C. and Waring, P. 2016, 'Competition law, regulation and trade: Implications for productivity and innovation in Singaporean manufacturing SMEs', in Schaper, M. and Lee, C. (eds.) *Competition law, regulation & SMEs in the Asia-Pacific: Understanding the small business perspective*, Singapore: ISEAS – Yusof Ishak Institute.

Bound, H. and Lin, M. 2011, *Singapore Workforce Skills Qualification (WSQ), workplace learning and assessment, (Stage One)*, Institute for Adult Learning Singapore, Research Paper.

Channel News Asia. 2016, 'Two new statutory boards formed for skills and employment', January 12.

Foo, X. Y. 2016, *Productivity and wage growth in Singapore*, Singapore: Ministry of Trade and Industry.

Ghesquire, H. 2006, *Singapore's success: Engineering economic growth*, Singapore: Cengage Learning.

Gov.sg. 2016, *About the committee on the future economy*. [online] Available at: www.gov.sg/microsites/future-economy/about-us/about-the-committee-on-the-future-economy [Accessed September 21, 2016].

Hui, W. T. and Toh, R. 2014, *Growth with equity in Singapore: Challenges and prospects*, Conditions of Work and Employment Series #48, Geneva: International Labour Organization. Available at: www.ilo.org/public/libdoc/ilo/2014/114B09_32_fren.pdf.

Lee, S. A 2015, 'Governance and economic change in Singapore', *Singapore Economic Review*, Vol. 60, no. 3, pp. 1–15.

Lim, L. 2016, 'Shake-up of trade bodies in Singapore: What could it look like?' *Channel News Asia*. [online]. Available at: www.channelnewsasia.com/news/singapore/shake-up-of-trade-bodies/2656112.html [Accessed September 21, 2016].

Ministry of Manpower. 2016, *Singapore yearbook of manpower statistics*. Available at: http://stats.mom.gov.sg/Pages/Singapore-Yearbook-Of-Manpower-Statistics-2016.aspx.

Ministry of Education (MOE). 2015, *Education Statistics Digest 2015*, Singapore. Ministry of Education

Murdoch University. 2015, *Singapore Innovation & Productivity Institute (SiPi) – Murdoch University: stakeholder report*, Singapore. [Online]. Available at: www.murdoch.sg/wp-content/uploads/SiPi-Benchmarking-Study-261115.pdf [Accessed September 21, 2016].

NRF.gov.sg. 2016, *RIE2020 plan*. [Online] Available at: www.nrf.gov.sg/rie2020 [Accessed August 21, 2016].

Pang, E. F. and Lim, L. Y. C. 2015, 'Labor, productivity and Singapore's development model', *The Singapore Economic Review*, Vol. 60, pp. 1–30.

Sin, Y. 2016, 'Singapore in 2035 to be inclusive and innovative: DPM Tharman', *The Straits Times*. [Online]. Available at: www.straitstimes.com/singapore/education/singapore-in-2035-to-be-inclusive-and-innovative-dpm-tharman [Accessed August 21, 2016].

Singapore Department of Statistics. 2016a, *Labour, employment, wages and productivity – tables*. Available at: www.singstat.gov.sg/statistics/browse-by-theme/labour-employment-wages-and-productivity-tables [Accessed September 17, 2016].

Singapore Department of Statistics. 2016b, *Singapore yearbook of statistics*. Available at: www.singstat.gov.sg/publications/publications-and-papers/reference/yearbook-of-statistics-singapore [Accessed September 17, 2016].

Skills Future. 2015, *Budget speech 2015 – Section C: Developing our people*. Available at: www.skillsfuture.sg/speeches.html/lbudget-speeche-2015.html [Accessed September 17, 2016].

Skills Future. 2016a, *Skills future*. [Online] Available at: www.skillsfuture.sg/factsheet.html/formation-of-the-council-for-skills-innovation-and-productivity [Accessed September 21, 2016].

Skills Future. 2016b, *Skills future*. [Online] Available at: www.skillsfuture.sg/factsheet.html/republic-polytechnic-launches-skillsfuture-earn-and-learn-programme-for-hotel-sector-with-largest-student-intake-to-date [Accessed September 21, 2016].

Skills Future. 2016c, *Skills future*. [Online] Available at: www.skillsfuture.sg/factsheet.html/retail-sectoral-manpower-plan-aims-to-drive-workforce-transformation-and-make-every-retail-job-better [Accessed September 21, 2016].

Ssg-wsg.gov.sg. 2016, *Annual WDA survey reveals that employers and individuals continue to benefit from WSQ training*. [Online]. Available at: www.ssg-wsg.gov.sg/new-and-announcements/20_Jul_2016.html [Accessed October 18, 2016].

Straits Times. 2015, *SIT to offer five new degrees and raise intake to a record 2,080 this year*. Available at: www.straitstimes.com/singapore/education/sit-to-offer-five-new-degrees-and-raise-intake-to-a-record-2080-this-year [Accessed September 17, 2016].

Sung, J., Chi Man Ng., M., Loke, F. and Ramos, C. 2013, 'The nature of employability skills: Empirical evidence from Singapore', *International Journal of Training and Development*, Vol. 17, no. 3, pp. 176–193.

TODAY online. 2014, *New CET masterplan to get employers more involved in building skills*. [Online] Available at: www.todayonline.com/singapore/new-cet-masterplan-get-employers-more-involved-building-skills [Accessed September 17, 2016].

United Nations Department of Economic and Social Affairs. 2015, *World population prospects: the 2015 revision*, accessed October 10, 2016. Available at https://esa.un.org/unpd/wpp/.

Waring, P. 2014, 'Singapore's global schoolhouse strategy: Retreat or recalibration?' *Studies in Higher Education*, Vol. 39, no. 5. pp. 874–884.

Willmott, G. and Karmel, A. 2011, *CET systems update: Developments in policy, systems and delivery: United Kingdom, Australia and New Zealand, Research Report*, Institute for Adult Learning, Singapore.

Wong, T. and Yeoh, B. A. 2003, *Fertility and the family: An overview of pro-natalist population policies in Singapore.* Working Paper. Asian Meta Centre For Population and Sustainable Development Analysis. Available at: http://hs-esl.ism-online. org/files/2011/03/SingaporePopulationReport.pdf [Accessed September 17, 2016].

Workforce Development Agency (WDA). 2016, *Adapt and grow.* [Online] Available at: http://wda.gov.sg/content/dam/wda/pdf/PressRelease/20160504/ AnnexA.pdf [Accessed September 21, 2016].

Yeoh, B. 2007, *Singapore: Hungry for Foreign workers at all skill levels.* Working Paper, National University of Singapore, Singapore.

8 Antecedents, consequences and strategic responses to graduate work-readiness

Challenges in India

Verma Prikshat, Sanjeev Kumar and Parinita Raje

Introduction

India is in a position to reap its prospective demographic dividends by 2020 by becoming one of the world's youngest countries with a median age of 27.3 and an estimated 28 percent contribution to the world's workforce (Ernst and Young 2014a; UN Habitat 2013). During this period, the prediction is that the labour force in the developed world will face a decline in its working age population by 4 percent (Bloom and McKenna 2015). Conversely, in India the workforce is set to increase by an estimated 32 percent, based on its lowest dependency ratio (i.e., number of children or elderly dependent on wage earners) (India Skills Report 2014). This is likely to catapult India and its workforce to the centre stage of the global labour market, due in part to the "ageing" challenge faced by the majority of developed nations (India Skills Report 2014). These favourable demographics show that the major portion of India's population will be active in the working age group of 15 to 50 years, indicating that by 2020 India will have a surplus in its active working population of approximately 47 million people (Bhattacharya et al. 2010). This presents a good opportunity for India to increase productivity in order to meet its needs and at the same time to contribute to the needs of the workforce globally, particularly in the Asian region. With the launch of the ASEAN Economic Community (AEC) in late 2015, and the impending increase in talent mobility across Asia, it is imperative for India to develop 'work-ready' graduates who can harness their skills to transcend the region with ease (Chia 2013).

Leveraging this 'demographic dividend' is easier said than done. The ever-competitive knowledge era will place increased emphasis on the quality as well as the quantity of skilled workers (Hajkowicz 2015). Major technological changes (megatrends) will also change the global industrial landscape significantly by 2030 (Hajkowicz 2015). This is the most significant challenge that India, among other emerging economies, will face in the wake of the relatively poor level of skills possessed and considerably higher level of unemployment of graduates, despite its large potential workforce (Chenoy 2012). This situation has arisen due to high rates of school dropouts, inadequate vocational education (VE) and higher education (HE) skills training capacities, negative perceptions of vocational skills in particular and relatively low levels of work-readiness of even those holding professional qualifications (Chenoy 2012; Majumder and Mukherjee 2013).

This is one of the most significant conundrums that India is likely to face into the future and has the potential to create a reverse economic impact leading to a "demographic disaster" instead of a "demographic dividend" (India Skills Report 2014, p. 17). The greatest challenge for India to reap the benefits of its demographic dividend is to create a skilled labour pool that is employable and 'work-ready' in response to the needs and demands of industry now and into the future (India Skills Report 2014). Considering that India will have the largest population in the world within the next fifteen years, and a large number of young people attempting to find worthwhile and satisfying employment will only exacerbate the scale of the problem.

This chapter discusses the antecedents and consequences of this challenge and identifies scalable solutions on the part of the stakeholders concerned. The first section of the chapter explores the scope and nature of these graduate work-readiness challenges in India, and the second section analyses the antecedents of these challenges. The third section considers the strategic responses initiated by government, industry and educational stakeholders, followed by the recommended strategies to drive effective change in the existing education system in order to meet these work-ready challenges.

Graduate work-readiness challenges in India

Human resource skills and knowledge are recognised as the primary determinants of the drivers of productivity, economic growth and social development for any country (ILO 2014). For the jobs of today and those of the future, countries with proportionately higher qualifications and superior skill levels will adjust more effectively to the challenges and opportunities of growth in a globalised world as opposed to those that are not as well positioned (ILO 2014). In contrast to the prolonged economic downturn in most Western countries, India's economy has grown faster than its pool of skilled workers, posing an immense challenge to its long-term sustainability (Chatterjee et al. 2014). The Indian economy has recorded high rates of GDP growth (7.6 percent) in 2015–2016, up from 5.6 in 2012–2013, spurred by strong growth in industrial and service sectors (ILO 2016). According to the latest economic survey, 2015–2016, the country has emerged as the fastest-growing major economy and a safe haven for long-term growth, due to improvement in its macroeconomic situation (KPMG 2016). India's 1.25 billion population is expanding at a rate of 17 percent annually, and India is predicted to become the world's most populous country, reaching almost 1.5 billion people, by 2030 (CRISIL 2010). India is also set to become the largest contributor to the global workforce, and its working-age population – 15–64 years – is likely to increase significantly, from 749 to 962 million, between 2010 and 2030 (CRISIL 2010). With respect to country demographic profiles and associated labour markets, India, Vietnam and Indonesia have amongst the youngest populations and labour markets in the world, whilst the populations of

Singapore, Taiwan and to a lesser extent Malaysia are ageing significantly, (Bruni 2013; di Gropello and Kruse 2011; ILO 2014).

Recently, 83 percent of India's educational institutions reported that they believed that their graduates were ready for the market, but only 51 percent of employers agreed (Mourshed et al. 2012, p. 40). Finding work-ready graduates to match job requirements has become a significant problem for many Indian employers (India Skills Report 2014). Given the current pace of economic growth, India is likely to face a staggering skills gap in which between 75 and 80 percent of graduates lack the skills for a growing labour market (India Skills Report 2014, p. 13). This is evident across all industry sectors (India Skills Report 2014), representing a paradox in which the country will have more than enough formally qualified people, but an insufficient quantity of work-ready or employable job candidates according to industry requirements (Goldin 2015).With an ever-increasing population, and its forecasted status as one of the 'youngest' countries in the world by 2020, it is imperative that India effectively addresses its graduate work-readiness challenges, for economic, productivity, growth and competitiveness purposes. With an ever-increasing population and an expected surge in workforce requirement in five key sectors (see Figure 8.1), it is clear that India faces a major challenge of creating a 'work- ready' workforce over the next few decades.

As one example of the scope of the challenge, of approximately three hundred thousand candidates who completed the Wheebox Employability Skill Test (WEST) (India Skills Report 2015), only 37.22 percent of participants were rated as employable. The test assessed the talent pool entering the job market on various parameters, including cognitive ability, numerical and logical ability, communication skills and behavioural traits (India Skills Report 2015). The WEST analysis revealed a disturbing proportion of graduates who were not work-ready across various qualifications/disciplines, as illustrated in Figure 8.2 (India Skills Report 2015).

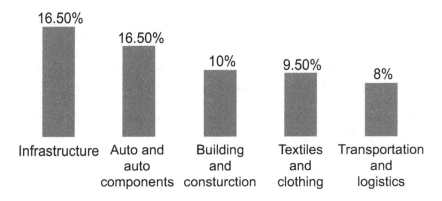

Figure 8.1 Estimated industry growth rate for India (Compound Annual Growth Rate: 2013–2021)

Source: Ernst and Young 2014a

Figure 8.2 Graduates not work-ready across various qualifications/disciplines
Source: Developed for this study on the basis of India Skills Report (2014)

Antecedents of the work-readiness challenges in India

The availability of an employable and skilled workforce is paramount to the economic development of any country, but the Indian economy is witnessing a divergent trend within which both critical levels of graduate unemployment and serious skill shortages coexist (Srivastava and Khare 2012; The Economist 2013). The employability of graduates can be directly related to the education system. It has been asserted that the Indian education system has prepared graduates poorly for the labour market (Khare 2014). Indian graduates lack the required skills, thus making them unsuitable for the competitive market (Srivastava and Chatterjee 2014). The growth in the Indian education sector, buoyed by more than a 7 percent per annum growth of gross domestic product (GDP) in the last decade, has witnessed a deficient array of haphazard policies that lack strategic and systemic planning (Sanghi et al. 2012). This has resulted in the vast majority of education service providers not being in a position to produce students equipped with a desirable skill-set for the job market (Khare 2014; Srivastava and Chatterjee 2014).The unemployment for "fresh" graduates from universities and affiliated colleges is four times (33 percent) higher than total country unemployment (8.5 percent) (The Economist 2014, p. 10).

The following sections outline the key factors suggested by the literature, which are antecedents to the lack of work-readiness of many Indian graduates.

Demand-supply mismatch

The work-readiness of a graduate is dependent on both the demand-side, that is the availability of jobs and the labour market signals, and the supply-side, including the availability of high-quality educational institutions that can generate matching academic knowledge and employability skills. Usually the industry that absorbs the graduates determines the criteria for employment in that particular industry. A disconcerting aspect of the Indian education system is the mismatch of demand and supply for graduate employment, resulting from the lack of work-readiness skills among many university graduates (India Skills Report 2015). Wheebox's report in association with Peoplestrong found that a gap exists between the productivity needs of employers and the skills available in the market today, resulting in a clear mismatch between talent and opportunity (India Skills Report 2015). This 'reality gap', as observed by Deloitte (2015), was attributed to the disconnection between the knowledge they gained in higher education (HE) and the skills their employers value most in the workplace.

As India approaches the year 2022, it is projected that India's Gross Domestic Product (GDP) will grow at a Compound Annual Growth Rate (CAGR) of approximately 8 percent (Ministry of Skill Development and Entrepreneurship 2015). On the demand side, there will be an additional net incremental human resource requirement of 109.73 million skilled employees (total projected employment – 560.46 million) in twenty-four key sectors except agriculture (Ministry of Skill Development and Entrepreneurship 2015). Some of the key industry sectors' incremental requirements are shown in Figure 8.3.

On the supply side, the projected requirements of the skilled workforce in 2022 is estimated to be 402.87 million, comprising 298.25 million of the existing workforce (farm and non-farm) and 104.62 million fresh entrants to the workforce over the next seven years (Ministry of Skill Development and Entrepreneurship 2015).

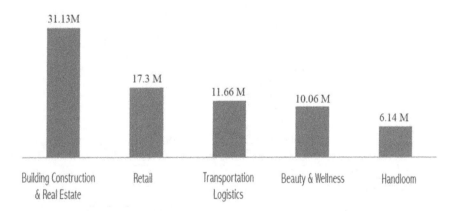

Figure 8.3 Break up of incremental requirement across some important sectors

Source: Developed for this study on the basis of Ministry of Skill Development and Entrepreneurship (2015).

Archaic/complex structure of the education system

Pertinent aspects of the Indian HE system are its ageing structure, archaic practices and processes (Agarwal 2010; Rath and Behera 2014). The funding is shared between government, the states and the private sector. According to the University Grants Commission (UGC) Report (2015), there are currently 46 central universities, 339 state universities, 225 private universities, 126 "deemed" universities and about 35,000 affiliated colleges (see Figure 8.4). A "deemed" university means an institute of higher education declared as having the academic status and privileges of a university by the central government on the advice of UGC, and working at a very high standard in a specific area of study (MHRD 2015c). A number of recent studies (Agarwal 2010; Shah 2015; Ernst and Young 2009, 2011, 2013) have suggested that the regulatory framework in Indian higher education is opaque, mired in complexity and tough to navigate (see Figure 8.4).

The prospect of universities and colleges making changes in obsolete curricula and adding new innovative courses of relevance are constrained by the rules, control and regulations of multiple agencies at the national and state levels. This necessarily inhibits the enhancement of graduate work-readiness or employability.

Stifling affiliation system

In India, the majority of undergraduate education is provided in affiliated colleges with state universities (Ernst and Young 2012). The affiliated college sector is huge, enrolling over 90 percent of undergraduates, 70 percent of postgraduates and 17 percent of doctoral students (Ernst and Young 2012). The

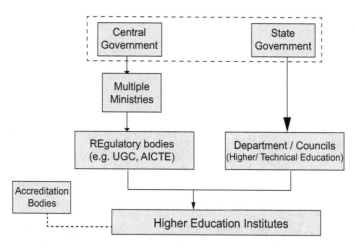

Figure 8.4 Structure of higher education system in India

Source: Ernst and Young 2009, p. 84

affiliating system that was useful for the rapid expansion of professional programs in engineering and medicine (for the uniformity of professional practices) has become a bottleneck, stifling innovation and experimentation (Agarwal 2010). The affiliation system is bureaucratic and stymied by over-centralisation and a lack of transparency and professionalism (Kumar and Ambrish 2015). Different state universities prescribe the courses for affiliated colleges, set the regulatory standards, conduct exams and award the degree, leaving very limited room for flexibility in teaching and innovation. Given the huge size of affiliated colleges, it has become difficult for the state universities to manage these colleges and ensure quality of output (Chopra 2010).

Lack of higher-order thinking (HOT) skills

Higher levels of thinking, as identified in Bloom's taxonomy (Bagchi and Sharma 2014; Bloom 1956), are important abilities to foster in graduates in order to prepare them for the future. It has been observed that priority and development of higher-order thinking (HOT) and skills – ability to analyse, logical reasoning, ability to evaluate and create and ability to solve problems – significantly heighten graduate work-readiness (Aman and Sitotaw 2014; Kim 2011). A major concern is that Indian graduates are relatively strong on lower-order thinking skills but weaker on higher-order thinking skills (Aspiring Minds Report 2013; Blom and Hiroshi 2011; Raman and Koka 2015; Tulsiand Poonia 2015). There appears to be minimum improvement in the higher-order thinking skills over the course of HE programs, and graduates accordingly leave with minimal employability skills, thus not coming up to the expectations of industry standards (Aspiring Minds Report 2013).

Employers expect their employees to be more attuned to an increasingly competitive external environment that requires creative thinking, problem solving and good communication skills in addition to sound academic skills (Postiglione 2012; Shafie and Nayan 2010; Smith and Krüger 2008; The Economist 2014). The deficiencies of Indian universities' education model (curriculum, teaching, learning process and assessment) and lack of focus on HOT skills in graduate programs can be held at least partly responsible for graduates who are 'not work-ready' (Rath and Behera, 2014). Moreover, academic pedagogy often reflects elements of rote learning and overemphasises factual learning (Abraham et al. 2008). It lacks the student-centred learning (SCL) approach (Dayal 2002), which is an effective learning approach that develops higher-order thinking skills and creative thinking skills (Zain et al. 2012).

Lack of industry – HE linkages

The problem of work-readiness of graduates in India can also be attributed to the missing link between industry and HE. There is a growing realisation among the government, academic institutions and industry of the urgent need to bridge these skill gaps (Singh 2010). There have been very limited instances of industry/

employer linkages with education providers until the last few years, thus creating gaps in terms of sectoral need and availability, and the competencies required by employers and those possessed by graduates (Ministry of Skill Development and Entrepreneurship 2015). This gap impacts on the work-readiness of graduates as they are deprived of a mutual exchange of practical and theoretical aspects of knowledge and subsequent supplementation of professional expertise (India Skills Report 2015). Insufficient levels of industry participation in aspects like curriculum development, placement services and research and lecturer exchange programs of universities/colleges results in a lack of co-ordination between employment-seeking graduates and prospective employers who are looking for suitably qualified candidates (Deloitte 2012).

Quality assurance issues in Indian education

Another prominent reason for the lack of work-readiness of Indian graduates is the perceived low quality of the education being imparted (The Economist 2014). Sumanasiri and colleagues (2015) observed that accreditation bodies appear to measure quality of education through the contributions made towards graduate employability. Despite the presence of designated bodies such as the National Assessment and Accreditation Council (NAAC) and the National Board of Accreditation (NBA) for quality assurance, less than one-third of all universities and around one-fifth of colleges are accredited in India (UGC 2011a). In 2011, the NAAC accredited only 548 institutions, resulting in a total of 5780 accredited institutions out of more than 35,500 institutions in India (Shah 2015). A complete lack of accountability by non-accredited institutions to the state and central governments, students and other stakeholders has resulted in graduates with low work-readiness skills (British Council Report 2014). Moreover, the relatively poor quality of HE is evident in the absence of any Indian HE institution in the top 100 ranked universities in world, and only a few (nine) rank among the top 100 universities in Asia (The Times Higher Education Rankings, 2015). These issues are further exacerbated by the increasing shortages of qualified and experienced teaching staff.

Lack/Shortage of teaching staff

Significant factors affecting the work-readiness of many Indian graduates is the shortage of quality lecturers, coupled with a lack of faculty mobility across the regions (Deloitte 2012; Ernst and Young 2012; Kurup and Arora 2010; Shaguri 2013; UGC 2011a). While enrolment in higher education has grown six-fold in the last thirty years, academic numbers have grown only four times in response, and there is a 35 to 40 percent shortage in central and state universities respectively (Ernst and Young, 2012). Apart from the lack of teaching staff, their industry exposure, qualifications, experience or proper training are also often criticised (Shaguri 2013). These shortages and the inability of different states' educational system to attract and retain well-qualified teachers have been posing challenges to quality education for decades (Deloitte 2012; Ernst and Young 2011). Poorly qualified and lowly paid contract lecturers employed as a stop-gap measure are unlikely to be able to effectively address these graduate work-readiness challenges (Varma 2013).

Out-dated curricula

Another major area of concern for the employability of Indian graduates is the out-dated curriculum for different courses in tertiary education. There is a mismatch between what the students study and future job tasks, rendering their skill sets obsolete (Ernst and Young 2014a; KPMG 2014). Given that the end goal of graduate education is gainful employment linked to study and qualifications, the curricula for different courses at Indian universities and affiliated colleges has limited relevance for students, as the skills being taught do not reflect the demand of the marketplace (India Skills Report 2015). There is a lack of autonomy with respect to framing course curriculum due to over-regulation, and it results in courses that are out-dated and devoid of new modes of learning or an entrepreneurship and innovation focus (Deloitte 2015). Moreover, the curriculum of most higher education courses is infrequently updated according to the changing needs of the workforce, resulting in significant gaps between industry expectations and graduates' capabilities (Shaguri 2013). This is particularly evident in the engineering curriculum in most colleges, which has persisted in focusing on mainframe computers despite the reality of hand-held devices and smartphones (Industry Skills Report 2014).

Emphases on generalist rather than specialist qualifications

The shortage of graduates with specialised skills is another issue affecting the work-readiness of Indian graduates. Arts and science courses account for more than 70 percent of the total enrolment in higher education (Rath and Behera 2014) and approximately 40 percent of graduate job seekers (Khare 2014). These courses impart generalised skills, with less focus on industry or vocational skills (Ernst and Young 2011). Only 20 percent of these, according to Ernst and Young (2009) and 10 percent according to NASSCOM (2005) are perceived to be work-ready, as they lack specific industry skills.

It is clear from the foregoing discussion that India's economic growth is likely to be constrained by a significant lack of work-readiness among many of its higher education graduates, and the biggest challenge is to ensure that the major proportion of educated graduates are work-ready for the emerging skill needs of employers and industry (Khare 2014).The following section considers some of the strategies which have been proposed and/or implemented by the multiple Indian stakeholders – government, industry and the higher education system – in their efforts to ensure increased graduate work-readiness, and is complemented later in the chapter with our own recommendations.

Strategic responses – a multiple-stakeholder approach

The present Indian government has attempted to build a supportive work-force development system in its new National Skills Policy (Goldin 2015). This policy takes into account the various economic and social factors that impact on India's labour force, which is comprised of 60 percent of the population aged between 15 to 50 years (Goldin 2015). Under this policy umbrella, the Indian government, industry and education institutions have taken the following initiatives in order to counter the problems outlined in this chapter.

Government initiatives

To leverage the approaching demographic dividend, the Modi national government has initiated several new flagship initiatives (see Table 1.1), including the new Education Bill, in order to revitalise the education sector (Deloitte 2012; GOI 2013).

Table 8.1 highlights the detailed initiatives of the government of India to improve access, equity, quality and work-readiness of graduates in the Indian higher education system. A *Joint Declaration of Intent* between the Ministry of Human Resource Development (MHRD) and the US Department of State (SWAYAM), upgrading the educational and research infrastructure of state universities (RUSA) and collaboration with foreign universities (GIAN), are likely to be effective steps in augmenting the country's existing academic resources, accelerating the pace of quality reform, and elevating India's scientific and technological capacity to global standards (GOI 2013, 2014b; Sharma 2014). The establishment of 127 bachelor of vocation (B.Voc) courses and master degree programs in vocational education has underlined the importance of departing from conventional courses such as the BA and BSc and making graduates work-ready for needed skills in the industry (Joshi 2015; MHRD 2015a).

Substantive academic and administrative reforms (consideration of the adoption of a semester system, a choice-based credit system and reforms regarding curriculum development, admissions processes and examinations) are intended, through the alignment of fifty collaborating colleges in the city or district to establish an independent university (College Cluster Universities) (UGC 2009, 2011b, p. 31). Restructuring and strengthening the technical education sector is also planned (AICTE review committee), paving the way for a strong mentorship role of AICTE focusing on research and intervention, provision of internships, robust accreditation and an increased focus on distance and life-long education to the AICTE Act (MHRD 2015b).

To bridge the gap between industry and higher education and enhance the work-readiness of graduates, the Planning Commission is set to roll out twenty National Knowledge Functional Hubs (NKFH) across the country by 2017 (Ernst and Young 2014b). Another peak body, the "Education Sector Skill Council

Table 8.1 Government of India initiatives for the higher education sector

SWAYAM (Study Webs of Active-learning for Young Aspiring Minds)	India-focused MOOC platform offering online courses in Management, Social Sciences, Basic Sciences, Engineering and Energy.
RUSA (RashtriyaUchchatarShiksha Abhiyan)	To provide an excellent opportunity to the state universities to upgrade educational and research ambience of infrastructure, knowledge resources and skill development expertise to produce international quality workforce.
GIAN (Global Initiative for Academic Networks)	For supporting Indian universities to invite eminent scholars and researchers both inside and outside the country as guest speakers/ scholars.
B.Voc/M.Voc (Bachelor/Master of Vocation courses)	Delivered under National Vocational Education Qualification Framework (NVEQF) Schemes.
College Cluster Universities	To facilitate greater autonomy and freedom of growth to affiliated colleges.
NKFH (National Knowledge Functional Hub)	A collaborative framework of academia and industry, focusing on multiple disciplines and sectors.
SSC/LMIS (Education Sector Skill Council/ Labour Market Information System)	To assist and plan in delivery of training to raise skill competency standards and work-readiness of the youth.
AICTE review committee	To restructure and strengthen the technical education sector.
IMPRINT India	For raising the quality of higher education through original research.
Private sector participation	Increased share of private sector in HE (60 percent)

Based on sources from 2014b; Ernst and Young 2014a; GOI 2013; Joshi 2015; MHRD 2015a, 2015b; Sharma 2014; Srinivasan 2015; UGC 2009, 2011b)

– SSC", was established in September 2014 to establish the Labour Market Information System (LMIS) that will assist in the planning and delivery of training to develop skill competency standards and qualifications in order to increase the work-readiness of youth (MHRD 2015a). Another ambitious project, IMPRINT India, a \$150 million project, was launched in 2015, to raise the quality of higher education through original research, in collaboration with Indian Institutes of Technology and Indian Institutes of Science (MHRD 2015a; Srinivasan 2015). Further, by actively promoting the participation of the private sector, the Indian government has ensured capacity-creation in Indian HE (Shaguri 2013). The share of the private sector in HE institutions has increased to around 60 percent, with over 53 percent of the total enrolments representing the under-represented communities (Ernst and Young 2014b).

Industry initiatives

The Indian information technology (IT) industry has been instrumental in setting the pace for tackling the problem of work-readiness, as many IT companies have collaborated with engineering colleges and universities (CISCO 2007). Various joint initiatives (Infosys' Campus Connect, Wipro's Academy of Software Excellence in association with BITS Pilani, Tech Mahindra's-Mahindra College of Engineering and CISCO's Networking Academy) by the industry and academia are trying to ensure that graduates are work-ready for industry jobs (CISCO 2007). The National Association of Software and Services Companies (NASSCOM) was instrumental in the Foundation Skills in Integrated Product Development (FSIPD) program that outlined curriculum for courseware and incorporated an internship program that aimed to help make students more employable, at fifteen Indian colleges (The Economist 2014). The School of Inspired Leadership (SOIL), founded in 2009 by a group of leading companies from across industry verticals like Nokia, Maruti, Dabur, Infosys, Asian Paints and L&T, is another step in this direction, which offers postgraduate management courses and executive education programs (Ernst and Young 2012).

Education institutional initiatives

Keeping in view that the private sector needs to be involved to complement and supplement the efforts of the government (Deloitte 2012), many of the private sector educational institutes have been instrumental in bringing forth innovative models and strategies for giving graduates exposure to global education, research and practical training (Ernst and Young 2011). Many market leaders (Manipal Education Group, Symbiosis International University, BITS Pilani, Narsee Monjee Institute of Management Studies) and new entrants (Shiv Nadar University and OP Jindal Global University) have embarked upon improving the status of work-readiness of graduates through value proposition measures (Ernst and Young 2011). These measures include collaboration with industry, industry-sponsored research, high-quality faculty, collaboration with foreign universities, a focus on distance education, innovative course design and pedagogy (Ernst and Young 2011).

Discussion

The importance of collaboration between the Indian government, industry and universities/colleges to produce work-ready graduates cannot be understated (Ernst and Young 2014b). There needs to be a conscious tripartite collaboration among these stakeholders to design and implement strategies based on a systematic review of roadblocks within the current education systems (Ernst and Young 2014b). The key challenge is to adopt a transformational and innovative approach to position India's HE system as a globally relevant and competitive collective to increase the quantity of work-ready graduates and to compete successfully at the higher end of the global knowledge economy (Carnoy et al. 2013; Ernst and Young 2014b).

Considering that the Gross Enrolment Ratio (GER) in India is considerably lower than its global peers (Ernst and Young 2011), the government must firmly monitor the 30 percent GER by 2020, to sustain high growth of the Indian economy and reduce the demand-supply gap with the help of private participation (Ernst and Young 2011). An independent body coordinating between the central and state governments, having a transparent mechanism and a legal capacity to take action against defaulting institutions (Ernst and Young 2009), would go a long way to meet the challenges of the demographic dividend in India.

There is an urgent need for systemic change in affiliated colleges to improve the quality of teaching and learning and enhance the work-readiness of graduates (British Council Report 2014). Removing the ban on the affiliation of colleges to private universities is another strategy which can have a flow-on effect and alleviate the burden of "affiliation" for government universities (Shah 2015), as it will relieve universities from the burden of affiliating colleges, thus potentially clearing the way for improved academic effectiveness (Skorton 2013; UGC 2011b).

A conscious change in curriculum, reflecting a shift in the focus of assessments, the teaching-learning process and curricula away from lower-order thinking skills and toward higher-order skills and creativity, needs to be introduced in undergraduate courses (Blom and Hiroshi 2011; Donawa 2011). Moreover, as Barman (2013) outlined, a pedagogical shift from a teacher-centred learning to a student-centred learning (SCL) approach is imperative. This will transform Indian students from being passive recipients of knowledge to active learners who are work-ready with HOT skills (Barman 2013).

The active participation of the industry is pivotal in realising the potential of the demographic dividend. Strategic interventions aimed at identifying employers' role as equally responsible partners in creating an employable workforce might be brought in to practice through work-integrated learning (WIL), industry placement programs (IPP), industry mentoring programs (IMP), industry-based projects (IBPs) and internship programs (IP). In this way, students can be supported through their formal academic training by providing a link to industry in a structured and tailored way. There is a need for joint initiatives to redesign the curriculum to meet the needs of today's industrial world, creating graduates who have the capabilities to perform well in the labour market (CISCO 2007). The interface between HE and the industry should act as a platform for sharing projects, conducting market and action research, developing curricula and engaging in discussion among and between academics and industry professionals, to formulate higher-quality education for students (Ernst and Young 2011; India

Skills Reports 2015; Ministry of Skill Development and Entrepreneurship 2015; Mourshed et al. 2012; Shaguri 2013; UGC 2013).

For ensuring quality education and work-ready graduates, the student-teacher ratio must be reduced to an appropriate level (Shaguri 2013); educational institutions must ensure that all academic and teaching staff possess adequate qualifications, experience and training before commencing teaching (Shaguri 2013). The emphasis should be on offering competitive remuneration, high-quality operational and research infrastructure and academic freedom to attract the best quality academics, and to collaborate with the highest-ranking international institutions for academic development and exchange (Ernst and Young 2014b).

Conclusion

This chapter has examined a wide selection of academic literature and industry reports to provide an insight into Indian graduates' work-readiness and the key changes needed to alleviate a complex and serious problem. Further research, outlining and identifying these challenges by creating an ongoing dialogue with HE educational institutions, governments and industry can help to overcome these significant graduate work-readiness challenges.

Table 8.2 Summary of key findings, India

	Summary
Demographics/ labour market	***Demographic dividend***: India is in a position to become one of the world's youngest countries by 2020. ***Demographic disaster***: Despite a large, much younger workforce, both critical levels of graduate unemployment and serious skill shortages coexist, which may create a reverse impact.
Economy	***High rates of GDP growth***: High rates of GDP growth spurred by strong industrial growth in industrial and service sectors. ***Contribution to the global workforce***: India is set to become the largest contributor to the global workforce, and its working age population – 15–64 years – is likely to increase significantly, from 749 to 962 million between 2010 and 2030 (CRISIL, 2010). ***Five key sectors***: Infrastructure, auto & auto components, building & construction, textiles & clothing, transportation & logistics.
Antecedents of the work-readiness challenges	***Demand-supply mismatch***: Existing gaps between the productivity needs of employers and the skills available in the market. ***Archaic/complex structure***: Regulatory framework in Indian higher education is opaque, mired in complexity and tough to navigate ***Stifling affiliation system***: The affiliation system is bureaucratic and stymied by over-centralisation and a lack of transparency and professionalism

Lack of HOT skills: Indian graduates are relatively weaker on higher-order thinking skills

Lack of industry-HE linkages: Limited instances of industry/ employer linkages with education providers, thus creating gaps in terms of sectoral need and availability.

Quality assurance issues: Less than one-third of all universities and around one-fifth of colleges are accredited in India

Lack/shortage of teaching staff: 35 to 40 percent shortage of faculty/staff in central and state universities respectively

Out dated curricula: A mismatch between what the students study and future job tasks, rendering graduates' skill sets obsolete

Emphasis on generalist rather than specialist qualifications: Arts and science courses account for more than 70 percent of the total enrolment in higher education

Work-readiness issues:	*Lack of skills*: Indian graduates lack the required skills, thus making them unsuitable for the competitive market. *Impact on employment*: The unemployment for "fresh" graduates from universities and affiliated colleges is four times 33 percent higher than total country unemployment 8.5 percent.
Government policy initiatives	*SWAYAM*: Study Webs of Active-learning for Young Aspiring Minds *RUSA*: Rashtriya Uchchatar Shiksha Abhiyan *GIAN*: Global Initiative for Academic Networks *B.VOC/M.VOC*: Bachelor/Master of Vocation courses *NKFH*: National Knowledge Functional Hub *SSC/LMIS*: Education Sector Skill Council/ Labour Market Information System *IMPRINT India*: Raising the quality of higher education
Recommended strategies	• Collaboration between the Indian government, industry and universities/colleges • Private sector participation in education • Systematic change in affiliated colleges • Conscious change in curriculum • Pedagogical shift from a teacher-centred learning to a student-centred learning • Reduction of student-teacher ratio • Strategic interventions aimed at identifying employers' role as equally responsible partners through work-integrated learning (WIL), industry placement programs (IPP), industry mentoring programs (IMP), industry-based projects (IBPs) and internship programs. (IP).

References

Abraham, R., RamNarayan, K., Vinod, P. and Torke, S. 2008, 'Students' perceptions of learning environment in an Indian medical school', *BMC Medical Education*, Vol. 8, no. 1, p. 20.

Agarwal, P. 2010, *Indian higher education: Envisioning the future*, London, New Delhi, Singapore and Washington, DC: Sage.

Aman, M. and Sitotaw, M. 2014, 'Perception of summer cooperative graduates on employers generic skills preference', *International Journal of Instruction*, Vol. 7, no. 2, pp. 181–190.

Aspiring Minds. 2013, *National employability report – graduates*. Annual Report. Available at: www.aspiringminds.in/docs/national_employability_report_graduates_2013.pdf.

Bagchi, S. N. and Sharma, R. 2014, 'Hierarchy in Bloom's Taxonomy: An empirical case-based exploration using MBA students', *Journal of Case Research*, Vol. 5, no. 2, pp. 57–79.

Barman, B. 2013, Shifting education from teacher-centred to learner-centred paradigm', *International Conference on Tertiary Education* (ICTERC 2013), Daffodil International University, Dhaka, Bangladesh 19–21', January 2013.

Bhattacharya, A., Srivastava, R. and Jain, N. 2010, 'Indian manufacturing: The next growth orbit aspiration and roadmap for Indian manufacturing', *Boston Consulting Group: The Confederation of Indian Industry Report*. Available at: www.bcgindia.com/documents/file157021.pdf.

Blom, A. and Hiroshi, S. 2011, 'Employability and skills set of newly graduated engineers in India', *The World Bank South Asia Region*. Available at: http://elibrary.worldbank.org/doi/abs/10.1596/1813-9450-5640.

Bloom, B. S. 1956, *Taxonomy of educational objectives: The classification of educational goals, by a committee of college and university examiners*, New York, NY: D. McKay.

Bloom, D. E. and McKenna, M. J. 2015, *Population, labour force and unemployment: Implications for the creation of (decent) jobs, 1990–2030*, UNDP Human Development Report Office Background Paper.

British Council Report. 2014, *Understanding India: The future of higher education and opportunities for international cooperation*. Available at: www.britishcouncil.org/sites/default/files/understanding_india_report.pdf.

Bruni, M. 2013, *Labor market and demographic scenarios for ASEAN countries (2010–2035): Education, skill development, manpower needs, migration flows and economic growth*, DEMB Working Paper Series, No. 6, University of Modena.

Carnoy, M., Loyalka, P. and Froumin, I. 2013, 'University expansion in the BRIC countries and the global information economy', *Change: The Magazine of Higher Learning*, Vol. 45, no. 4, pp. 36–43.

Chatterjee, S., Nankervis, A. and Connell, J. 2014, 'Framing the emerging talent crisis in India and China: A human capital perspective', *South Asian Journal of HRM*, Vol. 1, no. 1, pp. 25–43.

Chenoy, D. 2012, 'Skill development in India: A transformation in the making', India *Infrastructure Report*. Available at: www.idfc.com/pdf/report/2012/Chapter_18.pdf.

Chia, S. 2013, *The ASEAN economic community: Progress, challenges, and prospects*, ADBI Working Paper 440. Tokyo: *Asian Development Bank Institute*. Available at: www.adbi.org/working-paper/2013/10/25/5916.asean.economic.community.progress.challenges/.

Chopra, R. 2010, Planning Commission to junk university affiliation system? *Mail Today, 11 Jan*. Available at: http://indiatoday.intoday.in/story/planning-commission-university-affiliation-system/1/168293.html.

CISCO. 2007, *Bridging the skills gap with industry: Academia partnerships*. September 7, 2007. Available at: www.cisco.com/web/IN/about/network/academia_partnerships.html.

CRISIL. 2010, *Skilling India: The billion people challenge*, CRISIL Centre for Economic Research. Available at: www.crisil.com/pdf/corporate/skilling-india_nov10.pdf.

Dayal, I. 2002, 'Developing management education in India', *Journal of Management Research*, Vol. 2, no. 2, pp. 98–113.

Deloitte. 2012, *Indian higher education sector: Opportunities aplenty, growth unlimited!* Deloitte Education Sector Team. Available at: www2.deloitte.com/content/dam/Deloitte/in/Documents/IMO/in-imo-indian-higher_education_sector-noexp.pdf.

Deloitte. 2015, *Mind the gaps: The 2015 Deloitte millennial survey*. Available at: www2.deloitte.com/global/en/pages/about deloitte/articles/millennialsurvey.html.

di Gropello, E., Kruse, A. and Tandon, P. 2011, *Skills for the labor market in Indonesia: trends in demand, gaps, and supply*, Washington, DC, World Bank Publications.

Donawa, M. 2011, 'Critical thinking instruction and minority engineering students', In *2011 Annual Conference & Exposition*, Vancouver, BC, June 26–29, 2011. Available at: https://peer.asee.org/critical-thinking-instruction-and-minority-engineering-students.

The Economist. 2013, *Skills development in South Asia: Trends in Afghanistan, Bangladesh, India, Nepal, Pakistan and Sri Lanka*, The Economist Intelligence Unit Report. Available at: www.britishcouncil.org/sites/britishcouncil.uk2/files/south-asia-skills-report-summary.pdf.

The Economist. 2014, *High university enrolment, low graduate employment: Analysing the paradox in Afghanistan, Bangladesh, India, Nepal, Pakistan and Sri Lanka*, Economist Intelligence Unit report. Available at: www.britishcouncil.in/sites/default/files/british_council_report_2014_jan.pdf.

Ernst and Young. 2009, *Making the Indian higher education system future ready*, Higher Education Summit. Available at: www.edgex.in/resources/ficci_eyreport2009.pdf.

Ernst and Young. 2011, *Private sector participation in Indian higher education*, FICCI Higher Education Summit. Available at: www.ey.com/Publication/vwLUAssets/Private_sector_participation_in_Indian_higher_education/$FILE/Private_sector_participation_in_Indian_higher_education.pdf.

Ernst and Young. 2012, *Higher education in India: Twelfth five year plan (2012–2017) and beyond*. FICCI Higher Education Summit 2012. Available at: https://learnos.files.wordpress.com/2012/11/ey-ficc_higher_education_report_nov12.pdf.

Ernst and Young. 2013, *Higher education in India: Vision 2030*, FICCI Higher Education Summit 2013. Available at: www.ey.com/IN/en/Industries/India-sectors/Education/EY-Higher-education-in-India-Vision- 2030.

Ernst and Young. 2014a, *Reaping India's promised demographic dividend: Industry in driving seat*. India-Skills-Development 2013–2014 Report. Available at: www.ey.com/Publication/vwLUAssets/EY-Government-and-Public-Sector-Reaping-Indias-demographic-dividend/$FILE/EY-Reaping-Indias-promised-demographic-dividend-industry-in-driving-seat.pdf.

Ernst and Young. 2014b, *Higher education in India: Moving towards global relevance and competitiveness*, FICCI Higher Education Summit 2014. Available at: www. ey.com/Publication/vwLUAssets/EY_-_Higher_education_in_India/$FILE/ EY-higher-education-in-india.pdf.

GOI. 2013, *Rashtriya Uchchatar Shiksha Abhiyan for reforming state higher education system*, Press Information Bureau, Government of India, Ministry of Human Resource Development. 03-October-2013. Available at: http://pib.nic.in/news-ite/PrintRelease.aspx?relid=99842.

GOI. 2014a, *Joint declaration of intent for cooperation in the field of higher education for Indo-US partnership for Study Webs of Active-Learning for Young Aspiring Minds (SWAYAM), a program for online education*, Press Information Bureau, Government of India, Ministry of Human Resource Development, 2014 September 24. 20:42 IST. Available at: http://pib.nic.in/newsite/PrintRelease. aspx?relid=109984.

GOI. 2014b, *Joint declaration of intent between India and United States of America for cooperation in the field of higher education for implementation of Global Initiative of Academic Networks (GIAN) program*, Press Information Bureau, Government of India, Ministry of Human Resource Development, September 24, 2014. 20:42 IST. Available at: http://pib.nic.in/newsite/PrintRelease.aspx?relid=109981.

Goldin, N. 2015, *Key considerations in youth workforce development*, A Report of the CSIS Project on Prosperity and Development. Center for Strategic and International Studies Washington. Available at: http://csis.org/files/publication/150129_Goldin_YouthWorkforce_Web.pdf.

Hajkowicz, S. 2015, *Global megatrends seven patterns of change shaping our future*, Melbourne, Australia: CSIRO Publishing.

ILO. 2014, *Indonesia: Labour and social trends update*, Geneva: International Labour Organisation(ILO). Available at: www.ilo.org/wcmsp5/groups/public/-asia/-ro-bangkok/-ilo-jakarta/documents/publication/wcms_329871.pdf.

ILO. 2016, *India labour market update*, ILO country office for India, July 2016. Available at: www.ilo.org/wcmsp5/groups/public/-asia/-ro-bangkok/-sro-new_delhi/documents/publication/wcms_496510.pdf.

India Skills Report. 2014, *Wheebox in association with Confederation of Indian Industry (CII) and PeopleStrong*. Available at: https://wheebox.com/wheebox/resources/IndiaSkillsReport.pdf.

India Skills Report. 2015, *Wheebox in association with Peoplestrong: Confederation of Indian Industry (CII) and LinkedIn*. Available at: https://wheebox.com/logo/India%20Skills%20Report2015.pdf.

Joshi, P. 2015, 'UGC announces master's degree in vocational education', *The Times of India*, September 24, 2015, 05.22AM IST. Available at: http://timesofindia. indiatimes.com/city/aurangabad/UGC-announces-masters-degree-in-vocational-education/articleshow/49083789.cms.

Khare, M. 2014, 'Employment, employability and higher education in India: The missing links', *Higher Education for the Future*, Vol. 1, no. 1, pp. 39–62.

Kim, L. C. J. 2011, 'Enhancing the employability of and level of soft skills within tourism and hospitality graduates in Malaysia: The issues and challenges', *Journal of Tourism*, Vol. 12, no. 1, pp. 1–16.

KPMG. 2014, *Skilling India: A look back at the progress, challenges and the way forward*. Available at: www.kpmg.com/IN/en/IssuesAndInsights/ArticlesPublications/Documents/FICCI-KPMG-Global-Skills-Report-low.pdf.

KPMG. 2016, *Indian economic survey 2015–2016 – Key Highlights*, KPMG – Tax Flash News. February 26, 2016. Available at: https://home.kpmg.com/con tent/dam/kpmg/pdf/2016/04/KPMG-Flash-News-India-Economic-Survey-2015-16%E2%80%93Key-Highlights-3.pdf.

Kumar, A. and Ambrish, K. 2015, 'Higher education: Growth, challenges and opportunities', *International Journal of Arts, Humanities and Management Studies*, Vol. 1, no. 2, pp. 19–32.

Kurup, A. and Arora, J. 2010, *Trends in higher education: Creation and analysis of a database of PhDs in India*, National Institute of Advanced Studies, May 2010.

Majumder, R. and Mukherjee, D. 2013, *Unemployment among educated youth: Implications for India's demographic dividend*, Munich Personal RePEc Archive.10 May. Available at: https://mpra.ub.uni-muenchen.de/46881/1/.

MHRD. 2015a, *200 days: New vision, New approach (E-View) government of India – Ministry of Human Resource Development (MHRD)*. Available at: http://mhrd. gov.in/200-days-new-vision-new-approach-e-view-1.

MHRD. 2015b, *Report of the AICTE review committee*, April 2015, Government of India – Ministry of Human Resource Development (MHRD). Available at: https://mygov.in/sites/default/files/master_image/Report_of_the_Review_ Committee_of_AICTE.pdf.

MHRD. 2015c, *Deemed University*, University and Higher Education. Department of Higher Education. Ministry of Human Resource Development (MHRD). Government of India. Available at: http://mhrd.gov.in/deemed-university.

Ministry of Skill Development and Entrepreneurship. 2015, *National policy for skill development and entrepreneurship*. Available at: www.skilldevelopment.gov.in/ assets/images/Skill%20India/policy%20booklet-%20Final.pdf.

Mourshed, M., Farrell, D. and Barton, D. 2012, *Education to employment: Designing a system that works*, McKinsey and Company: Center for Government Report. Available at: http://mckinseyonsociety.com/downloads/reports/Education/ Education-to-Employment_FINAL.pdf.

NASSCOM. 2005, *Extending India's leadership of the global IT and BPO industries*, Nasscom McKinsey Report 2005, National Association of Software and Service Companies, New Delhi.

Postiglione, G. 2012, *Improving transitions: From school to university to workplace: Higher education in dynamic Asia*, Asian Development Bank. Available at: www. adb.org/publications/improving-transitions-school-university-workplace.

Raman, M. and Koka, A. 2015, 'The ever-increasing demand for soft skills at workplace: A study on IT professionals' perspectives', *International Conference on Management and Information Systems*, September 18–20, 2015, Bangkok. Available at: www.icmis.net/icmis15/icmis15cd/pdf/S5014-final.pdf.

Rath, S. and Behera, B. 2014, 'Implications of skill incongruity on leveraging India's demographic dividend', *International Journal of Humanities and Social Science Invention*, Vol. 3, no. 4, pp. 26–35.

Sanghi, S., Subbiah, M., Reddy, R., Ganguly, S., Gupta, G., Unni, J., Sarkar, S., Sarin, S., Chand, V. and Vasavada, M. 2012, Preparing a globally competitive skilled workforce for Indian economy: Emerging trends and challenges', *Vikalpa*. Available at: www.vikalpa.com/pdf/articles/2012/Vikalpa373-87-128.pdf.

Shafie, L. and Nayan, S. 2010, 'Employability awareness among Malaysian undergraduates', *International Journal of Business and Management*, Vol. 5, no. 8, pp. 119.

Shaguri, O. 2013, *Higher education in India: Access, equity, quality*. Global access to Post-Secondary Education (GAPS) Report. Available at: www.ean-edu.org/assets/highereducationindiashaguri.pdf.

Shah, P. 2015, 'Regulatory structure of higher education in India', *Centre for Civil Society Report*. Available at: http://ccs.in/sites/default/files/research/research-regulatory-structure-of-higher-education-in-india.pdf.

Sharma, S. 2014, 'Open online courses: A welcome step in Indian education system', *The Economic Times*, November 23, 2014. 03.44PM IST. Available at: http://articles.economictimes.indiatimes.com/2014-11-23/news/56385074_1_education-system-moocs-higher-education.

Singh, A. 2010, 'Industry-academia convergence: "Bridging the skill gap" management education in India-a case study', *Prabandhan: Indian Journal of Management*, Vol. 3, no. 4, pp. 30–35.

Skorton, D. 2013, *India's strategic importance: International briefs for Higher Education Leaders*. Developed by American Council of Education(ACE)s Center for Internationalization and Global Engagement (CIGE) in partnership with the Boston College Center for International Higher Education.No.3, 2013.

Smith, E. and Kruger, J. 2008, 'A critical assessment of the perceptions of potential graduates regarding their generic skills level: An exploratory study: management', *South African Journal of Economic and Management Sciences*, Vol. 11, no. 2, pp. 121–138.

Srinivasan, V. 2015, 'India launches Imprint-India project', *ZDNet*, November 8, 2015–23:58 GMT (10:58 AEDT). Available at: www.zdnet.com/article/india-launches-imprint-india-project/.

Srivastava, A. and Khare, M. 2012, *Skills for employability: South Asia*, Innovative Secondary Education for Skills Enhancement (ISESE), Results for Development Institute. Available at: www.changemakers.com/sites/default/files/south_asia_skills_for_employability_21aug.pdf.

Srivastava, D. and Chatterjee, S. 2014, 'India's readiness on innovation and economic growth: A strategic analysis', *Global Journal of Human-Social Science Research*, Vol. 14, no. 3, pp.47–57.

Sumanasiri, E., Yajid, M. and Khatibi, A. 2015, 'Review of literature on graduate employability', *Journal of Studies in Education*, Vol. 5, no. 3.pp. 75–88.

The Times Higher Education Raking. 2014–15, *World university rankings*. Available at: www.timeshighereducation.com/world-university-rankings/2015/regional-ranking#!/page/0/length/25

Tulsi, P. and Poonia, M. 2015, 'Expectations of industry from technical graduates: Implications for curriculum and instructional processes', *Journal of Engineering Education Transformations*, Vol. 28, pp. 19–24.

UGC. 2009, *Action plan for academic an administrative reforms*, New Delhi: University Grant Commission (UGC), 21March. Available at: http://gndu.ac.in/ugc_acad.pdf.

UGC. 2011a, *Report of the working group on higher education for the 12th FYP* (Five year plan), New Delhi: University Grant Commission (UGC). Available at: http://planningcommission.gov.in/aboutus/committee/wrkgrp12/hrd/wg_hiedu.pdf.

UGC. 2011b, *Inclusive and qualitative expansion of higher education*, 12thFive-Year Plan, 2012–17, New Delhi: University Grant Commission (UGC). Available at: www.ugc.ac.in/ugcpdf/740315_12FYP.pdf.

UGC. 2013, *UGC guidelines for B.Voc*, New Delhi: University Grant Commission (UGC). Available at: www.ugc.ac.in/pdfnews/8508026_Guidelines-on-B-Voc_Final.pdf.

UGC. 2015, *Total number of universities in the Country as on* 03.09.2015, India. University Grant Commission (UGC), New Delhi. Available at: www.ugc.ac.in/oldpdf/alluniversity.pdf.

UN Habitat. 2013, *State of the urban youth, India report*. Available at: www.academia.edu/3280639/State_of_Urban_Youth_India_Report_2013_by_UN_HABITAT.

Varma, S. 2013, 'Indian higher education: 40% of college teachers' temporary, quality of learning badly hit', *The Times of India*, November 10, 2013. Available at: http://timesofindia.indiatimes.com/india/Indian-higher-education-40-of-college-teachers-temporary-quality-of-learning-badly-hit/articleshow/25520250.cms.

Zain, S., Rasidi, F. and Abidin, I. 2012, 'Student-centred learning in mathematics – constructivism in the classroom', *Journal of International Education Research*, Vol. 8, no. 4, pp. 319–328.

9 Graduate employability in Australia

Time for a VET and HE overhaul?

Alan Montague, Julia Connell and Barbara Mumme

Introduction

This chapter explores the complexities Australia faces in sustaining its international influence and position as a competitive nation in numerous areas, such as exports and trade, as well as its stable political system and the overall wellbeing of its citizens. In common with other nations, the challenges relate to the need for improved educational policies in both vocational and higher education in order to support a nation that depends on the skilling and reskilling of it citizens. In addition, Australia has an ageing population alongside a low birth rate. Given Australia's goal is to provide "high quality skills training that will meet student needs, be valued by employers, and contribute skilled human capital to an economy in transition" (Braithwaite 2016, p. 1), the quality of education (acquired skills and job prospects) must be relevant for students and their families. Braithwaite (2016) maintains that the VET sector once held a proud place in Australia's education system, providing opportunities along a less academically and more practically oriented path. However, the VET sector is now under threat with "plummeting enrolments and a few rogue operators tarnishing the reputation of the sector" (CEDA 2016, p. 4).

Skill shortages and the work-readiness of graduates are just some of the areas where improvements are crucial. This is a challenge for Australia in common with all the countries reported in this text regardless of their national fiscal prosperity. The ability for Australian graduates to be work ready is a key factor for a range of different stakeholders and indeed, the nation as a whole. Stakeholders include the graduates themselves, their parents and families, education providers and prospective employers. However, a number of recent reports have indicated that there is a deficit and that new graduates, who face a rapidly changing and highly competitive employment sector, are not being effectively prepared to enter the workforce. To maximise their likelihood of employment, graduates need to be able to demonstrate the skills and qualities most valued by employers.

To place these challenges in context, this chapter provides an outline of the Australian labour market and demographics, government education policies and the structure of the education system. Emphasis is placed on the vocational education (VE) and higher education (HE) sectors, in terms of the specific graduate work-readiness challenges faced by students, employers and educational institutions. Regulations, along with practical strategies which have been developed, or it is proposed should be developed in order to meet these challenges, are analysed and suggestions made with regard to the potential approaches that could be adopted to prepare Australians for the jobs of the future.

Australian demographics and local labour market

Australia is a prosperous nation, rich in natural resources and human capital within its progressive diverse population. Its democratic institutions, underpinned by economic stability and a robust economy, have shaped the conditions for a productive creative society. Australia has experienced over twenty years of continuous growth, low levels of unemployment, limited inflation, fairly low public debt, and a strong and stable financial system (ABS 2015). On a comparative basis, Australia's economy was largely unaffected by the global financial crisis due to a robust banking system and inflation held in check (ABS 2015). In 2016 the Australian labour market faces numerous constraints in its growth, mainly induced by a severe global reduction in the major export commodities. The demand for energy (predominantly coal) and mineral resources, from Asia (particularly China) has subsided, and harsh drops in current prices have impacted on Australia's economic growth (ABS 2015).

Within the Australian economy the services sector is the most prominent and in June 2015 accounted for near 70 percent of GDP and 75 percent of paid employment (ABS 2015). In July 2016 Australia's workforce comprised 11,955,100 persons (ABS 2016a). This includes an unemployment rate of 5.7 percent which accrued to 731,000 persons (ABS 2016b). In December 2014 the ABS (2016c) estimated that Australia's population was 23,940,300 with a participation rate of approximately 64.9 percent of people available to work within the labour market (ABS 2016b). In the Australian labour force, agriculture employs 3.6 percent of the working population; industry employs 21.1 percent and services 75.3 percent (ABS 2015, 2016d).

According to the latest Industry Employment Projections Report (2017, p. 1):

> Employment is projected to increase in 16 of the 19 broad industries over the five years to May 2022. Health Care and Social Assistance is projected to make the largest contribution to employment growth (increasing by 250,500), followed by Professional, Scientific and Technical Services (126,400), Construction (120,700) and Education and Training (116,200). Together, these four industries are projected to provide more than half of total employment growth over the five years to May 2022.

The ABS (2015a) estimated that in May 2015, of the 15.7 million people who were aged 15 to 64 years in Australia, 3 million, or 19 percent were enrolled in formal study. Among the Australian citizens or residents studying, 'approximately 1.2 million (41 percent) were attending a higher education institution, 884,000

(29 percent) were at school, 474,400 (16 percent) were at Technical and Further Education (TAFE) institutions and 404,200 (13 percent) were at other educational institutions or organisations' (ABS 2015a, p. webpage).

Labour force status

In May 2015 the ABS (2015, p. webpage) stated that 'people with higher levels of educational attainment were more likely to be employed, with 81 percent of persons with a Bachelor degree or above and 76 percent of persons with an Advanced diploma, Diploma or Certificate III or IV being employed'.

The summary of skill shortages published in 2016 (Department of Employment 2016) found that skill shortages were, on a marginal basis, more likely to occur for trade and technical occupations than they were for professionals. Table 9.1 provides a summary of the most recent skill shortage list with some commentary in relation to specialist skills or, in particular, locations where skills are most sought after. There is also an evident shortage of experienced employees for some professions/trades. For example, employers generally consider those who hold fast-tracked hairdressing qualifications to be unsuitable employees.

Table 9.1 Skill shortage list, Australia

Occupation	Date Assessed	Spec requirements/ location shortages
Accountants	April 2016	Taxation accountants
Surveyor	March 2016	Cadastral surveyors.
Civil Engineering Professionals	April 2016	Senior positions/ specialised requirements.
Agricultural Consultant/ Scientist	February 2016	Agricultural consultants and scientists
Veterinarian	February 2016	Veterinarians with two years or more experience
Early Childhood (Pre-primary School) Teacher	April 2016	Long day care centres in a number of states and territories.
Sonographer	June 2016	All states and territories.
Optometrist	June 2016	Differences between locations.
Physiotherapist	June 2016	Differences between locations/specialisations.
Audiologist	April 2016	
Midwife	June 2016	Shortages of midwives regional locations
Web Developer	Dec2015	Senior developers.
Analyst and Developer Programmers	Dec 2015	Senior programmers.
ICT Security Specialist	Dec 2015	Senior ICT security specialists.

Occupation	Date Assessed	Spec requirements/ location shortages
Civil Engineering Draftspersons/ Technicians	April 2016	Some states
Automotive Electrician	Sept 2015	Automotive electricians
Motor Mechanics	Nov 2015	Differences in locations/ specialisations.
Sheet metal Trades Worker	Dec 2015	Differences in locations.
Vehicle Painter	Nov 2015	Shortages are widespread.
Stonemason	Aug 2015	Qualified stonemasons.
Glazier	Sept 2015	Qualified and experienced glaziers.
Wall and Floor Tiler	Sept 2015	Few applicants have skill level employers want
Air-conditioning and Refrigeration Mechanic	Sept 2015	Qualified, licensed, experienced workers
Pastry cook	Oct 2015	Experienced pastry cooks/ independent patisseries.
Butcher	Nov 2015	Regional areas – some states and territories.
Hairdresser	Sept 2015	Qualified/ experienced hairdressers.
Cabinetmaker	Sept 2015	Shortages in almost all states and territories.

Source: *Department of Employment, Skill Shortage Research 2016*

Structure of the Australian education and training system

The Australian education system is referred to as the Australian Qualifications Framework (AQF 2016). The AQF was formulated in 1995 as a national policy framework that accredits qualifications from the tertiary education sector (higher education and vocational education and training), in addition to the school-leaving certificate and the Senior Secondary Certificates of Education that operates throughout Australia (AQF 2016).

The AQF has 10 levels and links school, vocational and university education qualifications into one national system (AQF 2016). This allows progress from one level of study to the next, and from one institution to another, as long as individuals satisfy requirements (DET 2016). The AQF enables choice and flexibility in career planning. All qualifications in the AQF are designed to help prepare students for further study and connection to an adult vocational life (DET 2016). The AQF defines and describes all nationally recognised qualifications (AQF 2016) forming a single qualification framework from Certificate I level through to Senior Secondary Certification to doctoral level (DET 2016) as illustrated in figure 9.1.

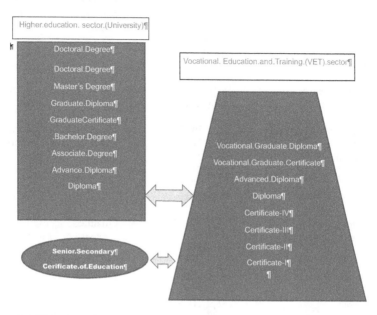

Figure 9.1 The Australian Qualifications Framework. Adapted from AQF 2016 (www.aqf.edu.au)

The Department of Education and Training (DET) is accountable for national policies and programs that assist Australian citizens in accessing the quality of early child care and childhood education, school education, higher education, vocational education and training, as well as international education and research (DET 2016).

School education is similar across the Australian nation with minor variations between states and territories. School education (primary and secondary) is required between the ages of six and sixteen (Year 1 to Year 9 or 10) (DET 2016). Compulsory school education comprises 11 years in total and is divided into primary school for seven to eight years, commencing at Kindergarten/Preparatory level, moving into Secondary (or high) school for another three or four years with years 11 and 12 not being compulsory (DET 2016).

Tertiary education embodies the academic and vocational/technical pathways in higher education (including universities) and includes vocational education and training (VET). Under the AQF, students who successfully prove that they are competent within a group of competencies can be awarded a VET qualification such as Certificate I; Certificate II; Certificate III; Certificate IV; Diploma and Advanced Diploma. The Certificate levels align to levels of attainment with a Certificate I graduate requiring supervision, and Certificate IV graduates being regarded as supervisors/managers of others. Certificate III, is common among apprentices with nearly 40 percent of students taking courses at that level and 30 percent at a higher level. The remaining 30 percent are enrolled in courses at lower levels, or in non-AQF programs (CEDA 2016). The awarding of HE qualifications (bachelor degree to PhD) is the domain of universities predominantly, but some VE institutions can also award degree level certificates (DET 2016). The AQF is comprised of 13 national qualifications in three sectors, with several cross-sectoral linkages (AQF 2016).

Government education policies

Australian education policy is a topic that has not been covered in great depth in the extant academic literature. With six Australian states and two territories, as well as, education systems that involve primary, secondary, VET and HE, amidst an array of government and independent systems, it is an area that is inhibited by a phalanx of mixed polices and assorted ideologies. Marginson (2013, p. 7) maintained that while:

> Australian politics are committed to the standard OECD policy mantras about the need for productivity advance, the importance of higher educational participation, and the economic role of the innovation benefits generated by research. The problem is that when ideas for long-term nation-building run up against the limitations imposed by a low tax-and-spend polity, in the short- term low tax wins every time. And the long-term in Australian politics and policy consists of the sum of all the short-terms.

The following section demonstrates that the VET sector in Australia is in what could be referred to as parlous circumstances due to inadequate neoliberal polices which have allowed an acquisitive private market to plunder public funds intended to prepare students for work- readiness.

Vocational education and training

VET is an integral feature of the Australian education system and is specifically designed to deliver workplace explicit skills and knowledge-based competencies that are predominantly practical (DET 2016). According to iVET (2016, p. web-page) 'VET is a sophisticated system governed by interconnected government and independent bodies functioning within a strict National Skills Framework of qualifications defined by Industry Training Packages and explicit quality delivery standards.' More than 1.2 million workers are represented in the technical and trade sector, which represents more than 13 percent of the entire Australian workforce (ABS 2016a). The VET sector is diverse: in 2014, there were 2865 private providers; 960 schools; 497 community education providers; 210 enterprise providers; 57 TAFE providers and 15 university providers (CEDA 2016).

To formulate effective educational policy for the VET Sector the Australian federal, state and territories met in 2012 to commit to a "National Partnership Agreement" on skills reform to establish goals and structures for national funding and reform for the period 2012–13 to 2016–17. This is about to expire and so requires urgent attention.

In 2012 the Gillard government decided with the Australian states and territories, to expose VET to the market with students able to access loans for "approved" diploma courses, up to a substantial sum of $95,000 (Manning 2016). This loan scheme is known as VET FEE-HELP and has elements of commodifying and commercialising training within the market as opposed to investing in training. This was not a strategy likely to support an era of major technical change, smart manufacturing and smart specialisation, referred to by the World Economic Forum and others (Ward 2016) as the Fourth Industrial Revolution. As noted by Manning (2016, webpage) 'Under this fully-contestable funding model, colleges were paid the entire fee up-front, it didn't matter if students finished the course'.

A 'user pays' system with students paying for their education, effectively, converted the Australian HE system into a consumer-orientated arrangement with heightened interest in vocational outcomes and associated skills for the new consumers – students (Thornton 2015). A loan scheme known as Higher Education Contribution Scheme (HECS) was instigated by the Australian federal government based on Friedman's neoliberal ideological bent (Thornton 2015). Notably, Australian students pay among the highest tuition fees in the OECD (DEEWR 2011).

HECS is now referred to as FEE-HELP and was extended in 2012 to students enrolling in VET (Thornton 2015). VET FEE-HELP and FEE-HELP loans require graduates to begin repayment when they earn a certain level of income (Thornton 2015).

Private training colleges raced to sign up as many students as possible and used brokers who threw in free laptops and iPads as incentives. Course completion rates plummeted. 'One college was costing taxpayers $1 million for every graduate' (Manning 2016, p. webpage).

To fund this initiative government finance escalated from $AUD325 million in 2012 to nearly $AUD1.8 billion by the end of 2014, and 75 percent of these funds were paid directly to private colleges, not the state-funded Technical and Further Education (TAFE) bodies (Manning 2016). As the VET FEE-HELP subsidies grew, the fiscal data was not being advised to the regulatory body, the Australian Skills Quality Authority (ASQA). This body accredited both VE courses and registered training organisations that provided the training, and was supposed to maintain a watchful eye over the billions of taxpayer dollars to ensure funds were well spent (Manning 2016). The policy framework worsened as ASQA did not have the necessary information to determine which proportion of public monies training organisations were using and which posed the greatest risk from a rorting perspective (Manning 2016).

By 2014 the system was so broken, the Coalition lost office in what was sometimes dubbed the 'TAFE election' (Technical and Further Education) (Manning 2016, p. webpage). The overall objectives according to ACIL, Allen Consulting (2015, p. ii) included a wide range of outcomes:

a)   *More accessible training for working age Australians and, in particular, a more equitable training system, which provides greater opportunities for participation in education and training;*

b)   *A more transparent VET sector, which enables a better understanding of the VET activity that is occurring in each jurisdiction;*

c) *A higher quality VET sector, which delivers learning experiences and qualifications that are relevant to individuals, employers and industry;*

d) *A more efficient VET sector, which is responsive to the needs of students, employers and industry.*

According to the Guardian (2016, p. 4) to a large extent these strategic objectives 'were not achieved, and in many cases (Australia has) gone backwards, although the report's authors (ACIL Allen Consulting 2015) tried hard to remain optimistic about some new trends and fragments of success'.

Manning (2016, p. webpage) argued, however, that the government policies led by the 'federal government's botched vocational education and training scheme has cost taxpayers $6 billion. TAFEs, unable to compete with the private institutions, have been forced to close and thousands of teachers have lost their jobs. The policies are characterised by extensive rorting and incompetence' (Manning 2016).

Thus, expected benefits have been overshadowed by unanticipated failures (Parliament of Australia 2015). The reputation of the VET sector has been marred by high incompletion rates, high student debt, bankruptcy among colleges and predatory behaviour by registered training organisations (RTOs) in the race to enrol students and obtain government funding. To outward appearances the intent of a significant proportion of providers has been profit maximisation with little regard for delivering educational objectives (Braithwaite 2016). As Braithwaite (2016, preface p. 2) argued "Industry and government domination over what was to be taught in VET was intended to create opportunity through growth and jobs, but domination is bound to be doomed when the guardians of delivery and quality are not engaged professionally in the process".

In short, education policies surrounding VET in Australia are so fraught with problems that the notion of work-readiness and skill development for industry competiveness is now at considerable risk. As a sector that has

> played a crucial role in equipping students with job- readiness, the ability to upskill and training for occupations that are not supplied by universities and other higher education institutions, it has been successful in changing the lives of many students from disadvantaged backgrounds through delivering employability skills.
>
> (CEDA 2016, p. 6)

Now it depicts a sector under threat, with plummeting enrolments in government supported providers, student exploitation, poor regulation and uncertainty about its future, post the upcoming expiration of the current National Partnership Agreement on Skills Reform.

Apprentices and trainees

In May 2015, 193,700 people aged 15 to 64 years were employed as apprentices or trainees within the Australian Apprenticeship Scheme (ABS 2015). According to a recent CEDA (2016) report, apprentices have excellent job outcomes, with about 84 percent of apprentices being employed after completing their training. This percentage rises to almost 91 percent for trade apprenticeships. Despite these success rates, apprenticeship numbers have been falling for some time now, with significant drops occurring post-2011 when incentives paid to employers to support apprentices were restricted to specific areas, namely the traditional trades and some non-trade areas deemed to be priority occupations.

For example, in 2014, 12,700 people who were employed in an apprenticeship/traineeship were not undertaking it in May 2015, while 27,400 people who applied for an apprenticeship/traineeship were unsuccessful in gaining a place in 2015 (ABS 2015). From 2013 until 2016 the total number of apprentices and trainees in Australia fell by '28 percent according to records held by the National Centre for Vocational Education Research' (Aston 2016, p. 1). Approximately half of apprentices did not complete their training, and this level of attrition has been consistently hovering around 50 percent since 2005 (Bednarz 2014).

Attrition in apprenticeships and traineeships stems from numerous reasons and problems with the workplace or employers including 'inferior employment conditions, such as excessive unpaid overtime, too few hours, not being allowed to take breaks, or not being paid correctly' (McDowell et al. 2013, p. 24). Other employment conditions are an issue, such as personal safety, bullying 'and unsafe work practices are also relatively common' (McDowell et al. 2013, p. 24). The issue of being treated as an inferior worker and a lack of meaningful work or training was an additional problem, along with low wages given 'the minimum award wages for first year Australian Apprentices are below the Henderson Poverty Line' (McDowell et al. 2013, p. 89). The Henderson Poverty Line stems from a 1973 Commonwealth Commission of Inquiry into Poverty (Saunders 2015). This poverty line is updated periodically using fiscal indexation rates to benchmark income to rate disposable income required to support basic needs (Saunders 2015).

Although McDowell et al. (2013, p. 79) indicated that employer surveys resulted in comments such as 'job seekers often do not have basic language, literacy, numeracy and work-readiness skills required for modern workplaces', as per the CEDA (2016) report findings, work- readiness was not an issue that was dominant in relation to the recruitment or sustained employment of apprentices.

Higher education in Australia

Australian universities reflect the traditional functions of universities in Western countries (Bradley and DEEWR 2008) and must demonstrate evidence of competitive performance when benchmarked on an international scale. Their key functions are to foster, develop and distribute innovative and advanced levels of knowledge and competence through scholarship and teaching (Bradley and DEEWR 2008). 'Self-fulfilment, personal development and the pursuit of knowledge are important outcomes, in addition to skills that enable 'critical analysis and independent thought to support full participation in a civil society' (Bradley and DEEWR 2008). HE has the additional role of generating new knowledge, preparing effective leaders for diverse global environments, as well as supporting and professionally invigorating the labour forces that build industry productivity (Bradley and DEEWR 2008).

Thornton (2015) maintained that higher education has been transformed incrementally from a predominantly public institution intended to serve the public good into an institution that is now an 'arm of industry'. In his view, the privatisation of universities was subtle, less overt, as 'public universities were not instantaneously privatised as a result of the neoliberal turn, as commonly occurred with other formerly public goods, such as utilities and public transport' (Thornton 2015, p. 3). Consequently, 'state disinvestment in higher education has caused the university's primary role to become more overtly instrumental, for it is now deployed by the state, specifically to serve the new knowledge economy' (Thornton 2015, p. 3).

The pressure on public universities is now directed towards producing large numbers of work-ready graduates at a low cost, in minimum time to serve the needs of industry. The private benefits of higher education are also invariably conceived in economic terms, emphasising vocationalism and wealth accumulation in order to justify a user pays regime (Thornton 2015, p. 3).

The HE sector is competing for funds on a global basis and is under stress (Thornton 2015). Circumstances indicate that the will to deregulate universities may result in HE courses being provided by private colleges in competition with universities (Rea et al. 2014; Rea and Maslen 2014). This could be problematic as the lessons learnt from the VE sector should act as a warning concerning the impact it may have on the work-readiness of HE students unless strong regulation and quality courses are maintained.

Returning to the topic of education policy, we argue that considerable care is necessary for strategic planning and policy implementation to drive HE as an investment in Australia's future. HE has many roles and ideological views, but employment is the most effective way to divide a nation's wealth. Students graduating from universities are paying for their courses and deserve a return on investment through the development of work-ready skills that lead to meaningful future employment.

Graduate work-readiness challenges

Thus far, this chapter has stressed some of the current problems and challenges evident in the contemporary Australian VET and HE sectors. Primarily, work-readiness has been inhibited by elements of the VET sector's focusing on profit maximisation, with little regard for delivering educational objectives. Moreover, the recent CEDA (2016) report states there is a need for a change in the VET training approach given VET qualifications are based on the concept of competency based training (CBT), leading to a set of narrowly defined qualifications. Given "the jobs of the future will require a more diverse set of skills, including creativity, social intelligence, patience, critical thinking and resilience" (CEDA 2016, p. 11), the VET sector should be equipping students with a broader set of skills and capabilities that would promote mobility of employment and flexibility to adapt to changing workforce needs. Turning to HE, it is argued that the HE sector has emerged from the threat of a neoliberal agenda for the time being (Hare 2016) but has suffered from inadequate government funding for some decades (Bradley and DEEWR 2008; Thornton 2015).

One way of addressing funding shortages has been to increase enrolments. In 2012, the Gillard government implemented the "demand-driven HE system" which stopped limits being placed on numbers, enabling unlimited bachelor degree level students enrolling at universities. This led to undergraduate enrolments growing by 26 percent between 2009 and 2014 (Knott 2016).

Thomson (cited in Knott 2016) indicates that work-readiness may be impacting on a labour market struggling to absorb large numbers of undergraduates. Students with Australian Tertiary Admissions Ranks (ATARs) as low as 30 were being admitted to courses where an ATAR of 75 was previously expected, and this has led to accusations that students were enrolled purely for financial reasons in some universities (Knott 2016). This situation is also grossly unfair to the enrolled students – if they struggle with the secondary curriculum, they are likely to be unsuited to HE courses (Thomson cited in Knott 2016), thus providing another dimension of complexity pertaining to work-readiness.

The *Graduate Outlook Survey*, a survey undertaken annually by Graduate Careers Australia (GCA 2014), considered employers' and recruiters' perceptions of graduates they have been exposed to during recruitment phases (GCA 2014). In 2014, 23.4 percent of employers surveyed reported that they would have recruited more graduates if a higher number of appropriate candidates had been available (GCA 2014). Almost one in three employers (30.3 percent) indicated they preferred to recruit graduates from a particular higher education institute, and of this number, 64.5 percent indicated that this was because of the quality of the graduate (GCA 2014). In addition, employers were asked to rate the three most important selection criteria for recruiting graduates, and table 9.2 outlines their responses. In 2014, 'communication skills' was ranked the most important in selection criterion by 48.6 percent of graduate employers. 'Academic results' and 'teamwork skills' were ranked second and third (24.3 percent and 22.4 percent, respectively). Around one-fifth of employers ranked 'aptitude' as a key selection criterion, followed by 'interpersonal skills', 'leadership skills' and 'work experience' as being their most important selection criteria in 2014 (GCA 2014).

The World Economic Forum (WEF) (2016) undertook a major global survey, and their results complement the findings reported by the Graduate Careers Council's (2015). The WEF findings also included what they referred to as 'cross functional skills' such as: social skills (i.e., emotional intelligence) and systems skills (i.e., decision making) – see figure 9.2 for more detail.

This report now turns to additional factors that substantiate the problems faced in the current Australian education landscape, emphasizing the urgent need for effective education and labour market policies.

In 2014/2015 30 percent of young people were unemployed (FYA 2015). As stated previously, graduates are experiencing difficulties in obtaining employment

Table 9.2 Most important selection criteria when recruiting graduates, 2014 (%).

Selection Criteria	2014	Selection Criteria	2014
Communication skills	48.6%	Relevant qualifications	14.0%
Academic results	24.3%	Willingness to learn	12.1%
Teamwork skills	22.4%	Problem-solving skills	11.2%
		Passion	10.3%
Aptitude	21.5%	Customer service	8.4%
Interpersonal skills	20.6%	Analytical skills	6.5%
Leadership skills	19.6%	Technical skills	6.5%
Work experience	19.6%	Integrity	3.7%
Cultural fit	18.7%	Organised	3.7%
Motivational fit	17.8%	Extra-curricular activities	3.7%

Source: Graduate Outlook 2014 (2014, p. 16)

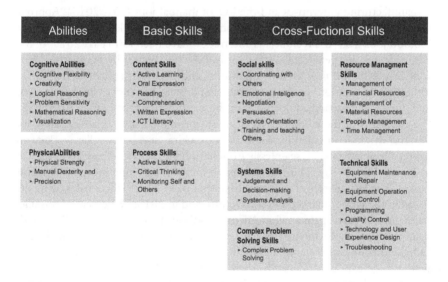

Figure 9.2 Core work-related abilities, basic and cross-functional skills
(Source: WEF, Figure 9, p. 21)

in the disciplines they studied in, and employers continue to report mismatches concerning the skills they are seeking to fill job vacancies. FYA (2016 citing Graduate Careers Australia 2015) claimed that 29 percent of recently employed HE bachelor graduates considered that their field of study was not important: for VET graduates, it was more than double that figure, with 62 percent claiming that their course of study was irrelevant to their jobs.

Another issue with skill mismatches is the issue of over-skilling which may result from workers being hired when the labour market is slack and jobs are hard to find. Mavromaras et al. (2010) warn that it is a strategy that is likely to have a negative effect on wages, job satisfaction and a higher propensity to quit.

It has been predicted that labour market disruptions lie ahead moving towards 2030 as the fourth industrial revolution gains momentum and global workplaces change, which will impact significantly on the vast majority of jobs in all industry sectors in all corners of the planet (FYA 2015; Ward 2016; Hajkowicz et al. 2016; WEF 2016).

Technological and economic changes are already having a vast impact on a global basis through automation (FYA 2015; FYA 2016; Hajkowicz et al. 2016; WEF 2016). Approximately 70 percent of graduates obtaining their first job will face exponential technological change, suggesting that training in higher and vocational education may be missing the mark (FYA 2015). The rise of computer technology has, however, led to a swathe of redundancies. Specifically, there have been 500,000 white-collar jobs dislodged, including people who worked in small business offices and corporate towers as secretaries and clerks as well as closures of manufacturing enterprises and the loss of manual jobs (FYA 2015). Approximately '100,000 machinery operator jobs, nearly 400,000 labourers, and nearly 250,000 jobs from the technicians and trades' have been lost (FYA 2015, p. 5).

From a positive perspective, these losses have been offset by significant expansion with '400,000 new jobs in community and personal services' and a further 700,000 new positions in the professional and business services fields being created due to heightened complexities in these industry sectors' (FYA 2015, p. 5). The problems of the labour market, whilst not immediately apparent, are complex and dynamic in equal measures as both white- and blue- collar workers are not readily able to switch seamlessly from hard hats, paper and pens to healthcare positions (FYA 2015). This has resulted in increasing competition in the labour market. The last quarter of a century has seen one in 10 unskilled males being displaced in the labour market, never to return, and in 2015, 25 percent of unskilled males did not participate at all in Australia's labour market (FYA 2015). In addition, youth unemployment rates have not improved and are at the same level as 1985, and young women remain disadvantaged as they continue to face the same gender wage gaps experienced by their mothers (FYA 2016).

A more obscure problem besetting the labour market for young people is underemployment as '3.4 times the number of young Australians are underemployed compared to 1985 and 2.8 times as many young people are employed in part-time positions compared to 1985' (FYA 2016, p. 2).

Addressing work-readiness challenges

Hajkowicz et al. (2016) and the WEF (2016) propose that jobs in the near future will be revolutionised as business enterprises acclimatise to the onset of the "Fourth Industrial Revolution". Moreover, the Hajkowicz et al. (2016) claims that the complexity of jobs will increase significantly with higher skills being demanded by a global vocational market for all positions, including entry level. This will require education systems to adapt and change to equip the workers of the future with the skills they need (Hajkowicz et al. 2016).

The Fourth Industrial Revolution (Ward 2016) will see massive developments that will feature artificial intelligence, machine learning, robotics, nanotechnology, 3D printing and genetics and biotechnology as factors that impact on individual jobs with their "interconnections" having an amplifying effect on one another (Hajkowicz et al. 2016; WEF 2016). Each of these factors signals the need for new skills. As Hajkowicz et al. (2016) and the WEF (2016) maintain, there is a need to drive a changing educational landscape. Additional technological factors, such as mobile supercomputing, renewable energy potential, artificially intelligent robots, self-driving cars, neuro-technological brain enhancements, genetic editing – the evidence of spectacular change is happening at "exponential speed" (Hajkowicz et al. 2016).

Industrial Revolutions one to three unhitched humans from animal power and made mass production possible and brought digital capabilities to billions of people. This Fourth Industrial Revolution fundamentally differs (WEF 2016). It is characterised by a broad range of different technologies that are already fusing physical, digital and biological worlds, impacting on all academic disciplines jobs and economies and industries (Hajkowicz et al. 2016; WEF 2016)

WEF (2016) and Hajkowicz et al. (2016) suggest that developed countries such as Australia are on the brink of a technological revolution that will profoundly revise the way people, live, work and interact unlike anything humankind has experienced previously.

To place the importance of this research on graduate work-readiness in perspective, an illustration of the rapidly changing labour market is presented based on research undertaken by the WEF (2016). Across the countries covered by the WEF Report (2016), current trends could lead to a net employment impact of more than 5.1 million jobs lost to disruptive labour market changes over the period 2015–2020. This may result in a total loss of 7.1 million jobs – two-thirds of which comprise routine white-collar office functions, such as office and administrative roles – and a total gain of 2 million jobs, in computer, mathematical, architecture and engineering related fields. Manufacturing and production roles are also expected to see a further decline but are also anticipated to have relatively good potential for upskilling, redeployment and productivity enhancement through technology.

The key recommendation from the CEDA (2016) report is that a comprehensive national review of the sector needs to be undertaken to underpin COAG (Council of Australian Governments) discussions and reach a new National Partnership on Skills Reform (NP), as the current NP will expire in 2017, as mentioned previously. Other recommendations include strategies to support a shift from narrowly defined qualifications to broader sets of skills transferable across occupational clusters. This means that service sector skills will be increasingly important in meeting Australia's skill needs, ensuring that VET instructors are appropriately qualified with relevant teaching and industry experience (CEDA 2016).

It is also clear that there is a need for a huge overhaul of the apprentice system and structure to reduce the attrition rate. One manufacturing manager interviewed for this chapter commented that this has "an economic cost and personal impact – if apprentices drop out and see themselves as a failure, as a result they then might struggle to get another job and retain their self-esteem".

It is clear that graduate work-readiness is a multifaceted concept consisting of a range of individual attributes, including disciplinary expertise, non-technical skills, life and work experience (Dacre Pool and Sewell 2007). Work experience is one of the elements built into the current Coalition Government's Youth Jobs Prepare-Trial-Hire (PaTH) program, announced in the 2016 budget (www.employment.gov.au/youth-jobs-path-infographic). The program involves an intensive, six-week pre-employment training period intended to support employability skills. The materials released so far do not specify that it be "nationally recognised training" that aligns to an existing AQF qualification (Oliver, in CEDA 2016 p. 39). There appears to be an implicit recognition by policy-makers that the traditional qualification framework doesn't fit the role of providing young people in particular with the range of skills (e.g., time management), attitudes (e.g., flexible, willing to take direction) and attributes (e.g., appropriately dressed and presented) required for work (Oliver 2016). The PaTH program comprises three key stages:

1   Employability skills training, due to commence on 1 April 2017 intended to help prepare young job seekers for the workplace and gain understanding of what employers expect of them and gain the skills, attitudes and behaviours required to be successful in a job.
2   From 1 April 2017, up to 30,000 young job seekers each year will be eligible to undertake an internship placement of 4 to 12 weeks. Internships will be voluntary and provide incentives of $1,000 up front to business to host an intern and a $200 fortnightly payment to job seekers on top of their income support.
3   From 1 January 2017 a Youth Bonus wage subsidy of between $6,500 and $10,000 will be available to businesses who take on an eligible young person as an employee or an apprentice (Parliament of Australia 2015).

As all of the PaTH initiatives are intended to commence in 2017, it is too early as yet to ascertain their effectiveness.

Turning to the HE sector, as universities have needed to respond to the pressures of developing employable graduates, many have started to include employability skills as part of the graduate skill set through curriculum redesign, course content and delivery strategy (Australian Qualifications Framework Council 2011; Bradley et al. 2008; Leong and Kavanagh 2013). Another way to address this in the HE sector is through Work Integrated Learning Programs, which have been one of the most evident forms of support for graduate work-readiness across Australian universities in recent years.

Jackson (2015) defines work-integrated learning (WIL) as the practice of combining traditional academic study, or formal learning, with student exposure to the world-of-work in their chosen profession. The aim of WIL is to better prepare undergraduates for entry into the workforce. WIL encompasses many forms, intended to support real world work practices and skill application. They can be work placements, internships, field work, job shadowing, action learning and more (Leong and Kavanagh 2013).

Evaluation of WIL programs in enhancing skill development remains predominantly outcomes-focused. To date, however, little attention has been paid to the process of what, how and from whom students acquire essential skills during work placements (Jackson 2015). Given students' comments from one study (Daniel and Daniel 2015) that industry practitioners are often too busy to engage with them or they do not respond at all as well as evidence from interviews gathered from one of the authors of this study where it was indicated that the quality of placements vary hugely and that some placement supervisors just 'tick a box' without really knowing what had been undertaken in the workplace or the effectiveness of the intern themselves, it is clear that it is not enough just to place a student in a workplace. It is possible that there is a need for interviews to be conducted with industry practitioners about possible mentoring and/or networking schemes between industry and educators put into place that might offer new insights and value for students as well as recent graduates (Daniel and Daniel 2015).

Further comments from industry interviewees were that "Any exposure that a graduate can have pre-employment to the world of work gives them an opportunity to benchmark their own development on the job. Without work placements there is an evidence gap." A manufacturing representative commented on the effectiveness of the ME Program launched in the Hunter, NSW region of Australia as a school to manufacturing pathway. The Regional Development Australia (RDA) Hunter's ME Program encourages young people to complete science, mathematics, physics and engineering subjects to better prepare them for a highly skilled future workforce. In 5 years, 7,500 senior students in 25 Hunter high schools have been engaged with 32 defence and manufacturing companies (Regional Development Australia 2016). Snapshot of results below:

- ME Program students 3 percent above state average for selecting HSC Physics
- 8 percent above state average ME Program students select HSC Engineering Studies
- 11 percent above state average ME Program students in Metals and Engineering Certificate II
- RDA Hunter's award-winning ME Program delivers smart schools for the Hunter's future.

Due to the success of the program, a 'mini-me' program has also recently been launched in primary schools, to engage children as young as eight years old in science, technology, engineering and maths. Demonstrations are conducted in Hunter primary schools and utilise technologies such as 3D printing, quadrocopters and robotics. Support from local industry partners ensures that students can understand the link between these engaging technologies and the STEM subjects they study at school.

Conclusion

This chapter has outlined a range of factors in both the VET and HE sectors that are currently inhibiting the work-readiness of graduates from both sectors. The evidence suggests that VET has been subjected to extremely poor policies, making observations about work-readiness quite complex. The frenzy to access VET fee funds without the provision of quality training has resulted in thousands of cases where VE graduates are not work ready and the system itself has been devastated. Given the critical role that VET plays in raising Australia's productivity, it is important to urgently address the problems outlined. HE also has its array of problems as it has been starved of public funding, and it has been argued that over enrolments have distorted the absorption of graduates into the labour market, calling into question the work-readiness of students when supply may well outstrip demand. What is needed in both the VET and HE education sectors are significant improvements in policy, stronger financial support from the government(s) along with sound regulatory practices, more innovative teaching and increased work integrated learning. Solving these policy problems may increase the capacity for Australian graduates to connect more successfully to their adult vocational and professional lives.

Table 9.3 Summary of key findings, Australia

	Summary
Demographics/ labour market	Population: 23,940,300. People employed 11,955.100. Unemployment rate 5.7 percent (731,000 people). Approximately 3 million enrolled in formal study. Local Labour Market (LLM): Agriculture employs 3.6 percent. Industry employs 21.1 percent. Services 75.3 percent. With the prediction that employment in services to continue to grow for at least the next five years. ***Demographic dividend***: Australia is a prosperous nation, rich in natural resources and human capital. Historically, Australia has been able to offset skills shortages through immigration policies which provides some level of security for industry where mismatches in LLM can be met through labour migration of both skilled and knowledge workers. ***Demographic Challenge***: Australia has an aging population with a low birth rate, placing pressure on the LLM to meet demands. Up-skilling and ensuring adequate numbers of graduates are educated to levels that meet specific industry challenges is an imperative.
Economy	Australia has experienced over 20 years of continuous growth with low levels of unemployment, limited inflation and reasonably low public debt. The recent downturn in demand for natural resources, accompanied by lower prices has put pressure on the economy. 2015 figures show the service sector is the most prominent, accounting for 70 percent of GDP and 75 percent of paid employment.

Educational Structure/ Work-readiness challenges	***Regulatory Framework:*** Australian Qualification Framework (formulated in 1995) is a national policy framework for tertiary and secondary students, and as such incorporates six Australian states and two territories. Recent policy changes allowing private market entry to the vocational education sector have seen public funds plundered and left some students with inadequate education qualifications. ***VET FEE-HELP and Higher Education Contribution Scheme:*** Australia has a 'user pays' system for tertiary education, with fees being deducted from employment salary once a certain monetary level is reached. This system will increasingly lead to students (and in some cases their parents) expecting more from their education, especially as Australia has some of the highest tuition fees in the OECD. ***VET Sector:*** The Australian Apprenticeship Scheme had 193,700 people employed as apprentices or trainees in 2015, with successful employment outcomes of 84 percent to 91 percent after training, depending on the trade. Challenging this is a fall in apprenticeship numbers post-2011 when incentives paid to employers were restricted, as well as the entry of rogue private education providers. ***HE Sector:*** 81 percent of people with a Bachelor degree or higher and 76 percent with Advanced Diploma, Diploma or Certificate III or IV obtain employment. Challenges include potential over-enrolments with supply outstripping demand, as well as, the growing need for education. Institutions to respond to rapidly changing industry demands by modifying courses/ reflecting new workplace skills required. ***Summary of Skill Mismatches/Shortages:*** Mismatches in skill level expectations between stakeholders has placed pressure on LLM, with a call for graduates to be more work-ready. Skill shortages are marginally more likely to occur in trade and technical occupations, than professional occupations. Identifying skill mismatches is an on-going challenge. ***Industry Links:*** Growing need for industry and education providers to establish closer links to rectify mismatches in work-readiness of graduates. Suggestions are that education needs to be less generic and more focused on specialist qualifications mindful of the nature of future jobs.
Work-readiness issues:	Whilst Australian employers point to mismatches in expectations of graduate work-readiness, Australian graduates are educated to a competitive standard on a global basis but there is a need for improvement to benefit Australian VE and HE graduates.

(*Continued*)

Table 9.3 (Continued)

	Summary
Policy Initiatives and recommended strategies for improved graduate work-readiness	• Greater collaboration between Industry and Education Institutions. • Pedagogical changes, more innovative teaching practices, coupled with more student-centered learning models, empowering students to adopt lifelong learning approach. • Improvements to Government policy and regulatory initiatives are required, such as: • Increased funding and improved management of funds by education providers; • Changes to Australian Education Framework to reflect a rapidly changing workplace; • Paid incentives and rebates to encourage businesses to offer business placements to both current students and recent graduates (including WIL, IPP, IMP, IBP and IP) and • Rigorous regulation of private sector education providers.

References

ABS. 2015, *Australian infrastructure statistics – yearbook 2015 and key Australian infrastructure statistics booklet 2015*. Canberra. Available at: https://bitre.gov.au/publications/2015/yearbook_2015.aspx [Accessed August 22, 2016].

ABS. 2015a, *6227.0 – education and work*, Australia. May 2015. Available at: www.abs.gov.au/ausstats/abs@.nsf/mf/6227.0 Australian Bureau of Statistics Canberra [Accessed August 22, 2016].

ABS. 2016a, *Trend employment growth continues*, OpenDocument Australian Bureau of Statistics Canberra. Available at: www.abs.gov.au/ausstats/abs%40.nsf/mediare leasesbyCatalogue/46DFE12FCDB783D 9CA256B740082AA6C? www.employ ment.gov.au/2016-17-budget-employment-overview [Accessed August 22, 2016].

ABS. 2016b, *July key figures*, Australian Bureau of Statistics Canberra. Available at: www.abs.gov.au/AUSSTATS/abs@.nsf/mf/6202.0 [Accessed August 22, 2016].

ABS. 2016c, *Australian demographic statistics*. Available at: www.ausstats.abs.gov.au/ausstats/subscriber.nsf/0/7645CB8797196A85CA257FDA00 1D5E87/$File/31010_dec%202015.pdf Australian Bureau of Statistics Canberra [Accessed August 22, 2016].

ABS. 2016d, *8155.0 – Australian industry, 2014–15*. Available at: www.abs.gov.au/ausstats/abs@.nsf/Latestproducts/8155.0Main%20Features32014–15?opendocument&tabname=Summary&prodno=8155.0&issue=2014–15&num=&view= Australian Bureau of Statistics Canberra [Accessed August 22, 2016].

ACIL Allen Consulting. 2015, *Review of the national partnership agreement on skills reform – final report*, ACIL Allen Consulting Pty Ltd, Melbourne. Available at: https://docs.education.gov.au/system/files/doc/other/final_report_npa_review.pdf [Accessed August 21, 2016].

Aston, H. 2016, 'Apprentice numbers dive: The áge', *News*, June 28, 2016. pp. 1 and 6. Fairfax Media Melbourne.

Australian Qualifications Framework (AQF). 2011, *Australian qualifications framework – first edition July 2011*, Australian Government, Canberra. Available at: www. aqf.edu.au/wp-   content/uploads/2013/05/AQF-1st-Edition-July-2011.pdf [Accessed September 26, 2016].

Australian Qualifications Framework (AQF). 2016, *Australian qualifications framework*, Australian Government, Canberra. Available at: www.aqf.edu.au/ [Accessed August 15, 2016].

Bednarz, A. 2014, *Understanding the non-completion of apprentices: National vocational education and training research program occasional paper*, NCVER, Adelaide. Available   at: www.ncver.edu.au/data/assets/file/0016/9520/understanding-non-completion- 2706.pdf [Accessed August 24, 2016].

Bradley, D. and Department of Education, Employment and Workplace Relations (DEEWR). 2008, *Review of Australian higher education: Discussion paper*, Department of Education, Employment and Workplace Relations, Canberra.

Braithwaite, V. 2016, *Transforming a race to the bottom to a ladder to the top: Regulatory support for excellence in Australian vet*. Power to Persuade, May. Australian National University – Research School of Social Sciences; School of Regulation & Global Governance (RegNet). Available at: http://papers.ssrn.com/sol3/papers. cfm?abstract_id=2825851 [Accessed February 9, 2016].

CEDA. 2016, *VET: Securing Skills for Growth, Committee for Economic Development of Australia*, Melbourne. Available at: www.ceda.com.au/research-and-policy/ research/2016/08/vet- skills-for-growth [Accessed February 9, 2016].

Dacre Pool, L. and Sewell, P. 2007, 'The key to employability: Developing a practical model of graduate employability', *Education + Training*, Vol. 49, no. 4, pp. 277–289.

Daniel, R. and Daniel, L. 2015, 'Enhancing capacity for success in the creative industries: Undergraduate student reflections on the implementation of work-integrated learning strategies', *Asia-Pacific Journal of Cooperative Education*, Vol. 16, no. 3, pp. 199–209.

DEEWR. 2011, *Higher education base funding review*. Available at: www.canberra. edu.au/research/faculty-research-centres/edinstitute/documents/HigherEd_ FundingReviewReport1.pdf.

Department of Education and Training (DET). *2015, FEE-HELP information for 2016.*

Department of Education and Training Canberra. 2016, Available at: www.studyassist.gov.au [Accessed August 27, 2016].

Department of Employment (DOE). 2016, *Skill shortage list – Australia*. Available at: https://docs.employment.gov.au/documents/skill-shortage-list-australia Department of Employment Canberra [Accessed September 21, 2016].

Department of Employment (DOE). 2016, *Industry employment projections report 2016*. Available at: http://lmip.gov.au/default.aspx?LMIP/EmploymentProjections.

Department of Employment (DOE). 2017, *Industry employment projections report 2017*, Australian Government, Canberra http://lmip.gov.au/default.aspx?LMIP/ EmploymentProjections.

FYA. 2015, *The new work order: Ensuring young Australians have skills and experience for the jobs of the future, not the past*, FYA Melbourne. Available at: www.fya.org. au/2015/08/23/the- new-work-order-report/ [Accessed June 10, 2016].

FYA. 2016, 'Renewing Australia's promise report card 2016', FYA Melbourne. Available at: www.fya.org.au/wp- content/uploads/2016/06/RenewingAusPromise_ReportCard_finalwebappend.pdf [accessed October 21, 2016].

Graduate Careers Australia (GCA). 2014, *Graduate outlook 2014*, Graduate Careers Australia, Melbourne. Available at: www.graduatecareers.com.au/wp- content/uploads/2015/06/Graduate_Outlook_2014.pdf [Accessed June 3, 2016].

Graduate Careers Australia (GCA). 2015, *Beyond graduation 2014 a report of graduate's work and study options three years after course completion*, Graduate Careers Australia, Melbourne. Available at: www.graduatecareers.com.au/wp- content/uploads/2015/07/Beyond_Graduation_2014.pdf [Accessed July 3, 2016].

Guardian. 2016, 'VET privatisation failures'. [online]. Guardian Sydney, Australia, p. 4, July 27, 2016, ISSN: 1325–295X. [cited 26 Aug 16]. Available at: http://search.informit.com.au.ezproxy.lib.rmit.edu.au/documentSummary;dn=242636995949877;res=IELAPA [Accessed August 26, 2016].

Hajkowicz, H., Reeson, A., Rudd, L., Bratanova, A., Hodgers, L., Mason, C. and Boughen, N. 2016, *Tomorrow's digitally enabled workforce*. Available at: www.acs.org.au/data/assets/pdf_file/0018/95103/16–0026_DATA61_REPORT_TomorrowsDigiallyEnabledWorkforce_WEB_160128.pdf.

Hare, J. 2016, *Budget 2016: 'Toxic higher education fee fund' plan bites the dust*, The Australian: Murdoch Press Sydney. National Affairs 2016 May 4, page webpage. Available at: www.theaustralian.com.au/budget-2016/budget-2016-toxic-higher-education-fee-fund- plan-bites-the-dust/news-story/8225af7ff36051ba9f1bef49f529fb02 [Accessed August 27, 2016].

iVET. 2016, *How VET Works – Australia's vocational and training (VET) system*, Department of Education Employment and Workplace Relations, Canberra. Available at: www.ivet.com.au/a/65.html [Accessed October 21, 2016].

Jackson, D. 2015, 'Employability skill development in work-integrated learning: Barriers and best practice', *Studies in Higher Education*, Vol. 40, no. 2, pp. 350–367.

Knott, M. 2016, *Unis blast 'degree factory' culture: The age*. Fairfax Media, Melbourne. August 1, 2016, News Page 1 and 4.

Leong, R. and Kavanagh, M. 2013, 'A work integrated learning (WIL) framework to develop graduate skills and attributes in an Australian university's accounting program', *Asia-Pacific Journal of Cooperative Education*, Vol. 14, no. 1, pp. 1–14.

Manning, P. 2016, *The TAFE plunder: Background briefing: Radio national*, Australian Broadcasting Corporation Sydney, February 28, 2016. Available at: www.abc.net.au/radionational/programs/backgroundbriefing/2016-02–28/7193402#transcript [Accessed August 19, 2016].

Marginson, S. 2013, *Tertiary Education Policy in Australia, Centre for the Study of Higher Education*, University of Melbourne. Available at: http://melbourne-cshe.unimelb.edu.au/data/assets/pdf_file/0007/1489174/Tert_Edu_Policy_Aus.pdf [Accessed February 9, 2016].

Maslen, G. 2014, 'Universities steel for anticipated overhaul', *The Age Education*, May 12, 2014, Fairfax Media Melbourne, p. 14.

Mavromaras, K., McGuinness, S., O'Leary, N., Sloane, P. and Fok, Y. K. 2010, 'The problem of overskilling in Australia and Britain', *The Manchester School*, Vol. 78, no. 3, pp. 219–241.

McDowell, J., Jak, D., Persson, M., Fairbrother, R., Wetzlar, S., Buchanan, J. and Shipstone, T. 2013, *A shared responsibility: Apprenticeships for the 21st century*,

Australian Government Canberra. Available at: www.australianapprenticeships.gov. au/publications/shared- responsibility-apprenticeships-21st-century [Accessed August 21, 2016].

Oliver, D. 2016, 'Getting over middle child status', *VET: Securing Skills for Growth, CEDA – Committee for Economic Development of Australia*, Melbourne. Available at: www.ceda.com.au/research-and-policy/research/2016/08/vet-skills-for-growth [Accessed February 9, 2016].

Parliament of Australia. 2015, *Final Report: The operation, regulation and funding of private vocational education and training (VET) providers in Australia Senate Inquiry Parliament of Australia Senate Inquiry*, Parliament of Australia, Australian Government Canberra. Available at: www.aph.gov.au/Parliamentary_Business/ Committees/Senate/Education_and_Employment/vocationaled/Final_Report [Accessed October 21, 2016].

Rea, J., Whyte, J. and Carnes, D. 2014, 'Federal budget: $100,000 degrees are no fantasy Advocate: Newsletter of the National Tertiary Education Union', Vol. 21, no. 3 (November), pp. 18–19, 23–24. Available at: http://search. informit.com.au.ezproxy.lib.rmit.edu.au/documentSummary;dn=733198602179 116;res=IELBUS [Accessed August 27, 2016].

Regional Development Australian. 2016, *Hunter valley ME program*. Available at: www.meprogram.com.au [Accessed September 26, 2016].

Saunders, P. 2015, 'Closing the gap: The growing divide between poverty research and policy in Australia', *Australian Journal of Social Issues*, Vol. 50, no. 1, p. 13.

Thornton, M. 2015, *Through a glass darkly: The social sciences look at the neoliberal university*, Canberra: ANU Press.

Ward, M. 2016, *4th industrial revolution, house of commons debate pack, number CDP 2016/0153*, September 2, 2016. Available at: www.parliament.uk/commons-library | intranet.parliament.uk/commons-library | papers@parliament.uk | @commonslibrary [Accessed February 9, 2016].

World Economic Forum. 2016, *The future of jobs employment, skills and workforce strategy for the fourth industrial revolution*. Available at: http://reports.weforum. org/future-of-jobs- 2016/ [Accessed July 13, 2016].

10 The state of higher education and vocational education and training sectors in Nepal

Implications for graduate work-readiness and sustainable development

Subas Dhakal

Introduction

Investment in human capital, embodied in the skills, knowledge and competencies that make people act in productive ways (OECD 1998), is one of the prerequisites for achieving sustainable development. The notion of sustainable development refers to balancing economic, social and environmental objectives for the betterment of society, now and in the future (see Dhakal 2012; UN 2015). The state of economic and human capital development in the South Asian region – Afghanistan, Bangladesh, Bhutan, India, Maldives, Nepal, Pakistan and Sri Lanka – is quite varied, and data indicate that these countries are collectively transitioning towards the middle-income bracket. For example, the Gross National Income (GNI) varies from US \$630 in Afghanistan to US \$6,670 in Maldives and only one country in the region – Sri Lanka with a GNI of US \$3,800 – is ranked 50th amongst 130 countries in the Human Capital Index (HCI) (WEF 2016; World Bank 2016a). The HCI assesses the result of past and current investments in education and offers insight into a country's talent base in the future (WEF 2016 p. 1). Although South Asian countries have made substantial investments in education and employment generation (Panth 2013; British Council 2014a; British Council 2014b), the work-readiness of graduates – the ability and capability to gain and maintain employment and obtain new employment when necessary (Hillage and Pollard 1998) – is yet to be a fully-fledged priority. Van Adams (2007) highlights four critical factors that influence employability: quality of education, work experience, training that fulfils labour market needs and labour market relevant policies. This chapter explores these elements in the context of employment opportunities and employability in Nepal.

Nepal is a small, landlocked country in South Asia, located between the two fastest-growing economies in the world, China and India. It is a democratic republic made up of 75 districts and Kathmandu is the capital city, located in central Nepal. The latest census data indicate a total population of nearly 27 million people, of which less than two-fifths (17 percent) live in urban areas (CBS 2012). A long history of power struggles between political parties and the now-abolished monarchy between the 1950s and 1990s and, more recently, a decade-long armed conflict between 1996 and 2006, have hindered the country's developmental progress. The deadly conflict left over 13,000 people dead and 1,300 missing (UNOHCHR 2012, p. 14). Nepal also experienced one of the biggest natural disasters in recent memory. The earthquake on 25 April 2015 claimed nearly 9,000 lives and injured over 22,000 people (NDRR 2015). Needless to say, the country remains one of the least-developed economies in the world and ranks 145th out of 187 countries on the Human Development Index (UNDP 2014). Over one-quarter (25.2 percent) of Nepal's population live in poverty, and the average life expectancy is 68 years (World Bank 2016b). Although neighbouring economies have grown rapidly over the past decade and a half, growth in Nepal has been rather subdued. The World Bank (2016b) data indicate that between 2001 and 2015 the average growth rates for China and India were 9.01 percent and 6.74 percent respectively, compared to 3.77 percent for Nepal. Since it is well-known that economic growth alone does not lead to poverty alleviation and sustainable development (Sachs and Reid 2006), it is the investment in higher education (HE) policies and institutions that leads to robust economic development (see Kruss et al. 2015; Neumayer 2012).

It is in this context that this chapter explores the state of the HE and vocational education and training (VET) sectors in Nepal through the lens of graduate work-readiness, contending that the concerted impetus on human capital policy must be a priority for the country. The chapter is structured in four parts, with the next section providing a background on labour market conditions. The structure and development of the education and training systems in the country are then reviewed. Next, the work-readiness challenges in specific industry sectors are discussed. Following this, the national policy environment on employment opportunities and work-readiness skills is reviewed. A positive example of an innovative work-readiness program currently being implemented is then discussed before making concluding remarks.

Labour market overview

It is estimated that the size of the Nepalese workforce is approximately 12 million people (ILO 2014), and that between 300,000 and 400,000 new employees enter the labour force every year (Islam 2014). The country has one of the highest (83.4 percent) labour force participation rates in the region (ILO 2014). Although the aggregate unemployment rate at the country level was 2.7 percent in 2014 (World Bank 2016c), a significant urban-rural divide exists. Rural unemployment is 1.2 percent compared to 7.5 percent for urban areas (ILO 2014). For youth (the 15- to 29-year age group constitutes 28 percent of the total population) unemployment is particularly concerning. The 2008 Labour Force Survey indicated that youth unemployment was at 19.2 percent (male=17.1 percent and female=22.2 percent) in 2014 (Serrière and CEDA 2014 p. 2), and over half of the employed youth (52.5 percent) hold vulnerable jobs (Sparreboom and Staneva 2014, p. 48). The low levels of overall unemployment in the context of sluggish economic growth suggest that workers might be willing to take up any available job, resulting in labour under-utilisation, for example not enough work, not enough pay and skill mismatches. For instance, 96 percent of the country's economically active population is employed within the informal sector (Suwal and Pant 2009, p. 2). The latest estimates suggest that over 10 percent of the potential workforce is gainfully employed outside the country (Shrestha 2016; MoLE 2014). As discussed earlier, the main labour market challenge for the country comes from the slow pace of economic development associated with political conflicts and natural disasters. For example, while the country's post-conflict average (2006–2015) gross domestic product (GDP) growth was 4.33 percent (World Bank 2016c), the 2016 forecast is a mere 0.5 percent (IMF 2016, p. 172), primarily because of the 2015 earthquake. The post-disaster policy for sustainable development has set a target of 7 percent growth by 2030 (NPC 2015).

The Labour Force Survey in Nepal is carried out every 10 years. Table 10.1 documents changes in the country's key employment sectors between 1998 and 2008. Almost three-quarters of the workforce in the country depend on agriculture/forestry to make a living. Nearly half (45.3 percent) of the youth workforce (15–29 age group) is employed in low-productivity activities in the agricultural sector (Serrière and CEDA 2014). When the youth workforce exits the

Table 10.1 Main employment sectors in Nepal

Sectors	1998[*]		2008[**]	
	%	Total ('000)	%	Total ('000)
1. Agriculture & Forestry	75.98	7190	73.87	8701
2. Manufacturing	5.84	553	6.56	773
3. Wholesale, Retail & Trade	4.31	408	5.87	692
4. Construction	3.64	344	3.12	367
5. Private Household Work	3.05	289	0.28	33
6. Education	1.73	164	2.42	285
7. Transport, Storage & Communication	1.43	135	1.68	198
8. Hotel & Restaurant	1.20	114	1.67	197
9. Public Administration & Defence	0.74	70	0.93	109
10. Health & Social work	0.35	33	0.65	77
Others	1.72	163	2.95	347
Total	100.00	9463	100.00	11779

Source: [*]CBS 1999; [**] CBS 2009

agricultural sector, it does so in foreign labour markets, particularly the Middle East (Basnett et al. 2014). For instance, over 500,000 labour permits were issued to Nepalese (mostly youth) planning to work abroad in 2014 (MoLE 2014). Manufacturing and construction are the second- and third-largest sectors overall, but with a modest youth participation of 7 percent and 5 percent respectively (Serrière and CEDA 2014). Although the Central Bureau of Statistics (CBS) does not capture travel and tourism (T&T) sector-specific employment data, T&T has emerged as one of the fastest-growing sectors in the country in recent years. Fuelled by the rising number of tourist arrivals from China and India, the World Travel & Tourism Council (WTTC 2015) estimated that the T&T sector generated more than a million direct and indirect jobs in 2014. This is substantiated by the fact that over 20 percent of youths are collectively employed in the wholesale, retail and trade, hotel and restaurants, transport, and business activities sectors (Serrière and CEDA 2014, p. 27). With the lacklustre private sector, some of the key labour market challenges recognised by the government and relevant to employability are: lack of employment opportunities, slow expansion of the non-agricultural sector and lack of skilled human capital (NPC 2015).

Vocational and higher education system

The formal modern education system in Nepal is relatively young. Tribhuvan University (TU), the first public HE institution, was established in 1959 (TU n.d.). The first non-government HE institution, Kathmandu University (KU), was established only in 1991 (KU n.d.). The parliament is currently in the process of finalising a policy framework for establishing the first Open University (CAN 2016). The latest data indicate that a total of 458,621 students are enrolled in 13 HE institutions across the country (MoE 2015, p. 22). The Ministry of Education (MoE) has the overall responsibility for primary, secondary and tertiary education, including VET in the country. Table 1.2 summarises the number of formal schooling years associated with the HE and VET pathways and the skills test level in the country. The Council for Technical Education and Vocational Training (CTEVT), established in 1989, is the national body for the VET sector with the purpose of technical and skilful human resources development (CTVET 2014). CTVET oversees the technical and senior secondary-level vocational education and training programs. The latest figures indicate that 16,024 students are enrolled across 387 VET providers in either post-secondary or diploma-level programs (MoE 2015, p. 19). Similarly, a total of 8,200 students are enrolled across 202 VET providers in the technical school leaving certificate (TSLC) program (p. 20).

The National Skill Testing Board, affiliated with CTVET, has developed National Occupational Skill Standards/Profiles for 265 different occupations with five levels of certification, ranging from basic to level 5 (MoE 2015; CTVET 2014). With the support of the Swiss government, the Training Institute for Technical Instruction was established in 1991. Since then it has evolved as a regional centre of excellence and has trained nearly 20,000 participants from

Table 10.2 Higher education and vocational education pathways in Nepal*

Schooling Years	HE Pathway	VET Pathway and Skills Test Levels
20+	PhD	n/a
19		
18		
17	Master's	
16		
15	Bachelor's	Level 4: Equivalent to
14		Bachelor's
13		Diploma/Level 3: Formal
12	Higher Secondary	Technical Education at the
11		Higher Secondary Level
10*	Secondary: *School	Technical SLC/Level 2: Formal
9	Leaving Certificate (SLC)	Technical Education at the Secondary Level
8	Lower Secondary	Level 1: Informal Grade 8
7		Equivalent
6		
5	Primary	Basic Level
4		
3		
2		
1		

*Sources: UNESCO 2008; CTVET 2014; MoE 2015

around the world (TIFTI 2016). Nepal also has a non-formal VET pathway, which is a short-term program (generally less than 12 months) with basic literacy as an entry requirement. However, the non-formal pathway does not provide a certificate of completion, and has no provisional pathway to enter formal HE or VET sectors (ADB 2015b).

Graduate work-readiness challenges

In recent years the academic literature, media coverage and industry reports have increasingly pointed out a gap between what employers are looking for in a graduate and what tertiary education providers are delivering (Docherty 2014; Kinash 2015; Lowden et al. 2011). This discrepancy is particularly noteworthy in Asia, as over one-third of employers have indicated that they are unable to recruit graduates who are work-ready (Manpower Group 2015). The challenges of graduate work-readiness are chronic in Nepal, where university graduates are three times more likely to be unemployed than uneducated youths (Serrière and CEDA 2014). Over a quarter (26.1 percent) of tertiary-educated youth and over half (60 percent) of VET graduates are unemployed. More importantly, although 7 percent of employed youths are overqualified, an overwhelming majority (51 percent) are underqualified (Sparreboom and Staneva 2014). Hence the concept of work-readiness is reviewed next before exploring graduate work-readiness challenges in the country.

The notion of work-readiness means many things to many people, as it has been labelled 'conceptually ambiguous' (Bennett and Kane 2009). One school of thought defines it as being able to secure employment after graduation (see Clark and Zukas 2013). However, it is often the case that changing local and global socio-economic environments impact labour markets and individuals' ability to be employed. Another school of thought focuses on the ability to gain and maintain employment and obtain new employment when necessary (Hillage and Pollard 1998). Connell and Burgess (2006) stress 'employability' rather than 'employment' as the new labour market reality. There are three broad components of graduate work-readiness: hard skills or discipline-specific knowledge, soft skills or interpersonal competencies and work experiences or work-integrated learning (Andrews and Higson 2008). The second chapter in this book extensively reviews the elements of work-readiness and adopts the six-skill-based work-readiness model in order to inform the country-level analysis.

The trend of graduate work-readiness (or lack thereof) is not well-captured in Nepal. The author's ongoing research in the country suggests that the construction, financial services, manufacturing, and tourism sectors are plagued by a lack of appropriately skilled HE or VET graduates. According to the ADB (2013), graduates not having adequate soft skills and the HE and VET programs not being aligned with market demand are two of the most important work-readiness challenges for the country. First, the construction industry is particularly suffering from skill shortages and often hires foreign workers (mainly from India) to fill the gap. For example, the professional skills of civil engineering graduates were overwhelmingly (80 percent) perceived as being inadequate by employers (Pahari 2009). This is ironic because thousands of Nepalese workers seek skilled jobs within the construction sector in the Middle East every year (ADB 2013). Second, the financial services sector has grown exponentially over the last decade. There are a total of 291 financial intermediaries (e.g., commercial banks, state banks, insurance companies) and over 13,000 savings and credit cooperatives in Nepal (MicroSave 2014; DoC 2014). These institutions specifically prefer graduates with a 4-year Bachelor of Business Administration (BBA) qualification, because this particular program offered by TU is aimed at equipping students with people skills when compared to the more popular three-year Bachelor of Business Studies (BBS) qualification with an emphasis on theoretical knowledge (Sthapit 2014). The competency gap between BBS and BBA qualification means that BBS graduates are disadvantaged in terms of work-readiness.

Third, the manufacturing sector is the second largest employer in the country. Although the share of employment in the manufacturing sector has slightly improved, the overall GDP contribution of the manufacturing sector has declined from 9 percent in 2001 to 6.2 percent in 2013 (CBS 2014). The 2011 survey of over 4000 manufacturing establishments revealed that a majority (60.3 percent) of businesses identified a lack of skilled manpower as one of the main problems facing the sector (CBS 2014, p. 9). Fourth, the T&T industry is often touted as the sector that can fast-track the country's sustainable development aspirations (ADB 2015c; World Bank 2015a). However, although studies have shown positive associations between tourism-specific academic competencies and work-readiness skills (Biswakarma 2016), the language proficiencies of graduates will be the key to employment in the tourism sector. With the rising Chinese and Indian economies, Nepal is suitably positioned to reap the benefits from outbound tourists from the two nations. Although English language proficiency is helpful to cater to the needs of Western tourists, it will be the personal qualities to deal with Chinese and Indian customers, as well as proficiency in Mandarin and Hindi, that ultimately enhance work-readiness in the tourism sector. These sector-specific challenges indicate that there is a gap between what is needed in the labour market and what is being produced by the HE and VET sectors.

Graduate work-readiness strategies in Nepal

The Nepalese government has prioritised the modernisation of the formal education system as a crucial vehicle for sustainable development, especially after the peaceful resolution of the armed conflict in 2006. For instance, on average, almost 17 percent of the national budget has been allocated to the education sector (World Bank 2015a). Several major policy initiatives or reforms have been undertaken at the national level. On the one hand, the National Skill Development Policy approved in 2012 places emphasis on strengthening and extending the authority of CTEVT and making it effective through a national vocational qualifications framework (Panth 2014; ILO 2014). On the other hand, the 2010 Youth Employment Policy focuses on more market-driven HE and VET programs to help graduates secure employment opportunities in high-demand sectors such as tourism and construction. The following section discusses some of the relevant policy mechanisms and shortcomings in the HE and VET sectors.

Higher education sector

The Innovative Strategies in Higher Education for Accelerated Human Resource Development in South Asia Nepal Report (ADB 2015a) highlighted the fact that the country lacks a clear policy framework or regulations related to the HE sector that link to the country's sustainable development aspirations (p. xii). An advisory body under the MoE, the Universities Grants Commission (UGC), has the mandate to take appropriate steps to promote and maintain standards of HE (UGC, n.d.). The UGC launched the Quality Assurance and Accreditation (QAA) program as a part of accreditation reform in 2007, with five specific purposes: (a) quality assurance, (b) continuous improvement, (c) ease of transfer amongst institutions, (d) recognition and (e) employers' confidence (UGC 2012, pp. 4–5). The fifth purpose makes an attempt to address the issue of graduate work-readiness by gaining employers' confidence in terms of hiring graduates, as well as further fulfilling the capacity development needs of already-employed workers. Despite the UGC-driven quality assurance scheme, the quality and credibility of the HE sector remains questionable (ADB 2015a, p. 12). This is reflected in a number of global statistics. For example, Nepal is ranked 108th in the HCI index (WEF 2016), and none of its universities are listed in the global rankings (Bhatta 2012). Consequently, thousands of Nepalese students decide to pursue university qualifications overseas each year. As evidence of this phenomenon, the ICEF Monitor (2015) considered Nepal as one of the fastest-growing markets for international education. Figure 10.1 shows that, on average, nearly 23,000 students went abroad to pursue HE between 2011 and 2015 (MoE 2015 p. 18). This is only a modest estimate as it is based only on the number of 'no objection' letters/certificates to study outside the country issued by the MoE. Since most HE institutions abroad do not require this, the utility of such certificates is for obtaining foreign exchange and primarily to avoid corrupt bureaucracy at airport immigration. Hence, not all outbound students request such certification. Figure 10.1 also depicts the top destinations of choice and the number of Nepalese students going abroad between 2011 and 2015. Although there are multiple reasons for Nepalese students deciding to study abroad (see Mathema 2007; Sijapati 2005), continuous political interference and uncertainties in the HE sector (Shrestha and Khanal 2016), poor employment prospects (Shrestha 2010) and the lack of technology integration (Shields 2011) for local graduates remain the top challenges.

The country clearly needs a HE policy that can provide guidance on how to institutionally address some of the identified challenges within the HE sector. The Nepalese government has initiated a National Program for Higher Education Reform and Development and drafted the HE policy. Based on the commentary of those who have reviewed the draft policy (Uprety et al. 2015), it is not clear that the issue of graduate work-readiness has become a matter of priority yet. The UGC has recently received a World Bank loan worth US$65 million for the Higher Education Reforms Project to tackle the country's human

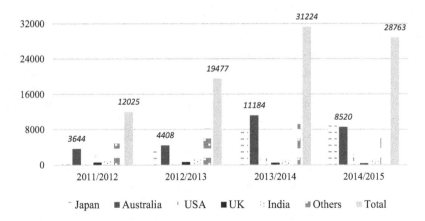

Figure 10.1 Main destinations and the number of Nepalese students going abroad for HE each year

capital needs (World Bank 2015b). Although the agenda and the impact of donor agencies in the region has been questioned as being too structural (see Dhakal and Mahmood 2014; Regmi 2016), the World Bank project does aim to put in place knowledge-based mechanisms to increase graduate employability and incomes with relevant skills and diminish human resource constraints to sustainable development.

Vocational education sector

The Innovative Strategies in Technical and Vocational Training and Education for Accelerated Human Resource Development in South Asia Nepal Report (ADB 2015b) considered that the involvement of industry and business are critical to a market-responsive VET sector in order to enhance the employability and productivity of the workforce. However, linkages between industry and VET service providers in Nepal are missing, or weak where they exist (p. 10). The country promulgated the Council for Technical Education and Vocational Training Act (CTEVT) in 1998 (CTVET 2014). Since then policy frameworks and institutional arrangements have been much better developed for the VET sector compared to the HE sector.

There are four sets of government policies for the VET sector: (a) the 1999 National Technical and Vocational and Education and Training Policy, (b) the 2007 Technical Education and Vocational Training Policy Framework, (c) the 2007 Technical Education and Vocational Training and Skills Development Policy and (d) the 2012 Nepal Technical and Vocational Education and Training (TVET) Policy. These policy frameworks emphasise training youth and adults who either did not attend school or lack trade skills. Although the main purposes of these policies are to invest in human capital development and facilitate employment, past and current programs have not been able to make a significant impact on the labour market, primarily due to a lack of demand-driven training programs (Sinha 2010). It is in this context that the ADB has provided a grant of US$20 million for the Skills Development Project (SDP), to help achieve the 2012 TVET Policy outcomes. One of the key objectives of this five-year project (2013–2018) is to increase private sector engagement in training delivery and job placement (SDP n.d). The preliminary labor market enquiry (with inputs from over 300 employers) identified construction, services and manufacturing as being priority sectors for additional training and employment (ADB 2013). More importantly, the construction sector has become an utmost priority for the country's recovery after the 2015 earthquake, as millions of houses, schools, government buildings and residential dwellings need to be rebuilt. It has been estimated that over 2 million construction-related skilled and unskilled jobs will be required for the reconstruction and recovery efforts alone (NEA 2015).

Nevertheless, the construction sector is facing skill shortages not only because of outbound migration but also because of the lack of semi-skilled professionals such as surveyors and overseers. To date there have been no programs announced for construction-related training with maximum employability. Second, on average, nearly 400,000 people seek overseas employment each year (Figure 10.2)

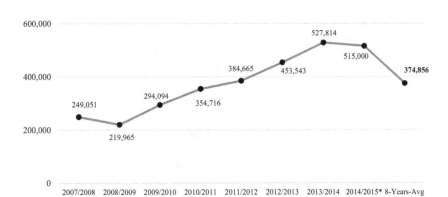

Figure 10.2 Number of overseas employment permits issued in post-conflict Nepal
(*estimate)

and the number of outbound employment permits has doubled since the peaceful resolution of armed conflict (Shrestha 2016; MoLE 2014). Most of these outbound workers are in low-skilled or semi-skilled professions. Specialised skills-training programs that enhance the employability of outbound workers in high-paying, semi-skilled and skilled professions (Paoletti et al. 2014) has the potential to not only benefit the workers but also the economy via remittance flow-back.

This trend reveals that although there are institutional mechanisms in the TVET sector, they are not agile but overly bureaucratic. Although there are multiple reasons for the mediocre success of the VET sector the following remain the top challenges: the lack of access due to fewer spaces as well as post-training support, relevant training courses and quality (ILO 2008; Panth 2014; Panth 2014). Sustainable disaster recovery and sustainable development benefits from the VET sector can only be reaped through quality training, and national and international recognition that can lead to higher employability in relevant sectors. Hence industry support mechanisms before and after vocational training are necessary for trainees. Nonetheless, despite a substantial number of government policies, integrated support mechanisms to connect trainees with potential employers do not exist (ADB 2015b) under the government programs. In this regard, one of the innovative initiatives – the Employment Fund Program (EFP) – funded by donor agencies has made an attempt to establish effective industry linkages. This initiative is discussed in the following section, as an illustration of a positive approach to resolving Nepal's graduate work-readiness challenges.

Innovation in skills for employability: the case of the employment fund program

Donor agencies have increasingly focused on skills-based education and training programs in order to facilitate graduate work-readiness capabilities towards economic transformation and sustainable development (Fraser 2014). This is particularly important in countries like Nepal, where the capacity to institution-alise such programs is lacking. Donor agencies can play a key pivotal role by working with government agencies to coordinate their funds to offer training services via private sector providers with direct links to the local labour market (UNESCO 2012). The EFP in Nepal reflects this trend. The EFP commenced in 2008, shortly after the decade-long armed conflict, as a joint effort between the Nepalese Government, the Swiss Agency for Development and Cooperation and HELVETAS Swiss Inter-cooperation Nepal (HELVETAS hereafter), the UK Department for International Aid and the World Bank (World Bank 2015c). It is an ongoing program that targets underemployed or unemployed youth from socially disadvantaged backgrounds to build skills that enhance employability (Paudel et al. n.d.).

The EFP competitively contracts training and employment service providers such as VET institutions, private-sector providers and skilled artisans to deliver training in mobile or fixed settings such as established training centres. The ser-vice providers are selected on an annual basis through a competitive procurement process (HELVETAS 2016). According to the World Bank (2015c), the innova-tive feature of this program is that EFP-funded training courses are market-driven instead of adopting a 'training for the sake of training' approach. For example, service providers must complete a rapid market assessment as a part of the com-petitive process. Once contracted, the service providers recruit and select train-ees according to the EFP guidelines. The trainees are encouraged to complete appropriate levels of skills certification conducted by the National Skill Testing Board. Financial incentives for service providers are higher for trainees that are from the most disadvantaged backgrounds. In addition, financial incentives are higher for trainees who are gainfully employed (earning US$40 per month) fol-lowing the training (p. 2). Since its inception, the EFP has trained nearly 92,000 youths, of whom more than 70 percent are gainfully employed (HELVETAS 2015, p. 5). In the aftermath of the 2015 earthquake, skills for reconstruction became a prominent component of the EFP in order to foster the skills required in earthquake-resilient construction and support, and owner-led reconstruction (HELVETAS 2016).

Conclusion

This chapter has explored labour market conditions and the state of the HE and VET sectors in Nepal. While acknowledging that the trends in graduate work-readiness challenges have not been well-documented in the country, the chapter discussed the particular issues in the construction, financial services, manufactur-ing and tourism sectors. It is clear that given the size of the informal economy and the state of socio-economic progress, work opportunities at the bottom of the pyramid, rather than the work-readiness of graduates, has been a priority for the government and donor agencies. Against the backdrop of resounding evidence that each additional year the educated population is associated with a substantial higher growth rate (Cuaresma et al. 2014, p. 307), the lack of human capital policy impetus remains a major impeding factor to realise Nepal's sustainable development aspirations. If human capital is to make a significant impact, the relevancy of the educational content to changing national labour market needs is necessary but inadequate for achieving sustainable development in the globalised world. What this means is that the desired economic transition necessitates an international outlook and substantial investment in education, employment and employability. The fact that Nepal, along with most of the South Asian countries, ranks poorly in the HCI ranking means that there are opportunities to integrate economic and education strategies through regional learning and cooperation (Maclean et al. 2013). This strategic intervention is particularly pivotal in the case of Nepal if it is to benefit from its proximities to the growing economies of China and India. Meanwhile, the issues raised in this chapter are a reminder that post-conflict and post-disaster sustainable development in Nepal looks much more sanguine with concerted policy efforts and investment in HE training and upskilling the working-age population than without them.

Table 10.3 Summary of key findings, Nepal

	Summary
Demographics/ labour market:	The size of the workforce is approximately 12 million people, and between 300,000 and 400,000 new employees enter the labour force every year. The country has one of the highest (83.4 percent) labour force participation rates in the region. The aggregate unemployment rate at the country stands at 2.7 percent in 2014.
Economy:	Country's post-conflict average (2006–2015) GDP growth was 4.33 percent. the 2016 forecast is a mere 0.5 percent, primarily because of the 2015 earthquake. Almost three-quarters of the workforce in the country depend on agriculture/forestry to make a living. Nearly half (45.3 percent) of the youth workforce (15–29 age group) is employed in low-productivity activities in the agricultural sector. When the youth workforce exits the agricultural sector, it does so in foreign labour markets, with over 500,000 labour permits were issued to Nepalese (mostly youth) planning to work abroad in 2014.
Educational structure:	The Ministry of Education (MoE) has the overall responsibility for primary, secondary and tertiary education, including VET in the country. The latest data indicate that a total of 458,621 students are enrolled in 13 HE institutions across the country and 16,024 students are enrolled across 387 VET providers in either post-secondary or diploma-level programs.

(Continued)

Table 10.3 (Continued)

	Summary
Work-readiness issues:	The trend of graduate work-readiness (or lack of) is not well-captured in Nepal. The author's ongoing research in the country suggests that the construction, financial services, manufacturing, and tourism sectors are plagued by a lack of appropriately skilled HE or VET graduates.
Policy initiatives/ strategies:	The country lacks a clear policy framework or regulations related to the HE sector that link to the country's sustainable development aspirations. The linkages between industry and VET service providers in Nepal are missing, or weak where they exist. The Employment Fund Program (EFP) is a specific strategy that has made an attempt to establish effective industry linkages. EFP is an ongoing program that targets underemployed or unemployed youth from socially disadvantaged backgrounds to build skills that enhance employability.

References

ADB. 2013, *Labor market assessment of demand for skills summary*, Manila: Asian Development Bank [ADB]. Available at: www.adb.org/sites/default/files/linked-documents/38176-015-nep-oth-01.pdf.

ADB. 2015a, *Innovative strategies in higher education for accelerated human resource development in South Asia Nepal*, Manila: Asian Development Bank [ADB].

ADB. 2015b, *Innovative strategies in technical and vocational education and training for accelerated human resource development in South Asia Nepal*, Manila: Asian Development Bank [ADB].

ADB. 2015c, *ADB-Nepal partnership for inclusive development*, Manila: Asian Development Bank [ADB].

Andrews, J. and Higson, H. 2008, 'Graduate employability, 'soft skills' versus 'hard 'business knowledge: A European study', *Higher education in Europe*, Vol. 33, no. 4, pp. 411–422.

Basnett, Y., Henley, G., Howell, J., Jones, H., Lemma, A. and Pandey, P. R. 2014, *Structural economic transformation in Nepal*, London: Overseas Development Institute.

Bennett, R. and Kane, S. 2009, 'Employer engagement practices of UK business schools and departments: An empirical investigation', *Journal of Vocational Education and Training*, Vol. 61, no. 4, pp. 495–516.

Bhatta, P. 2012, *Global ranking a dream too far for Nepal's long-degraded universities*, 2012 April 1, University World News. Available at: www.universityworldnews.com/article.php?story=20120328082036102.

Biswakarma, G. 2016, 'Relationship of tourism academic, employability abilities & skills and human resource development in Nepalese tourism industry', *International Journal*, Vol. 20.

British Council. 2014a, *High university enrollment, low graduate employment: Analyzing the paradox in Afghanistan, Bangladesh, India, Nepal, Pakistan and SriLanka*, London: An Economist Intelligence Unit Report for the British Council.

British Council. 2014b, *South Asia and higher education revolution and realities in the new economic order*, London: British Council.

CAN. 2016, *Open university bill*, Kathmandu: Constituent Assembly of Nepal [CAN]. Available at: www.can.gov.np/np/bills/passed-bills.html.

CBS. 1999, *Nepal labour force survey report 1998*, Kathmandu: Central Bureau of Statistics [CBS].

CBS. 2009, *Nepal labour force survey report 2008*, Kathmandu: Central Bureau of Statistics [CBS].

CBS. 2012, *Nepal in figures 2012*, Kathmandu: Central Bureau of Statistics [CBS].

CBS. 2014, *Development of manufacturing industries in Nepal: Current state and future challenges*, Kathmandu: Central Bureau of Statistics [CBS].

Clark, M. and Zukas, M. 2013, 'A Bourdieusian approach to understanding employability: Becoming a 'fish in water', *Journal of Vocational Education & Training*, Vol. 65, no. 2, pp. 208–219.

Connell, J. and Burgess, J. 2006, 'The influence of precarious employment on career development: The current situation in Australia', *Education + Training*, Vol. 48, no. 7, pp. 493–507.

CTVET. 2014, *National Skill Testing Board (NSTB)*, Kathmandu: The Council for Technical Education and Vocational Training [CTEVT]. Available at: http://ctevt.org.np/page.php?pagecat=7.

Cuaresma, J. C., Lutz, W. and Sanderson, W. 2014, 'Is the demographic dividend an education dividend?' *Demography*, Vol. 51, no. 1, pp. 299–315.

Dhakal, S. P. 2012, 'Regional sustainable development and the viability of environmental community organisations: Why does inter-organisational social capital matter?' *Third Sector Review*, Vol. 18, no. 1, pp. 7–27.

Dhakal, S. P. and Mahmood, M. N. 2014, 'International aid and cyclone shelters in Bangladesh: Adaptation or maladaptation?' *Contemporary South Asia*, Vol. 22, no. 3, pp. 290–304.

DoC. 2014, *Statistics of cooperative enterprises, 2014*, Kathmandu: Department of Cooperatives [DoC].

Docherty, D. 2014, 'Universities must produce graduates who are ready for any workplace', *The Guardian*, May 22, 2014. Available at: www.theguardian.com/higher-education-network/2014/may/22/universities-must-produce-graduates-who-are-ready-for-workplace.

Fraser, S. 2014, 'The role for technical and vocational education and training and donor Agencies in developing economies', *Global Policy*, Vol. 5, no. 4, pp. 494–502.

HELVETAS. 2015, *Annual report 2014 employment fund secretariat*, Kathmandu: HELVETAS Swiss Intercooperation Nepal.

HELVETAS. 2016, *Employment fund – skill for reconstruction*, Kathmandu: HELVETAS Swiss Intercooperation Nepal. Available at: https://nepal.helvetas.org/en/programmes___projects/employment_fund.cfm.

Hillage, J. and Pollard, E. 1998, *Employability: Developing a framework for policy analysis*, London: Department for Education and Employment.

ICEF Monitor. 2015, *Nepal emerging as an important growth market for international education*, Bonn, International Consultants for Education and Fairs

[ICEF]. Available at: http://monitor.icef.com/2015/12/nepal-emerging-as-an-important-growth-market-for-international-education/.

ILO. 2008, *Major skills challenges facing SKILLS-AP member countries in 2008 and strategies to address them*. Geneva: International Labour Organisation [ILO]. Available at: www.tesda.gov.ph/uploads/file/ilo_korea.pdf.

ILO. 2014, *Nepal labour market update November 2014*, Kathmandu: International Labour Organisation [ILO].

IMF. 2016, *World economic outlook update April 2016 too slow for too long*, Washington DC: International Monetary Fund [IMF].

Islam, R. 2014, *Nepal: Addressing the employment challenges. A report prepared for the International Labour Organisation [ILO]*, Kathmandu: International Labour Organisation [ILO].

Kinash, S. 2015, *8 ways to enhance your students' graduate employability*, Gold Coast: Bond University. Available at: https://bond.edu.au/files/627/8%20ways%20to%20enhance%20your%20students%20graduate%20employability.pdf.

Kruss, G., McGrath, S., Petersen, I. H. and Gastrow, M. 2015, 'Higher education and economic development: The importance of building technological capabilities', *International Journal of Educational Development*, Vol. 43, pp. 22–31.

KU. (n.d.). *History of KU in brief*, Banepa: Kathmandu University [KU]. Available at: www.ku.edu.np/university/index.php?go=his.

Lowden, K., Hall, S., Elliot, D. and Lewin, J. 2011, *Employers' perceptions of the employability skills of new graduates*, London: Edge Foundation.

Maclean, R., Jagannathan, S. and Sarvi, J. 2013, *Skills development for inclusive and sustainable growth in developing Asia-Pacific*, Manila: Asian Development Bank and Springer.

Manpower Group. 2015, *10th annual talent shortage survey*, Milwaukee: Manpower Group. Available at: www.manpowergroup.com/wps/wcm/connect/db23c560-08b6-485f-9bf6-f5f38a43c76a/2015_Talent_Shortage_Survey_US-lo_res.pdf?MOD=AJPERES.

Mathema, K. B. 2007, 'Crisis in education and future challenges for Nepal', *European Bulletin of Himalayan Research*, Vol. 31, pp. 46–66.

MicroSave. 2014, *Understanding the demand for financial services in Nepal*, Kathmandu: UN Capital Development Fund.

MoE. 2010, *TEVT skill development policy, 2064*, Kathmandu: Ministry of Education. Available at: www.moe.gov.np/article/193/tevt-skill.

MoLE. 2014, *Labour migration for employment A status report for Nepal: 2013/2014*, Kathmandu: Ministry of Labour and Employment.

MoE. 2015, Nepal education in figures 2015 at-a-glance, Kathmandu: Ministry of Education. Available at: http://www.moe.gov.np/article/520/nepal-education-in-figures-2015.html

NDRR. 2015, *Incident report of earthquake 2015*, Kathmandu: Nepal Disaster Risk Reduction Portal [NDDR]. Available at: http://drrportal.gov.np/.

NEA. 2015, *Presentation on construction sector in Nepal*, Kathmandu: Nepal Engineering Association [NEA]. Available at: www.sheltercluster.org/sites/default/files/docs/presentation_nepali_congress-june_15_2015.pdf.

Neumayer, E. 2012, 'Human development and sustainability', *Journal of Human Development and Capabilities*, Vol. 13, no. 4, pp. 561–579.

NPC. 2015, *Sustainable development goals 2016–2030 national (preliminary) report*, Kathmandu: National Planning Commission [NPC].

OECD. 1998, *Human capital investment: An international comparison*, Paris: Organization for Economic Cooperation and Development [OECD].

Pahari, B. R. 2009, 'Competency level of engineering graduates and quality of engineering education in Nepal', *Journal of the Institute of Engineering*, Vol. 7, no. 1, pp. 65–75.

Panth, B. 2013, 'Skills training and workforce development with reference to under-employment and migration', in *Skills development for inclusive and sustainable growth in developing Asia-Pacific*, The Netherlands: Springer, pp. 195–212.

Panth, B. 2014, 'Skills development for employability and inclusive growth: Policy dilemmas and priorities in South Asia', *Prospects*, Vol. 44, no. 2, pp. 167–182.

Paoletti, S., Taylor-Nicholson, E., Sijapati, B. and Farbenblum, B. 2014, *Migrant workers' access to justice at home: Nepal*, New York, NY: Open Society Foundations.

Paudel, B. R., Bettina, J., Hofstetter, S. and Porten, P. (n.d.), *Skills for gainful employment: The employment fund in Nepal*, HELVETAS Swiss Intercooperation Nepal. Available at: https://assets.helvetas.org/downloads/sde_employmentfundposter. pdf.

Regmi, K. D. 2016, 'World Bank in Nepal's education: Three decades of neoliberal reform', *Globalisation, Societies and Education*, vol. 15, no.2, pp. 1–14.

Sachs, J. D. and Reid, W. V. 2006, 'Investments toward sustainable development', *Science*, Vol. 312, no. 5776, p. 1002.

SDP. n.d., *Recent news*, Kathmandu: Skills Development Project [SDP]. Available at: www.sdp.org.np/about-us.

Serrière, N. and Centre for Economic Development and Administration [CEDA]. 2014, *Labour market transitions of young women and men in Nepal: Work4Youth Publication Series No. 12*, Geneva: International Labour Office [ILO].

Shields, R. 2011, 'ICT or I see tea? Modernity, technology and education in Nepal', *Globalisation, Societies and Education*, Vol. 9, no. 1, pp. 85–97.

Shrestha, B. K. 2010, *Perception of differences in quality of graduates: Employers versus students*, 16th International Conference in Quality, Asia Pacific Quality Organization, September, 18–20, 2010, Kathmandu, Nepal.

Shrestha, I. M. and Khanal, S. K. 2016, 'Indigenization of higher education: Reflections from Nepal', in *Indigenous culture, education and globalization*, Berlin. Springer, pp. 137–157.

Shrestha, R. 2016, 'Number of migrants leaving for foreign jobs on the decline', *The Himalayan Times*, July 19, 2016. Available at: http://thehimalayantimes.com/business/number-of-migrants-leaving-for-foreign-jobs-on-the-decline/.

Sijapati, B. 2005, 'Perils of higher education reform in Nepal', *Journal of Development and Social Transformation*, Vol. 2, pp. 25–32.

Sinha, R. 2013, 'TEVT policies in developing countries', Technical and Vocational Education and Training Development Journal, Vol. 1, no. 13, pp. 23–29.

Sparreboom, T. and Staneva, A. 2014, *Is education the solution to decent work for youth in developing economies? Identifying qualifications mismatch from 28 school-to-work transition surveys*, Work4Youth Publication Series No. 23, Geneva: International Labour Office [ILO].

Sthapit, A. 2014, 'Bank Jobs for BBA graduates: Revisiting market dynamics', Management Vision: *Journal of Management and Economics*, Vol. 2, no. 1, pp. 1–6.

Suwal, R. ad Pant, B. 2009, *Measuring informal sector economic activities in Nepal*. In Special IARIW – SAIM Conference on Measuring the Informal Economy in Developing Countries, Kathmandu.

TIFTI. 2016, *Introduction*, Kathmandu: Training Institute for Technical Instruction [TIFTI]. Available at: www.titi.org.np/.

TU. (n.d.), *About us*, Kathmandu: Tribhuvan University [TU]. Available at: http://tribhuvan-university.edu.np/about-us/.

UGC. 2012, *Quality assurance and accreditation for higher education in Nepal: A brief guideline*, Kathmandu: University Grants Commission [UGC].

UGC. (n.d.), *A brief Introduction of UGC*, Kathmandu: University Grants Commission [UGC]. Available at: www.ugcnepal.edu.np/page-detail/a-brief-introduction-4609.

UN. 2015, *Transforming our world: The 2030 agenda for sustainable development*. A/RES/70/1. July 25, 2015 from the United Nations [UN] Available at: https://sustainabledevelopment.un.org/post2015/transformingourworld.

UNDP. 2014, *Nepal human development report 2014 beyond geography unlocking human potential*, Kathmandu: United Nations Development Programme [UNDP].

UNESCO. 2008, *Secondary education regional information base: Country profile*, Bangkok: United Nations Educational, Scientific and Cultural Organization [UNESCO].

UNESCO. 2012, *Youth and skills putting education to work*, Bangkok: United Nations Educational, Scientific and Cultural Organization [UNESCO].

UNOHCHR. 2012, *Nepal conflict report*, Geneva: United Nations Office of the High Commissioner for Human Rights [UNOHCHR].

Uprety, D., Bhatta, P. and Onta, P. 2015, *The proposed higher education policy: It will not do!* 2015 August 21, SETOPATI. Available at: http://setopati.net/opinion/8720/The-Proposed-Higher-Education-Policy:-It-Will-Not-Do!/.

Van Adams, A. 2007, *The role of youth skills development in the transition to work: A global review*, Washington, DC: World Bank.

WEF. 2016, *The human capital report 2016*, Geneva: The World Economic Forum [WEF].

World Bank. 2015a, *Nepal country snapshot*, Washington, DC: World Bank.

World Bank. 2015b, *Higher education reforms project (P147010)*, Washington, DC: World Bank. Available at: http://documents.worldbank.org/curated/en/610541468060551481/pdf/PAD10190PAD0P1010Box385414B00OUO090.pdf.

World Bank. 2015c, *The role of skills training for youth employment in Nepal: An impact evaluation of the employment fund: Results series*. Washington, DC: World Bank. Available at: https://assets.helvetas.org/downloads/ef_result_series.pdf.

World Bank. 2016a, *GNI per capita, PPP (current international $)*, Washington, DC: World Bank. Available at: http://data.worldbank.org/indicator/NY.GNP.PCAP.PP.CD.

World Bank. 2016b, *Poverty*, Washington, DC: World Bank. Available at: http://data.worldbank.org/topic/poverty.

World Bank. 2016c, *Nepal*, Washington, DC: World Bank. Available at: www.worldbank.org/en/country/nepal.

WTTC. 2015, *Travel & tourism economic impact 2015 Nepal*, London: World Travel & Tourism Council [WTTC].

11 Work-readiness in Lao PDR

Vipapone Aphayvanh

Introduction

Lao People's Democratic Republic (Lao PDR) has been experiencing a fast-growing economy, and there is a need for productive human capital to ensure sustainable growth in the future (World Bank 2014a). However, the country is still listed as one of the least-developed nations in Southeast Asia (World Bank 2012). Hence, it is essential to have skilled human resources in order to ensure individuals are able to seek good-quality employment, and to therefore improve their quality of living and in many cases, escape from poverty (World Bank 2013b). The Lao government has been investing in education at all levels (DFAT 2014; World Bank 2013c). Despite the fact that more young people acquire tertiary qualifications in Technical Vocational Training Education (TVET) and Higher Education (HE) than before, graduates face difficulties in gaining employment after the completion of their studies (Jariangprasert and Kantabutra 2012). This is particularly problematic as the country's demographic comprises a large proportion of young people who can potentially be the powerhouse of labour for the country (ADB 2011).

The underlying course of the problem is rather complex. At present employers suggested that it is challenging to recruit highly skilled candidates for job vacancies since those who graduated from the educational institutions, both in TVET and HE, were poorly equipped with skills and knowledge required in the jobs (World Bank 2013c). Students, on the other hand, found themselves enrolled in outdated courses that do not reflect the skills and technical knowledge needed by the employers in industry (DPEM 2008). The major gap of skills between the supply side and the demand side contributes to a persisting problem of youth unemployment and underemployment, which in turn can hinder the development of the country as a whole (World Bank 2013c).

This chapter will examine the current employability situation in Lao and investigates the challenges that the country faces amidst rapid social changes and economic growth. The chapter will then present the current major strategies and policy implemented to address the skill shortage problems.

Country background

Lao is a small landlocked country situated in the Southeast Asia region (Lao Statistics Bureau 2016). With the population of 6.8 million people, the government is attempting to graduate the country from being on the Least Developed Country (LDC) list by 2020 (UNFPA 2015). Laos is also categorised as a lower-middle-income country (World Bank 2017b), with GDP per capital of only $1740 per year, among the lowest in the South East Asia region next to Myanmar ($1,160) and Cambodia ($1,070) (World Bank 2015). Nevertheless, the country has progressed significantly in the past few decades, and this can be seen through the fact that the population living under the poverty line reduced from 46 percent in 1993 to 16.5 percent in 2011 (World Bank 2017a). However, a fact which cannot be neglected is that a large number of the population is still living near the poverty line, especially those in rural areas (World Bank 2012).

Laos was affected by foreign colonisations and recently became independent in 1975 at the end of the Vietnam War (Stuart-Fox 2008). Since then, Laos is a single party-led government which is centralised under the guidance of the Lao People's Revolutionary Party (Soukamneuth 2006). Until the 1980s, the country transitioned the economy from a centrally-planned to a free market economy. However, the free market is not to the same degree as in Western countries, and the country is unlikely to transit into a liberal-democratic state (UNFPA 2015), even though there is an increase in foreign investments in the country due to current political stability (Ministry of Education and Sports 2015).

Laos has experienced economic progress with the fast growth rate of GDP ranging between 7.5 percent and 7.8 percent since 2007, due to an increasing economic integration within the region such as ASEAN Economic Community (AEC), East-West Economy Corridor (Myanmar, Lao and Vietnam), and the Emerald Triangle (Lao, Vietnam and Cambodia) (Lao Statistics Bureau 2016; Ministry of Planning and Investment 2015; World Bank 2013c). The dramatic economic growth was partly due to the boom in mining and hydropower constructions, which account for 2.5 percent of GDP growth in 2007 (out of 7.5 percent growth rate) (World Bank 2008). Despite the high proportions from the GDP, the natural resources sector created only 22,000 jobs in 2013 (World Bank 2014a). On the other hand, the tourism sector has a balanced contribution to the GDP and job creation, especially for the poor (Turner 2015). There is a climbing number of tourists coming into Laos each year, and in 2013 the number reached 3.7 million. This accounts for a direct contribution to the national GDP at 14.7 percent and total employment of 12.8 percent in 2014 or around 400,000 jobs supported by the tourism industry (Turner 2015).

When breaking down the composition of the GDP, 42.0 percent is from the service sector, 30.3 percent is from agriculture and 27.7 percent is from industry (Jones 2015). Nevertheless, the labour force distribution to each sector is not aligned with productivity levels generated by the sector. The majority of the workforce is in agriculture (71 percent), while 20.2 percent and 8.3 percent are in services and industry respectively (Jones 2015). This shows that the labour force engaging in the agricultural sector has a relatively low productivity level. This makes Laos the most agrarian economy in Southeast Asia (Ministry of Education 2008), and there is the need for productivity improvement in this sector in order to increase population's income (World Bank 2013b). Hence, this is how the need for a semi-skilled and skilled workforce comes into the picture, and this can be achieved by skill upgrading through tertiary educational training to enable the workforce to engage in other economic sectors, as well as contributing to increasing productivity in the agricultural sector (ADB 2011).

Lao labour market

It is undeniable that Laos has an advantage in terms of its demographic as more than 50 percent of the population are under 25 years. Those members of this population segment are of working age and are the powerhouse of the country's labour force (UNFPA 2015).

The unemployment rate in Laos is relatively low. For instance, the rate was only 0.4 percent in 2012 (World Bank 2013c) and 1.4 percent in 2014 (World Bank 2014b). As mentioned earlier, this trend is partly explained by the fact that most of the working population is engaging in the agricultural sector (71 percent), either full-time or part-time (Jones 2015). The workforce engaging in agricultural sector are generally unpaid workers involved in agricultural production, for the purpose of assisting their family with subsistent rice production and self-employed individuals in private business (Ministry of Planning and Investment 2008). However, as per the STEP Household Survey 2011/12, when excluding unpaid workers and self-employed individuals; and only including those who are actively seeking jobs in wage-earning occupations, the unemployment rate can be as high as 2.7 percent (World Bank 2013c).

It is suggested by an influential body such as the World Bank that in order to ensure alleviation of poverty, people should be able to gain access to job opportunities that help them to financially sustain themselves and their families, and improve their well-being (World Bank 2013b). Evidence shows that those who are working poor are likely to be unskilled labour, and on the other hand, skilled workers are likely to earn more wages than unskilled individuals (King and Van de Walle 2007). Therefore, in order to escape from poverty, upskilling the labour force through education is a necessity by providing them a safeguard to secure higher paid employment.

Education system in Laos

According to Figure 11.1, the Lao formal educational system comprises of 19 years in total. In the formal education pathway to the higher education, the system starts with kindergarten and students can be as young as three years old when they first start at this level. This early childhood education is not compulsory due to the unavailability in many locations around the country (UNESCO 2013). The next level is primary school education, which is compulsory. Despite the fact that primary school students account for the largest number of student enrolments, the completion rate of 73 percent is still significantly lower than the target of 95 percent as mentioned in the 8th National Socio-Economic Development Plan (Ministry of Planning and Investment 2015). Then, successful

Table 11.1 The overview of Lao's national education system

Level of Education	Year	Formal Education		Non-formal Education Stream
		Higher Education Stream	TVET Stream	
	3	PhD	-	-
Tertiary	2			
Education	1			
	2	Master		
	1			
	5	Bachelor Degree		
	4	(4–5 years)	Continuing to Bachelor Degree (>1.5 years)	
	3		High TVET	
	2		Diploma	
	1		(1–3 years)	
Secondary	12	Upper Secondary	Secondary	Upper Secondary
Education	11	Level (3 years)	Vocational	Level G10–12
	10		(1–3 years)	
	9	Lower Secondary	IVET Certificate III	Lower Secondary
	8	Level (4 years)	(> 2 years)	Level G6–9
	7		IVET Certificate II	
	6		(> 1 year) IVET Certificate (3–6 months)	
Primary	5	Primary Level	Primary Level	-
Education	4	(5 years)	(5 years)	
	3			Primary Level
	2			B1–3 (3 years)
	1			
Pre-education	-	Kindergarten (3 years) (not compulsory)	-	-

Source: (Sisongkharm et al. 2014; UNESCO 2013; World Bank 2013c)

students proceed into four years of lower secondary school education. The third year of secondary school (year 12) was recently added in 2010 as a part of major educational reform by the Ministry of Education (World Bank 2013c). The next level is higher education, which includes bachelor programs (5 years) and master and PhD programs (2–5 years) (UNESCO 2013).

In the TVET pathway, students can commence their studies in three levels, namely first level, secondary level and high level (at post-secondary level) (see Table 11.1) (Sisongkharm et al. 2014). It is noted that students can commence their TVET pathway after the primary level. Though for adults who do not have any prior formal education but need TVET training, students are eligible to enrol in primary education through a non-formal education stream, which takes a shorter period of time to complete compared to the formal pathway (UNESCO 2013). In total, the non-formal program includes primary level (3 years), secondary level (grade 6–9) and upper secondary level (grade 10–12) (Sisongkharm et al. 2014).

The delivery of the non-formal education system is for the purpose of providing education for adults (UNESCO 2013). This is due to the fact that the low number of enrolments at the primary level in the formal education pathway has a ripple on effect on the number of students eligible for TVET training later on in that educational pathway. Hence, TVET becomes a short-term solution for the labour shortage problem, meaning that those who do not follow the formal education pathway (including primary and secondary level) can also enrol in TVET programs to upgrade their skills (World Bank 2013c).

As seen in Table 11.2, higher education institutions in Laos consist of four universities in Vientiane Capital, Luangprabang and Champasack. Apart from universities, the country also has five Teacher Training Colleges and 83 private higher education institutions (DPEM 2008).

The biggest university of the country, the National University of Laos, was established in 1996 in accordance with The Prime Minister's Decree to rationalise the higher educational system by combining various institutions (DPEM 2008; NUOL 2013). Since 2001, there has been a significant number of enrolments in bachelor degrees, from 22,605 in 2001 to 76,332 in 2007. However, there are still some challenges associated with the inadequate higher educational facilities. Around 44,700 students completed their upper secondary level education in 2006, and only over 18,000 students can gain entrance into the tertiary level every year due to the limited capacity (DPEM 2008).

TVET institutions in Laos are delivered by ministries and organisations (as seen in Table 11.3). International donors also assist with the implementation of various projects to enhance the effectiveness of TVET institutions. There are two types of vocational training, TVET and IVET (UNESCO 2013). The differences between the two system is that TVET programs are for those who follow the formal educational pathway (starting from primary school to upper secondary

Table 11.2 Higher education institutions in Laos (DPEM 2008)

Higher Education Institutions (Universities and Colleges)*	Provinces
National University of Laos (NUOL)	Vientiane Capital
Souphanouvong University (SU)	Luangprabang
Champasack University (CU)	Champasack
University of Health Sciences (UHS)	Vientiane Capital
5 Teacher Training Colleges	In many provinces
83 Private Colleges	In many provinces

Table 11.3 TVET Institutions in Laos (UNESCO 2013)

Ministry and Organisation	TVET Institutions	Assistance
Ministry of Public Health	University of Health Science and 12 Nursing schools	– Lux – Development – World Bank – ADB (Asian Development Bank) – JICA (Japan International Cooperation Agency)
Ministry of Finance	3 training institutes	– Vietnam (2004–2010)
Ministry of Agriculture and Forestry	5 specialist training institutes	– Swiss Cooperation (2009–2012) – Rockefeller Foundation (2008–2009)
Ministry of Information and Culture	5 training institutes	
Ministry of Justice	3 training institutes	
Bank of Lao	1 training institute	
Lao Women's Union	3 training centres	
Lao Revolutionary Youth Federation	10 training centres	
Community Learning Centres	321 centres across the country	

school), while IVET or Integrated Vocational Education Training primarily targets adults who do not have formal education qualifications but need vocational trainings to improve their skill level. Currently, there are eight IVET schools operates in Laos under the supervision of MOE and the support from GIZ International (UNESCO 2013).

The education system in Laos is relatively centralised in which the central government has the control and responsibilities ranging from determining school curricula to appointing board members and instructors. Schools do not have control over setting tuition fees, and institutions do not have other income apart from budget allocated per number of students from the government (Benveniste et al. 2007). At a vocational training as well as higher educational level, the government is the main body to design pedagogical approaches, meaning that the skills produced are supply driven rather than be in accordance with the labour market demand.

There are two ministries that regulate and manage higher education and TVET institutions, Ministry of Education and Sports (MOES) and Ministry of Labour and Social Welfare (MOLSW) (UNESCO 2013). The two ministries form the National Training Council (NTC), which has the purpose of implementing various activities, such as forming and recommending policies, being the coordinator between public representatives of enterprises' occupations and the private sector in relation to skills development; and determining and developing occupational standards (Ministry of Education 2009).

Graduate work-readiness challenges

The definition of employability is relatively broad, and currently there is no conclusive definitions for the term. A general definition signifies that 'Employability is about having the capability to gain initial employment, maintain employment and obtain new employment if required' (Hillage and Pollard 1998, p. 1). However, some scholars have pointed out that employability definitions vary in accordance to a particular group of workforce in the labour market. For example, Yorke and Knight (2006, p. 4) defined employability for graduates, the group of individuals who are likely to be at early stage in their career, as 'the potential a graduate has for obtaining, and succeeding in graduate-level positions.' The boundary of graduate employability expands from the acquisition of technical skills, soft skills to career development skills and work experience (Dacre Pool and Sewell 2007).

In Lao PDR, evidence shows that there is a lack of skills regarding the quality and quantity of graduates. The quality problem means that the pool of graduates is not adequately trained during their time in universities, and employers found their skills mismatched with their expectations (World Bank 2013c).The quantity problem is referred to as employers are facing challenges in seeking the right number of employees both in high-skilled jobs and elementary-level jobs as many are seasonal workers who seek employment only in off-farming seasons (World Bank 2013c). To break down the proportion of skilled labour in the Laotian workforce, 74 percent of the population is active labourer, but only 12 percent are classified as skilled labour. This means Laos faces labour shortages as the qualified and productive human resources do not meet the national labour demand (ILO 2007). This finding is in accordance with the STEP Employer Survey and Enterprise Survey, which illustrates that employers face challenges in finding qualified candidates, despite the fact that there are many job seekers in the labour market (World Bank 2013c).

Manufacturing is the industry that is heavily affected by the labour shortage and unskilled labour problems due to the nature of the manpower attracted to this industry. Most of the workers are seasonal, who temporarily seek employment outside their farming work in off-seasons, though this group of the workforce would migrate back to rural areas in harvest seasons (World Bank 2013c). Therefore, the manufacturing industry faces severe shortages of applicants during farming season, and the applicants are mostly unskilled. Due to the frequent turnover, employers in manufacturing are reluctant to provide training to their employees. Moreover, due to proximity and linguistic similarity, a large number of young workers, as many as 200,000, emigrated to Thailand to seek employment opportunities in factories, which further exacerbates the current labour shortage problem (Lintner 2008).

On the other hand, the services sector also faces skills shortage but in a different form compared to the manufacturing sector. Unlike the industry, companies in services sector are able to find applicants for advertised vacancies. However, companies have difficulties in selecting suitable candidates for the positions due to skills mismatch and candidates' high expectation in wages. The cause of skills mismatch can be explained by looking at the supply side of the workforce (e.g., choosing a field of study, quality of training). For instance, despite the fact that there is a high skill demand in technical skills such as engineering and science disciplines, business administration, accounting and finance are the most popular degrees both in public and private universities and colleges (DFAT 2014; Planco Consulting 2010; World Bank 2013a). Data from 2011–2012 shows that all of master degree students in Laos obtain a Master of Business Administration (MBA), and this could be as high as 85 percent (DFAT 2014).

As seen in Figure 11.1, countries with developed economies such as South Korea have a more balanced skill composition than in Laos, where the skewed human resources may lead to the oversupply of skills in certain areas, such as business, social science and law (43.4 percent in Laos compared to 21.8 percent in

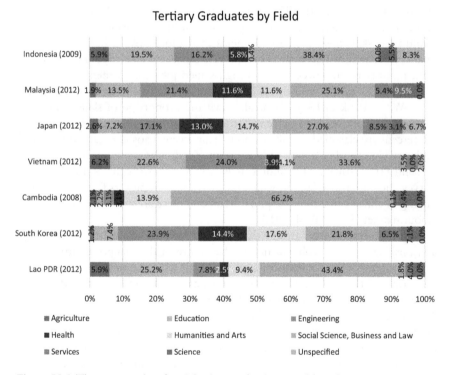

Figure 11.1 The oversupply of social sciences, business and law degrees in Lao PDR (World Bank 2013a)

Source: World Bank Data, cited in (World Bank 2013a)

South Korea). However, business- and economics-related occupations are among the lowest-income professions in Laos (World Bank 2014a).

The antecedents to this trend may lie within the discrepancy in expectations between students, universities and employers. Students choose a field of study not on a market-driven basis but possibly due to peer pressures (World Bank 2013c). Institutions' lack of connections with the industry means that they do not obtain adequate information on workforce forecast regarding degrees in demand, which then can be used in university advertisements accordingly (World Bank 2013c). Consequently, the mass-produced nature of business degrees compromises the quality of graduates (ADB 2011).

The underlying issues of such a problem may be due to the lack of link between industries and educational institutions. The design of teaching content is supply based and centralised from the government under the control of the Ministry of Education. The lack of collaboration with the industry has an adverse impact on the level of productivity of human resources, as shown in the STEP survey indicating that graduates feel that they are not capable in performing their jobs, even though they mention that their degrees add value to their skill set (World Bank 2013c). The implication of this is that the industry does not have confidence in the effectiveness of training accreditations provided by educational institutions (ILO 2007).

One of the reasons for the quality problem is due to the limited resources in higher education institutions and TVET. For instance, at a higher educational institution level, the budget can range from USD$ 0.9 to 1.2 million per faculty. Compared to developing countries, the allocation of budget as per proportions from the GDP is relatively low (3.6 percent in developing countries versus 2.7 percent in Laos in 2007) (DPEM 2008). It can be seen from reports that the expenditure of budgets is mostly allocated to teacher salaries and student stipends and there is minimal investment in infrastructure, teacher training and curriculum improvements (DPEM 2008).

Moreover, there is a prominent inadequacy of qualified trainers and instructors to facilitate students' learning, especially instructors and teachers specialised in industrialised areas, such as modern process and technology (World Bank 2014a). The main problem is that the instructors do not have the access to appropriate teaching materials and teaching techniques, as mentioned earlier. Another issue is that they do not have adequate industry experience and technical expertise for effective teaching (GIZ 2014). Therefore, the lack of innovative pedagogical approaches affects the quality of courses and training.

Addressing the challenges

The Lao government has been enacting policies to strengthen the capability and management of the education sector. The main themes of action plans are aimed at ensuring equitable access to education, improving quality and relevance of curricula, increasing efficiency and effectiveness in terms of management and collaboration between different departments (Ministry of Education 2009; UNESCO

2013). For example, recent policies and strategies focusing on increasing investment in education include the National Growth and Poverty Eradication Strategy in 2006, the National Socio-Economic Development Plan 2006–2015 and the Education for All (EFA) National Plan for Action 2003–2015 (UNESCO 2013).

As mentioned in the previous section, the creation of human capital in Laos is relatively complex and would need a substantial amount of resources to improve the tertiary education system. Hence, the government needs to strategically allocate the budget to address the existing skill issues. Asian Development Bank (ADB), one of the major donors for educational projects in Laos, pointed out that the short-term approach to the ongoing labour shortage problem is to increase funding in TVET sector (ADB 2011). Therefore, since 2011, there has been a significant rise in funding TVET education, and the sources of the funding are from the government budget and international donors (World Bank 2013c). The major donors include ADB, German government, Luxembourg governments, Thai NGOs, Swiss cooperation agency and GIZ International (see Table 11.4). It is noted that the majority (65 percent) of the tasks related to developing TVET and HE sector was carried out by international donors, though the Lao government facilitates the process in terms of the legislation and policies (Ministry of Education and Sports 2015).

There is also evidence of cooperation with countries in the region to address the skilled labour issues. In 2013, the governments of Vietnam, Thailand and Laos are cooperating in developing vocational training for young people (Saengpassa 2013). This cooperation includes sharing teaching resources and equipment. The program has a purpose to respond to the labour demand in the market in which the challenges, such as skill shortages and human resource capacity, are shared between the three countries. The project is still at a trial stage, and if successful, the future plan is to include the rest of ASEAN nations (Saengpassa 2013). Moreover, the project is also developing a unified qualification system that allows students from the three countries to use their accredited qualifications to apply for jobs between the countries (Saengpassa 2013). However, despite the increased partnership between the countries, problems still exist in terms of having qualified teachers and good teaching techniques to deliver the knowledge effectively and efficiently (Saengpassa 2013).

Each donor has different plans to implement the project to enhance the quality of TVET education and create high-quality human resources. For instance, the US$23.0 million worth of projects funded by the ABD through the so-called Strengthening Technical and Vocational Education and Training project aims to equip 20,000 students with TVET qualifications in line with the need of the labour market (ADB 2010). The project timeline from 2011 to 2021 also has the purpose to empower women in order to increase their participation in the workforce by having a goal of increasing females with TVET qualifications and diverse skills by 50 percent by the end of the project (ADB 2010). On the other hand, teaching trainings, as a part of the GIZ Teacher Training project (TTEP), would focus on training vocational teachers in order to multiply the number of qualified graduates in the future (GIZ 2014). However, international donors experienced

Table 11.4 Main donors for TVET in the period 2008–2015 (Ministry of Education and Sports 2015, p. 48)

Organization	Projects	Amount contracted during the period 2008–2015	Period	Future Plan
ADB	Strengthening Technical and Vocational Education and Training (STVET)	23 million USD (remaining for 2015–2016: 4,000,000 USD)	2010 – mid 2016	Project Preparatory Technical Assistance in 2016, around same amount expected
Swiss Agency for Cooperation	Vocational Education in Laos (VELA)	10.5 million EUR + 4.5 million EUR	2013–2018	
Federal Ministry for Economic Cooperation and Development (BMZ) GIZ International	TVET Teacher Education Programme (TTEP)	4.1 million EUR	2012–2016	Under discussions
Thailand International Development Cooperation Agency (TICA)	Strengthening Lao National Good Agricultural Practices (GAP) in Lao PDR	3 million USD	2015	Under discussions
Swiss Agency for Cooperation Luxembourg cooperation	Lao National Institute of Tourism and Hospitality (LANITH)	15 million EUR	2016–2020	
Francophonie	Capacity building	0.15 million USD per year	2015	Under discussions
Bank aus Verantwortung (KfW)	Capacity building	6 million EUR	2015–2019	

some overlaps in terms of implemented activities, and the resources could have been improved and being optimised. This is the area of improvement in the next course of project implementation (Ministry of Education and Sports 2015).

Implication of policies

The target with the TVET sector has helped to increase the number of enrolments in TVET institutions (ADB 2010). However, data from *Skills & Knowledge for Greater Growth and Competitiveness in Lao PDR* (World Bank 2013c) shows that due to the strategic nature of the project, the higher educational sector has not been the main priority. Evidence shows that the number of enrolments at universities decreased between 2010 and 2011. This is partially due to the decrease in quota of student enrolments in public universities, meaning that there are less students able to gain access to scholarships at the higher education level, though students outside the quota still can enrol in classes but have to pay for tuition fees. Another implication to the increased funding on the TVET project is that graduates for TVET institutions found themselves not being qualified for jobs. According to Employer/Enterprise surveys, employers expressed that they prefer graduates who obtain a university degree over TVET students due to the perceived higher qualifications of the former group (World Bank 2013c).

Conclusion

At present, in order to address the skills shortages, the Lao government, as well as international donors, have been increasingly investing in the educational sector in order to improve the skills of the workforce. However, the question remains whether the current approach to the problem is appropriate and whether the challenges will be addressed by primarily focusing on the TVET sector. This is due to the fact that the preference of young people in choosing their educational disciplines still remains the same over time. This means that young people want to obtain a higher educational degree with the goal of gaining higher paid employment, working in an office, and being prestigious in society; more than working in vocational areas which are perceived to be a manual work in manufacturing and lower-pay jobs when compared to HE. However, jobs in the services area are limited. Therefore, every year, several thousand graduates from HE could not find jobs, and they are in surplus. On the other hand, in the manufacturing sector, there is a major shortage of semi-skilled and skilled labour due to the minimal interests from young people to be engaged in employment in this area. In reality, those who are working in the manufacturing sector are mostly unskilled due to the fact that these people migrate from rural areas to find jobs, some of them only seeking temporary work in the farming off season and they would then return home in the harvest seasons. Hence, employers would not want to invest in training and development to upskill their employees due to the uncertainty in turnover. This exacerbates the skill shortage in the industry among the increasing foreign investment in the construction of hydropower stations and mining operations. Nonetheless, time will tell and Lao may see if the increase funding in TVET will yield a satisfactory outcome in the near future.

Table 11.5 Summary of key findings, Lao PDR

	Summary
Country Background	Lao PDR is a landlocked country in South East Asia with the population of 6.8 million people. A large proportion of the population is still living under the poverty line (16.5 percent). The country has an aim to graduate from the least poverty list by 2020. To achieve that, there is a need to improve the quality of human capital of the country. The country's economy has progressed dramatically in recent years, with 7.8 percent growth rate in 2007. However, it is mainly due to the boom in mining and hydropower production, which creates smaller number of jobs compared to other sectors such as agriculture and tourism.
Labour Market	50 percent of Lao population are under 25 years old, in which the group is considered to be the powerhouse of the labour force. Unemployment rate is relatively low (1.4 percent in 2014), though the majority of working population (71 percent) is engaging in agricultural production which yield very small financial returns. Meaning that people have jobs but they are 'working poor'. Hence, there is a need to equip them with skills in order to provide them opportunities to seek employment in wage earning occupations or improve productivity in agricultural sector.
Education System	Lao education system comprises of formal education pathway to academic qualification (i.e., higher education) and vocational training pathway (i.e., TVET). Due to the low enrolments at primary school level, a large group of the workforce has low literacy and not able to receive formal trainings, both at higher education and vocational training. Therefore, the non-formal and integrated system provides a fast-track for adult learners to gain access to vocational trainings, even without basic education. The education in Laos is centralised, meaning government is the main support for almost all aspects of the management and operation of educational institutions.
Work-readiness challenges	The country experiences labour shortages both in quality and quantity. The manufacturing sector in particular faces difficulties in recruiting work force at all levels of skills due to the nature of the industry that mostly attracts temporary workers from rural areas who are away in their off-farming seasons. On the other hand, skills in services sector has a surplus in supply, especially in business, social science and law disciplines. However, employers are still experiencing some challenges in recruiting candidates with adequate skill set in these areas. This shows the lack of link between industries, educational institutions and students' needs. The lack of resources is the main hindrance to addressing the skill shortage problem.
Addressing the challenges	International donors have been funding projects to support and improve the effectiveness and capacity of the tertiary education system. The approach to the problem is to primarily focus on increasing investment in TVET sector due to the apparent skill needs in the labour market. However, evidence shows that employers prefer graduates from universities to TVET due to perceived higher quality of the former.

References

ADB. 2010, *Lao people's democratic republic: Strengthening technical and vocational education and training project*, Management Learning, Asian Development Bank, Manila.

ADB. 2011, *Addressing skill shortages in the Lao people's democratic republic*, Social Protection Project Briefs, Asian Development Bank, Manila.

Benveniste, L., Marshall, J. H. and Santibañez, L. 2007, *Teaching in Lao PDR*, Human Development Sector, East Asia and the Pacific Region, the World Bank and Ministry of Education, Lao People's Democratic Republic.

Dacre Pool, L. and Sewell, P. 2007, 'The key to employability: Developing a practical model of graduate employability', *Education + Training*, Vol. 49, no. 4, pp. 277–289.

DFAT. 2014, *Australia-laos education delivery strategy 2013–18*, Department of Foreign Affairs and Trade, Canberra.

DPEM. 2008, *The current situation of higher education in Lao PDR*, Department of Private Education Management, Vientiane.

GIZ. 2014, *TVET Teacher Education Programme (TTEP)*, Deutsche Gesellschaft für Internationale Zusammenarbeit, Vientiane.

Hillage, J. and Pollard, E. 1998, *Employability: Developing a framework for policy analysis*, London: DfEE.

ILO. 2007, *Major skills challenges facing SKILLS-AP member counties in 2008 and strategies to address them*, Incheon: International Labour Organization [ILO].

Jariangprasert, N. and Kantabutra, S. 2012, 'The exploratory of student's job selection factors and job candidate attributes in Luang Prabang, Laos', *World*, Vol. 2, no. 2, pp. 84–95.

Jones, G. 2015, *Population and development in Lao PDR: Understanding opportunities, challenges and policy options for socio-economic development*, Vientiane, UNFPA.

King, E. M. and Van de Walle, D. 2007, *Schooling, poverty, and disadvantage in the Lao People's Democratic Republic*, New York, NY: World Bank.

Lao Statistics Bureau. 2016, *Home*, Lao Statistics Bureau, Vientiane, viewed Available at: www.lsb.gov.la/en/index.php [Accessed December 21, 2016].

Lintner, B. 2008, 'Laos: At the crossroads', *Southeast Asian Affairs*, Vol. 2008, no. 2008, pp. 171–183.

Ministry of Education. 2008, *The development of education: National report Lao PDR*, Ministry of Education, UNESCO, Vientiane.

Ministry of Education. 2009, *Second Education Development Project (EDPII): Economic relevance study report*, Technical Assistance and Capacity Building in Education Policy Analysis, Ministry of Education, Vientiane.

Ministry of Planning and Investment. 2008, *Social and economic indicators: Survey results on expenditure and consumption of household 2007/2008*, Department of Statistics, Vientiane.

Ministry of Planning and Investment. 2015, *Five year national socio-economic development plan VIII (2016–2020)*, Ministry of Planning and Investment, Vientiane.

Ministry of Education and Sports. 2015, *Technical and vocational education and training development Plan 2016–2020*, Ministry of Education and Sports, Vientiane.

NUOL. 2013, *About us: History of national university of laos*, National University of Laos, viewed. Available at: www.nuol.edu.la/index.php/en/about-nuol-4/2013-02-12-08-18-58/2013-02-12-07-57-13.html [Accessed October 1, 2017].

Planco Consulting. 2010, *Demand-oriented vocational training in Lao PDR: Sector analysis, criteria-based evaluation of training institutes, and design recommendations for a new program under lao-German financial cooperation*, Lao-German Financial Cooperation, Vientiane.

Saengpassa, C. 2013, 'ASEAN countries join forces to boost vocational education programmes', *The Nation*, viewed. Available at: www.nationmultimedia.com/news/national/aec/30211884 [Accessed December 12, 2016].

Sisongkharm, A., Xayalueth, C., Banmanivong, L., Khuangvichit, V., Homsombat, K., Pathoomvan, A., Sibounhueang, K., Soysouvanh, K., Vilay, P., Phengsavatdee, M., Koulabouth, K., Thammavongsa, V., Lattanavong, S., Soudachan, S., Khammounhueang, N., Sitphaxay, N., Mahasai, D., Inthaxoum, V., Sisavang, A., Chanthalath, A., Phoumasavat, N., Phommachanh, X. and Chanthabuala, S. 2014, *College majors guidebook & web*, Vientiane: College Guidebook Publisher.

Soukamneuth, B. J. 2006, *The political economy of transition in laos: From peripheral socialism to the margins of global capital*, Ithaca, Cornell University.

Stuart-Fox, M. 2008, *Historical dictionary of Laos*, Plymouth: Scarecrow Press.

Turner, R. 2015, *Travel & tourism: Economic impact 2015 laos*, London: World Travel & Tourism Council.

UNESCO. 2013, *Policy review of TVET in Lao PDR*, Paris: United Nations.

UNFPA. 2015, *Population situation analysis: Lao PDR*, Vientiane: United Nations Population Fund.

World Bank. 2008, *Lao PDR economic monitor*, Vientiane Office: World Bank.

World Bank. 2012, *Country gender assessment for LAO PDR: Reducing vulnerability and increasing opportunity*, Vientiane: Asian Development Bank and World Bank.

World Bank. 2013a, *East Asia Pacific at work: Employment, enterprise and well-being*, Washington, DC: World Bank East Asia and Pacific Regional Report, International Bank for Reconstruction and Development.

World Bank. 2013b, *Jobs*, Washington, DC: World Bank.

World Bank. 2013c, *Skills for quality jobs and development in Lao: A technical assessment of the current context PDR*, Lao People's Democratic Republic Skills & Knowledge for Greater Growth and Competitiveness in Lao PDR, World Bank, W Bank, Vientiane.

World Bank. 2014a, *Expanding productive employment for broad-based growth*, Lao Development Report 2014, Vientiane: World Bank.

World Bank. 2014b, *Unemployment, total (% of total labor force) (modeled ILO estimate)*, World Bank, viewed. Available at: http://data.worldbank.org/indicator/SL.UEM.TOTL.ZS?locations=LA [Accessed January 21, 2017].

World Bank. 2015, *Gross national income per capita 2015, atlas method and PPP*, World Development Indicators database, Washington, DC, World Bank.

World Bank. 2017a, *Country dashboard: Lao PDR*, World Bank, viewed. Available at: http://povertydata.worldbank.org/poverty/country/LAO [Accessed October 1, 2017].

World Bank. 2017b, *World bank country and lending groups*, World Bank, viewed. Available at: https://datahelpdesk.worldbank.org/knowledgebase/articles/906519-world-bank-country-and-lending-groups [Accessed January 23, 2017].

Yorke, M. and Knight, P. 2006, *Embedding employability into the curriculum*, vol. 3, York: Higher Education Academy.

Part III

Comparative analysis and conclusions

12 A comparative perspective on work-readiness challenges in the Asia Pacific region

Subas Dhakal, John Burgess, Roslyn Cameron and Alan Nankervis

This chapter presents a brief comparative overview of the higher (HE) and vocational education and training (VET) sectors and their associated graduate work-readiness challenges across the nine Asia Pacific economies included in this book. The chapter is structured into four parts, beginning with a brief introduction to the socio-economic and demographic trends in the region and a review of the common threads in their work-readiness challenges. This is followed by comparative discussions on the history of the HE and VET sectors, and the magnitude of the skills shortages and associated issues, policy gaps and challenges, and innovative work-readiness initiatives in the region. The chapter ends with a summary of the key findings.

Introduction

The primary objective of the book is to explore contemporary labour market–related challenges across the Asia Pacific region. It is in this context that the successful transition of graduates from education to employment in the labour market is a pivotal aspect of sustainable economic development. And yet graduates are facing increasing difficulty in finding work despite substantial, if diverse, investments in education (Burgess et al. 2017). This book focuses on graduate work-readiness and job-related challenges in nine Asia Pacific countries – Australia, Indonesia, India, Lao People's Democratic Republic (PDR), Malaysia, Nepal, Singapore, Taiwan and Vietnam. With over 4 billion people, the Asia Pacific is one of the most populous regions of the world (UNESCAP 2016). Home to two of the largest democracies – India and Indonesia – the region has achieved impressive economic growth in the past five decades. However, the countries that are the focus of this book are at varying stages of economic development. For example, according to the recent World Bank's (2017) Gross National Income (GNI) based classification, Nepal is considered a low-income economy; whereas Australia, Singapore and Taiwan are categorised as high-income countries. The following table (Table 12.1) illustrates the classifications for all countries explored in the book.

There are substantial differences in labour market participation rates across these nine nations (Figure 12.1). The rate varies from 59 percent in Taiwan,

Table 12.1 Income classification of case countries in Asia and the Pacific level of income

Low ($1,025 or less)	Lower Middle ($1,026 and $4,035)	Upper Middle ($4,036 and $12,475)	High ($12,476 or more)
Nepal	India Indonesia Lao PDR Vietnam	Malaysia	Australia Singapore Taiwan

(Source: World Bank 2017)

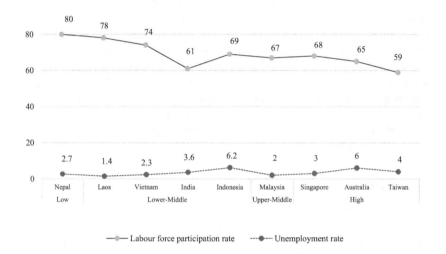

Figure 12.1 Labour force participation and unemployment rates
(Source: *World Bank 2017*)

with an unemployment rate of 4 percent, to 78 percent in Lao PDR, with an unemployment rate of 1.4 percent in 2014 (World Bank 2016; Taiwan Statistics Bureau 2016). Indonesia has the highest unemployment rate of 6.2 percent, and Nepal has the highest labour force participation rate of 80 percent. On the one hand, late entry, early retirement, excessively selective local workers and increasing numbers of foreign workers have kept the labour force participation rate low in high-income economies like Taiwan. On the other hand, the low levels of overall unemployment in the context of Lao PDR and Nepal suggests that workers might be willing to take up any available job, resulting in labour underutilisation, for example not enough work, not enough pay and skill mismatches.

The other burgeoning issue is that the populations in high-income economies such as Australia, Singapore and Taiwan are ageing significantly, whereas the low- and lower-middle economies – India, Nepal, Vietnam and Indonesia – have amongst the youngest populations and labour markets in the world, often called a 'demographic dividend'.

Work-readiness: an overarching framework and the common thread

Work-readiness as a concept remains ambiguous and means many things to many people (Bennett and Kane 2009). Nonetheless, the concept signifies three-pronged abilities: the ability to gain employment, the ability to maintain employment and the ability to make transitions between jobs and roles (Wickramasinghe and Perera 2010). Consequently, Connell and Burgess (2006) suggest that work-readiness rather than the job itself is the new labour market reality. Drawing upon Andrews and Higson (2008), Nankervis et al. (2017) discussed three broad components of graduate work-readiness: hard skills or discipline-specific knowledge, soft skills or interpersonal competencies and work experiences or work-integrated learning, and adopted the ten skill-based competencies ranging from teamwork and political skills to system thinking skills in order to inform the country-level analysis.

The diverse stages of economic development in the region also mean dissimilarities in terms of competencies required, the nature of work-readiness and the work itself. For instance, service-oriented sectors provide the majority of jobs in high-income economies, and agriculture and manufacturing employ the most people in low and lower middle economies. Health care and social assistance, professional, scientific and technical services, education and training and retail trade are the fastest-growing sectors for employment in Singapore and Australia (see Waring et al. 2017; Montague et al. 2017). In the lower and lower middle economies of Nepal, Lao PDR and Vietnam, the agriculture, forestry and fisheries sectors are the largest employers (Dhakal 2017; Vipapone 2017; Nguyen and Nguyen 2017). This division in economic development also means that there is an increasing reliance on foreign workers in the upper middle and high-income countries such as Malaysia, Singapore and Taiwan. For instance, more than one-third and one-tenth of the labour force in Singapore and Taiwan respectively, is comprised of foreign workers (see Min-Wen and Connell 2017; Waring et al. 2017). Conversely, countries such as Lao PDR and Nepal primarily export cheap labour, resulting in low unemployment rates in these countries (Dhakal 2017; Vipapone 2017). Recognising this divergence in the labour market, chapter 2 adopts a stakeholder perspective as a common framework and persistent thread for reviewing work-readiness challenges, and more importantly, to address government, industry and educational institutions' policy responses.

The nature and scope of work-readiness often depends on how well a particular country's educational system allows stakeholders to build, maintain, and harness interrelationships. Stakeholders represent groups or individuals who can be affected, or are affected, by the functioning of an organisation (Freeman 2010). However, as chapter 2 pointed out, engaging with stakeholders and managing relations is challenging and multi-faceted and often requires compromise on conflicting and competing interests. Key stakeholders associated with graduate work-readiness challenges in the region are broadly categorised as: (a) government agencies which include national, provincial and local governments; (b) the private sector, encompassing local, small and medium, and large enterprises, and multi-nationals; (c) educational services providers including HE and VET institutions; (d) graduates and their families; and (e) aid organisations, including development agencies and banks. Although there are substantial variations in terms of changing vocational and higher education imperatives as well as graduate and employer prospects, as Cameron et al. (2015) argued, stakeholder contributions are pivotal for addressing work-readiness-related challenges in the region. Consequently, the stakeholder lens provides a common thread to compare key work-readiness issues across the region. As noted earlier in this book, only the three main stakeholder groups – namely, governments, industry and educational institutions – are discussed in detail here.

Comparative perspectives: key issues

Although many countries in the region face considerable challenges linked to ageing populations and skill shortages, graduates reportedly are experiencing significant difficulties in securing appropriate employment in all countries discussed in this book (Burgess et al. 2017). This is due, at least partially, to a disconnect between tertiary education outcomes and the needs of employers in the middle- and high-income economies in the region (World Bank 2012). In this context, four of the key issues: (a) the history and scope of educational sectors, (b) skills-shortages and associated issues, (c) policy gaps and challenges and (d) innovative employability initiatives across the region, are compared next.

The history and scope of educational sectors

The history of educational institutions in Asia and the Pacific region goes back several hundred years. The Nalanda University in India was established in the 5th century and was fully functional until the 12th century. It was a truly a global university of the time with 2,000 teachers and 10,000 students from countries across the region. Recognised now as a UNESCO World Heritage Site, the university is now being revived with the support of the Indian government (Nalanda University 2016). Most of the countries in the region established their first modern universities around the mid-1850s. As table 12.2 depicts, the University of Indonesia was the first one to be established, in 1849, whilst the National University of Laos was established much later, in 1996.

The number of HE institutions varies extensively across the region. On the one hand, with over 35,000 HE institutions, India has the highest number of education providers (see chapter 9). Given that the country is expected to produce

Table 12.2 First modern universities of case countries in Asia and the Pacific

GNI	Country	First university	Year established
Low	Nepal	Tribhuvan University	1959
Lower Middle	**Lao PDR**	**National University of Laos**	**1996**
	Vietnam	National University of Vietnam	1955
	India	University of Calcutta	1857
	Indonesia	**University of Indonesia**	**1849**
Upper Middle	Malaysia	University of Malaya	1959
High	Singapore	Nanyang University	1956
	Australia	University of Sydney	1850
	Taiwan	National University of Taiwan	1928

20 million high school graduates by 2017 (Cooper et al. 2012), the number of institutions is not surprising. On the other hand, Taiwan has an oversupply of HE institutions (a total of 159) that guarantees university placement for virtually all students who sit the entrance exam (see chapter 4). The size and scope of VET providers in the region also vary to a large extent and are generally tied to the overall labour market trends and economic realities. For instance, as indicated in chapters 10 and 11, Australia has a large VET sector, with a total of over 4000 institutions primarily focused on delivering services-sector skills, whereas Nepal has about only 400 VET institutions that are primarily focused on low-skills development. In line with the view of Agrawal (2013), it is clear that the extensive network of HE and VET providers in the upper middle and high-income countries has played a much more pivotal role in their economic growth when compared to low and lower middle-income nations. More importantly, although the region as a whole is predicted to grow continuously and even more rapidly in the immediate future, a recurring challenge has been to find ways to address country-specific labour demands, as well as skill shortages and to support effective transitions from HE and VET sectors into meaningful jobs.

Skill shortages and associated issues

The fact that nine nations in the region are at different stages of economic development translates into diverse labour mobility opportunities and skill shortages. In this context, the recently established ASEAN Economic Community (AEC) has been viewed as a potentially positive step towards increasing flows of trade and investment as well as enabling the freer movement of skilled workers (ILO/ADB 2014). However, it is likely that there will be winners and losers in this increasingly competitive labour market. As a result, the dynamics of the challenges related to employment, employability, capacity building and intra-regional migration are likely to remain volatile. As indicated in table 12.3, construction, tourism, manufacturing and professional services are the top four sectors facing acute skill shortages.

Although the construction sector is facing broad skill shortages across the region, the extent of these challenges varies to a large extent even within the same sector. For example, the construction sector has become a priority in Nepal after the 2015 earthquake because over two million jobs will be required for the reconstruction and recovery efforts. With an unemployment rate of less than 3 percent, primarily because of outbound migration, the government is facing difficulties to find and train local workers (Dhakal 2017). In contrast, nearly one-third of construction sector labour is comprised of foreign workers in Singapore, which is facing increasing competition from within and outside the region to secure labour (see Waring et al. 2017). In Australia, construction is the third-largest employing sector that provides jobs to over a million workers, accounting for nearly 10 percent of the workforce (Department of Employment 2015). Consequently, skill shortages are more prevalent here than in any other sector (Department of

Table 12.3 Skill shortages sectors across case countries

GNI	Country	Skill shortages	Main issues
Low	Nepal	Construction, Tourism	Outbound migration
Lower Middle	Lao PDR	Construction, Agriculture/ Forestry	Mis-alignment between skills needed and VET graduates
	Vietnam	Manufacturing, IT sector	Mis-alignment between skills needed and VET graduates
	India	Infrastructure, Auto-manufacturing, Construction	Demand supply mismatch, Low enrolment in vocational courses
	Indonesia	Tourism, Agriculture/ Forestry	Differences in the quality of training between private and public sectors
Upper Middle	Malaysia	Healthcare, Finance	Reliance on foreign labour
High	Singapore	Construction, Tourism	Reliance on foreign labour
	Australia	Construction, Professional Services	Maintaining employment rate
	Taiwan	Manufacturing, Professional Services	Attracting foreign labour; long hours low pay

Employment 2016), and the state and federal government policies in the country are often geared towards overcoming shortages as well as ensuring employment within the sector. A one and half billion–dollar stimulus package for the construction sector is believed to have saved the country from going into recession post 2008 Global Financial Crisis (Thangaraj and Chan 2012).

It is obvious that the varied nature of skill shortages has been a burgeoning issue for both HE and VET sectors across the region. The VET sector in general appears to be struggling to overcome industry-specific skill shortages. For example, our research indicates that lower middle economies such as India and Indonesia suffer from the lack of ability to provide students with appropriate industry-relevant skills, mainly because of outdated curriculum together with a lack of industry engagement (see chapter 9). These challenges, albeit slightly different, also exist in other countries of the region, including the higher-income ones such as Australia and Taiwan (Nankervis et al. 2012). For example, an ageing population and the late entry of the young people into the workforce in Taiwan means that it has had to change its foreign labour policy (see Min-Wen and Connell 2017). In addition, "long hours and low pay" have emerged as the main challenges to attract and retain workers in Taiwan because of practices such as: paying workers less than a minimum wage, making employees work thirteen consecutive days in a row and longer than twelve-hour days. Nonetheless, the misalignment between labour market needs and VET sector graduates, to varying degrees, can be identified as the single most important common thread across the countries, especially in the lower middle-income economies.

Policy gaps and challenges

ADB (2011) posits that although the demand for expanding Education Service Providers (ESP) has increased in the region, concerns about the quality and relevance of the ESPs have equally spread. In this context, it is imperative to assess the state of educational policies and priorities in order to better serve the needs of labour markets and foster or sustain economic growth. Several similarities as well as differences in policies in terms of gaps and innovation can be noted across the region. Based on our recent research (Cameron et al. 2015) of the nine nations in the region, three countries – Lao PDR, Nepal and Vietnam – do not have a national qualification framework (NQF). Since the primary purpose of a NQF is to raise quality and drive continuous improvement and consistency in education services, its absence suggests that policy frameworks are rather under-developed. In addition, as table 12.4 indicates, there is no comprehensive recognition of prior learning (RPL) mechanism in Lao PDR and Nepal. RPL is generally more effective and efficient in overcoming skills-shortages than additional VET training in areas that educational services beneficiaries already have the necessary experiences and knowledge. Once again, the absence of RPL is an indication of the need for improving policy implementation mechanisms. Since appropriate policies and strategies are necessary to encourage employers to improve employee skill utilisation and skills alignment; to formulate NQFs and provide flexible RPL

Table 12.4 The policy gaps and issues across the case countries

Country	NQF	RPL	VET policy	HE Policy	Prominent Challenges
Nepal	No	No	Under-developed	Under-developed	Lack of political will
Lao PDR	No	No	Under-developed	Under-developed	Conflicting priorities of donor agencies
Vietnam	No	Yes	Fairly developed	Fairly developed	Conflicting interests of government agencies
India	Yes	Yes	Under-developed	Under-developed	Outdated curriculum
Indonesia	Yes	Yes	Fairly developed	Fairly developed	Outdated curriculum
Malaysia	Yes		Well-developed	Well-developed	Slow bureaucracy
Singapore	Yes	Yes	Well-developed	Well-developed	None, perhaps one of the most innovative in the region
Australia	Yes	Yes	Well-developed	Well-developed	Political interference; commodification
Taiwan	Yes	Yes	Fairly developed	Fairly developed	Quality of education

opportunities, HE and VET sectors' related policies in each nation can be cat-egorised into three stages: well developed; fairly developed and under-developed.

The conventional mindset in many of the lower and lower middle-income countries such as Indonesia and India has been such that university education is often deemed more important and valuable than vocational training (Soegeng and Nankervis 2017; Verma et al. 2017). Although there have been significant changes in this regard based on the evidence of linkages between a vibrant VET sector and economic development (for example, in Malaysia – Rasul et al. 2015), the VET sector specific related policy reforms remain sluggish in the region. This mindset at least partially explains the lack of an adequate emphasis on developing VET policies. However, one of the main reasons behind under-developed edu-cational policies in both HE and VET in low-income economies such as Nepal is the lack of political will (Dhakal 2017). In countries like Lao PDR, it is the conflicting priorities of diverse donor agencies that have been the main obstacle to the development of such policies (see Vipapone 2017). Nonetheless, even a high-income economy like Australia has had its fair share of political interference, especially with respect to a focus on the privatisation of VET, which has had a significantly adverse impact on policy formulation and implementation, as well as graduate outcomes (see Montague et al. 2017). Although sectoral policies are well-developed in Malaysia, bureaucratic processes are not keeping pace with changes on the ground (see Noorziah et al. 2017). In lower-middle economies like India and Indonesia, it is the inability to make curriculum contemporary that is considered the main drawback (see Soegeng and Nankervis 2017; Verma et al. 2017). Singapore is ahead of many other economies by making significant investments in research and innovation activities and complementing rhetoric with action, thus preparing its workforce more effectively for the future. Both HE and VET policies in the country are geared toward creating a flexible lifelong system of education with a focus on futuristic skills (see Waring et al. 2017).

Innovative employability initiatives

Despite significant skill shortages and policy challenges, there have been several innovative employment initiatives across the region. The high-income economies of Singapore and Australia have demonstrated substantial progress in this area. For instance, the Singaporean government has actively encouraged Workforce Skills and Qualifications (WSQ) that focus on skills upgrading and competency enhancement to future-proof employability during recessionary as well as non-recessionary periods (see Waring et al. 2017). The country has focused on identifying particular industry needs every five years and adopting specific measures, such as competency frameworks; online education and training; blended learning; and financial support for structured workplace-based learning, which has resulted in productivity growth. Table 12.5 shows a summary of range of such initiatives from the countries explored in this book, which are discussed in greater detail in each country chapter.

In terms of outcomes, the Australian Apprenticeship Scheme (AAS), for example, has trained nearly 200,000 people, with 84 percent being employed after completion (see chapter 10). To the contrary, the Collaborative Apprenticeship Program (CAP) in the other high-income economy of Taiwan has had mixed outcomes and has even been blamed for exploiting the young trainees (see chapter 4). The upper middle economy of Malaysia has clearly recognised the importance of VET in its goal to become a high-income economy by 2020 (ETP 2013). As table 12.5 indicates, the Economic Transformation Program (ETP) is targeting a 2.5-fold increase in VET sector enrolment in order to supply an adequate workforce to the twelve key locations and industry sectors in Malaysia: Greater Kuala Lumpur/Klang Valley; oil, gas and energy; financial services; wholesale and retail; palm oil and rubber; tourism; electrical and electronics; business services; communications content and infrastructure; education; agriculture; and health care (ETP 2013).

The lower middle economies in general have gradually begun to pay attention to educational sector reform. For example, under the National Vocational Education Qualification Framework (NVEQF) scheme, India has established over 125 undergraduate and postgraduate VET courses (see Verma et al. 2017). This is a clear departure from an excessive investment in conventional courses such as the Bachelor of Arts and Bachelor of Science degrees and has begun to improve graduates' work-readiness for key industry skills. Similarly, the VET sector has not been the preferred option of school leavers in Indonesia, and the government has launched national promotional campaigns in order to change negative

Table 12.5 A snapshot of innovative employability initiatives by country

GNI	Country	Programs	Outcomes
Low	Nepal	Employment Fund Program (EFP)	Underemployed or unemployed youth from socially-disadvantaged backgrounds to build skills
Lower Middle	Lao PDR	Strengthening Technical and Vocational Education and Training (STVET)	VET qualifications for 20,000 students in line with the needs of labour market
	Vietnam	National Fund for Employment (NFE)	Support youth in starting a business; dissemination of employment information and workplace availability
	India	National Vocational Education Qualification Framework (NVEQF)	Development of undergraduate and postgraduate VET courses
	Indonesia	Public Employment Program (PEP)	Short-term work opportunities for vulnerable and marginalised workers in the informal economy
Upper Middle	Malaysia	Economic Transformation Program (ETP)	2.5-fold increase in VET enrolment by 2025 to supply workforce to the 12 National Key Economic Area (NKEA) sectors
High	Singapore	Workforce Skills and Qualifications (WSQ)	Perhaps, most futuristic and innovative in the region, productivity growth, employability during recession and non-recession periods
	Australia	Australian Apprenticeship Scheme (AAS)	Nearly 200,000 trained with 84 percent employed after completing the scheme
	Taiwan	Collaborative Apprenticeship Program (CAP)	Better industry engagement with limited tangible benefits

perceptions. In addition, the Public Employment Program (PEP) provides short-term work opportunities for vulnerable and marginalised workers in the informal economy (see Soegeng and Nankervis 2017). In Vietnam, the government has recently proposed a National Fund for Employment (NFE) with a mandate to support youth in starting a business, together with boosting labor market forecasts and the dissemination of employment information and workplace availability to help youth and students to obtain suitable jobs after graduation (see Nguyen and Nguyen 2017). The Lao PDR is working with donor agencies in the Strengthening Technical and Vocational Education and Training (STVET) project which aims to equip 20,000 students with qualifications more aligned with labour market needs (see Vipapone 2017). Similarly, in Nepal, various donor agencies have helped establish the creation of Employment Fund Program (FEP) that targets underemployed or unemployed youth from socially disadvantaged backgrounds to build skills that enhance employability (see Dhakal 2017).

Conclusion

This chapter has presented a comparative overview of the higher and vocational education and training sectors across the nine Asia Pacific economies included in this book, and their associated work-readiness challenges. The World Bank's (2017) GNI-based classification was utilised to rank the nine countries as low, lower-middle, upper-middle and high-income economies. The comparative assessment revealed that service-oriented sectors provide the majority of jobs in high-income economies, whilst agriculture and manufacturing employed the most people in low and lower-middle economies. The construction sector is facing skills shortages across all the nations regardless of income categories. However, there was a strong association between income classification and the maturity of HE/VET policies. In addition, donor agencies have played a key role in influencing government policies and devising innovating employability initiatives in the low and lower-income countries. Meanwhile, the issues raised in this comparative chapter are a reminder that addressing work-readiness challenges in the Asia Pacific region is likely to be much more effective, with a concerted emphasis on stakeholder engagement than without it.

References

Agrawal, T. 2013, 'Vocational education and training programs (VET): An Asian perspective', *Asia-Pacific Journal of Cooperative Education*, Vol. 14, no. 1, pp. 15–26.

Andrews, J. and Higson, H. 2008, 'Graduate employability, 'soft skills' versus 'hard 'business knowledge: A European study', *Higher Education in Europe*, Vol. 33, no. 4, pp. 411–422.

Asian Development Bank (ADB). 2011, *Higher education across Asia: An overview of issues and strategies*, Asian Development Bank, Manila, Philippines.

Bennett, R. and Kane, S. 2009, 'Employer engagement practices of UK business schools and departments: An empirical investigation', *Journal of Vocational Education and Training*, Vol. 61, no. 4, pp. 495–516.

Burgess, J., Cameron, R., Dhakal, S. and Brown, K. 2017, 'Introduction', in Cameron, R., Dhakal, S. and Burgess, J. (eds.) *Transitions from education to work: Workforce ready challenges in the Asia Pacific.* Chapter 1, London: Routledge.

Cameron, R., Nankervis, A., Burgess, J., Brown, K., Connell, J. and Dhakal, S. P. 2015, *Enhancing work-readiness of vocational and higher education graduates: Asia-Pacific region*, International Conference on Researching Work and Learning. December 9–11, 2015. Singapore.

Connell, J. and Burgess, J. 2006, 'The influence of precarious employment on career development: The current situation in Australia', *Education + Training*, Vol. 48, no. 7, pp. 493–507.

Cooper, D., Hersh, A. and O'Leary, A. 2012, *The competition that really matters comparing U.S., Chinese, and Indian investments in the next-generation workforce*, Washington, DC: Centre for American Progress. Available at: www. americanprogress.org/issues/economy/reports/2012/08/21/11983/ the-competition-that-really-matters/.

Department of Employment. 2015, *Industry outlook construction*, Canberra: Commonwealth of Australia. Available at: https://cica.org.au/wp-content/ uploads/2015-Construction-Industry-Outlook.pdf.

Department of Employment. 2016, *Labour market research – construction trades.* Available at: https://docs.employment.gov.au/system/files/doc/other/ausconstructiontrades_0.pdf.

Dhakal, S. P. 2017, 'The state of higher education and vocational education and training sectors in Nepal: Implications for graduate work-readiness and sustainable development', in Cameron, R., Dhakal, S. and Burgess, J. (eds.) *Transitions from education to work: Workforce ready challenges in the Asia Pacific.* Chapter 10, London: Routledge.

Economic Transformation Program [ETP]. *2013, annual report*, Kuala Lumpur: Malaysian Government. Available at: http://etp.pemandu.gov.my/annualreport2013/upload/BM/ETP2013_BM_full_version.pdf.

Freeman, R. E. 2010, *Strategic management: A stakeholder approach*, London: Cambridge University Press.

ILO/DB. 2014, *ASEAN community 2015: Managing integration for better jobs and shared prosperity*, Bangkok, International Labour Organization and Asian Development Bank.

Min-Wen, S. and Connell, J. 2017, 'Labour market and work readiness challenges: The case of Taiwan', in Cameron, R., Dhakal, S. and Burgess, J. (eds.) *Transitions from education to work: Workforce ready challenges in the Asia Pacific*, Chapter 3, London: Routledge.

Montague, A., Connell, J. and Mumme, B. 2017, 'Graduate employability in Australia: Time for a VET and HE overhaul?' in Cameron, R., Dhakal, S. and Burgess, J. (eds.) *Transitions from education to work: Workforce ready challenges in the Asia Pacific*, Chapter 9, London: Routledge.

Nalanda University. 2016, *History and revival.* Available at: www.nalandauniv.edu. in/about-nalanda/history-and-revival/.

Nankervis, A., Cooke, F. and Chatterjee, S. 2012, *New models of HRM in China and India*, London and New York: Routledge.

Nankervis, A., Verma, P. and Cameron, R. 2017, 'Literature analysis of job readiness: challenges and solutions', in Cameron, R., Dhakal, S. and Burgess, J. (eds.) *Transitions from education to work: Workforce ready challenges in the Asia Pacific*, Chapter 2, London: Routledge.

Nguyen, D. N. and Nguyen, B. N. 2017, 'Enhancing graduate work-readiness in Vietnam', in Cameron, R., Dhakal, S. and Burgess, J. (eds.) *Transitions from education to work: Workforce ready challenges in the Asia Pacific*, Chapter 4, London: Routledge.

Noorziah, M. S., Emeleonwu, J., Winterton, J. and Chan, K. M. 2017, 'Work-readiness in Malaysia', in Cameron, R., Dhakal, S. and Burgess, J. (eds.) *Transitions from education to work: Workforce ready challenges in the Asia Pacific*, Chapter 5, London: Routledge.

Rasul, M. S., Ashari, Z. H. M., Azman, N. and Abdul Rauf, R. 2015, *Transforming TVET in Malaysia: Harmonizing the governance structure in a multiple stakeholder setting*. Available at: www.tvet-online.asia/issue4/rasul_etal_tvet4.pdf.

Soegeng, P. and Nankervis, A. 2017,' "The perfect storm": Constraints on Indonesian economic growth posed by graduate work-readiness challenges', in Cameron, R., Dhakal, S. and Burgess, J. (eds.) *Transitions from education to work: Workforce ready challenges in the Asia Pacific*, Chapter 6, London: Routledge.

Taiwan Statistics Bureau. 2016, *Unemployment rate*. Available at: https://eng.stat.gov.tw/np.asp?ctNode=1543.

Thangaraj, R. K. and Chan, T. K. 2012, 'The effects of the global financial crisis on the Australian building construction supply chain', *Construction Economics and Building*, Vol. 12, no. 3, pp. 16–30.

UNESCAP. 2016, *Population dynamics challenges and opportunities*. Available at: www.unescap.org/our-work/social-development/population-dynamics/about.

Verma, P., Kumar, S., and Raje, P. 2017, 'Antecedents, consequences, and strategic responses to graduate work-readiness: Challenges in India', in Cameron, R., Dhakal, S. and Burgess, J. (eds.) *Transitions from education to work: Workforce ready challenges in the Asia Pacific*, Chapter 8, London: Routledge.

Vipapone, A. 2017, 'Work-readiness in Lao PDR', in Cameron, R., Dhakal, S. and Burgess, J. (eds.) *Transitions from education to work: Workforce ready challenges in the Asia Pacific*, Chapter 11, London: Routledge.

Waring, P., Vas, C. and Bali, A. S. 2017, 'Work-readiness in Singapore', in Cameron, R., Dhakal, S. and Burgess, J. (eds.) *Transitions from education to work: Workforce ready challenges in the Asia Pacific*, Chapter 7, London: Routledge.

Wickramasinghe, V. and Perera, L. 2010, 'Graduates', university lecturers', and employers' perceptions towards employability skills', *Education and Training*, Vol. 52, no. 3, pp. 226–244.

World Bank. 2012, *Putting higher education to work skills and research for growth in East Asia*, Washington, DC: World Bank.

World Bank. 2016, *Unemployment, total (% of total labor force) (modeled ILO estimate)*. Available at: http://data.worldbank.org/indicator/SL.UEM.TOTL.ZS.

World Bank. 2017, *World Bank country and lending groups country classification*. Available at: https://datahelpdesk.worldbank.org/knowledgebase/articles/906519-world-bank-country-and-lending-groups.

13 Conclusion

The future for work-readiness and graduate employability in the Asia Pacific

Roslyn Cameron, John Burgess, Subas Dhakal and Barbara Mumme

This concluding chapter reviews findings and provides a broader regional context, which highlights the complexity of the challenges of work-readiness and employability of VET and HE graduates in the ASEAN region. The contribution and research for this volume have examined the contemporary landscape of nine countries within the Asia Pacific region, namely, Taiwan, Vietnam, Malaysia, Indonesia, Singapore, India, Australian, Nepal and Lao PDR, in terms of their respective policies related to labour market challenges, skill mismatches and human capital development, with specific reference to the vocational education and training (VET) and higher education (HE) systems.

Key issues and challenges identified for the region

The data collected and synthesised for this book reveals the many complexities and challenges facing the ASEAN region. The region can take comfort in that the issues of graduate work-readiness are being felt globally and much can be learnt from the international community. The following paragraphs highlight some of the key issues and challenges for the ASEAN region. This section will first seek to bring some clarity to regional megaforces and challenges; second, the urgency of finding solutions to mismatches cannot be understated and some of the reasons for this are discussed; third, stakeholder responsibilities are considered, especially in relation to skills mobility and international skills recognition; and last, ASEAN regional partnerships are examined in light of Internationalisation of Higher Education.

Regional megaforces and challenges in the ASEAN region

Megaforces, as described by Batalova et al. (2017), operating in the ASEAN region will greatly influence the future supply and demand and mobility of professionals. These megaforces include: diverging demographics (reduced fertility and increased life expectancy), rising educational levels and aspirations and continuing economic disparities and opportunities in the region. The demographics of ASEAN countries are diverse, with, for example, countries like Singapore,

Thailand and Brunei having declining and aging workforce projections while Lao PDR and Indonesia will see a growth in labour force numbers over the coming decades. Both forces provide impetus for skilled mobility within the region. In terms of education levels and aspirations, Batalova et al. (2017, p. vii) point to increased investments in education and increased numbers seeking international educational opportunities:

> In the past few decades, all ASEAN countries have made large investments in secondary and tertiary education. Larger cohorts of ASEAN citizens with a vocational or college education mean a greater pool of skilled workers who are likely to migrate, given the right incentives. In addition, more students from ASEAN countries are seeking an international education.

The report refers to the phenomenon of brain circulation and two key pressing challenges for the region: brain waste (skills underutilization) and brain drain (emigration of highly educated/skilled). Despite these challenges, the mega-forces are creating "unique opportunities for human capital development and brain circulation" within the region (Batalova et al. 2017, p. ix). For low-income ASEAN countries such as Lao PDR:

> even a small increase in the absolute number of high-skilled foreigners can raise the number of needed professionals and expand access to critical services. For middle income countries such as Malaysia, a greater number of highly skilled workers might propel the nation toward becoming a high-income economy and thus avoid the middle-income trap. Finally, the wealthiest ASEAN countries, Brunei Darussalam and Singapore, would benefit from tapping skilled regional talent to compensate for a declining labor supply and to sustain economic vitality and growth.

The level of complexity and diversity of challenges for work-readiness and employ-ability in the Asia Pacific region may seem overwhelming. However, this volume has captured this complexity and at the same time has synthesised the issues and challenges and to present strategies for combating these challenges. The key to these strategies lies within the countries themselves and the engagement of key stakeholders, working together to find solutions, but also in regional strategies that take on board the megatrends at play and the increasing circulation of skilled human capital within and across the ASEAN and Asia Pacific region.

The urgency to address skill mismatches in the ASEAN region

There is no mistaking the urgency in relation to investing in human capital to sustain economic growth in the Asia Pacific region. The matching of skills is the nexus or interface between education and training skills supply, and industry skills demands and requirements. Panth (2014) investigated skills development for employability and inclusive growth in developing countries in the South Asian

Region (India and Nepal) and suggested critical ways the training systems in these countries need to improve to meet the contemporary demands. Opportunities in the region for future growth stem from globalization, advances in technology and unprecedented labour mobility.

As discussed in chapters 1 and 2, we arguably stand on the brink of a technology revolution, the fourth industrial revolution, which is evolving at an unprecedented pace and disrupting industry globally (WEF 2016; 7. This digital disruption is reported to open up opportunities in less-developed countries in the region, increasing demand for skilled employees at a rapid pace (Schwab 2017). The demand for employee skills is changing. Industries are experiencing a significant shift in the quality, speed and price of their products and services, often creating ambiguity as to the skills required (Schwab 2017). On the demand side, graduates need a greater range of employability skills to meet these new demands, but to ascertain what these skills are can be illusive.

The World Economic Forum's Future of Jobs Report (2015) suggests that around 60 percent of children entering primary school may work in jobs that do not exist at the moment. Planning for the unknown is creating unprecedented challenges for legislators and regulators (Schwab 2017), suggesting that a framework of stakeholder engagement, will help to provide Governments, Industry and Educational Institutions with a platform to come together to address these pressing issues. The urgency and importance to national economies of graduate work-readiness cannot be over emphasised, the OECD (2016, p. 129) sums up the global significance of the skills matching challenge as:

> Ensuring a good match between the skills acquired in education and on the job and those required in the labour market is essential if countries want to make the most of their investments in human capital and promote strong and inclusive growth. It is also a desirable outcome for individuals who have, themselves, invested in education. A mismatch between workers' skills and the demands of their job has potentially significant economic implications. At the individual level, it affects job satisfaction and wages. At the firm level, it increases the rate of turnover and may reduce productivity. At the macroeconomic level, it increases unemployment and reduces GDP growth through the waste of human capital and/or a reduction in productivity."

The McKinsey Global Institute (2017) proposes that one of the most significant society challenges will be labor redeployment and urge governments, industry and educational institutes to develop strategies to skill up for the future of automation and associated digital disruptions. It is important that when people make educational choices, they are aware of the skills that will be required for the future. Highly skilled workers will be in most demand and best positioned to take advantage of opportunities presented. Policy makers working with educational institutions and industry need to improve basic skills sets, with a new emphasis on creativity and critical thinking. Furthermore, resilience, flexibility and the ability to respond with dexterity will be essential attributes when jobs are likely to change over time (McKinsey 2017).

Stakeholder responsibilities: skills mobility and international skills recognition

In line with major donor organisations like the World Bank (2011) and the Asian Development Bank (2011), Panth (2014) also views the top three constraints to economic growth for South Asia as: transport, energy and skills. In relation to the latter, he suggests the following to combat the skills constraint: more effective education and training funding models, strong and effective coordination between education and training institutions, improvements in the delivery and modes of deliver of education and training and the need for improved and increased engagement with the private sector. These all need to be overseen with strong quality assurance (QA) policies and bodies tasked with the QA brief and industry councils, which could oversee sector based skills and training coordination. Panth (2014, p. 168) refers to infrastructure as a key priority:

> South Asian countries are growing quickly and have the potential to grow even faster if they systematically address the binding constraint linked to skills. For all of them, investing in infrastructure is a top priority. But the only additional way to move up the value chain in South Asia is to invest more in training and upskilling the working-age population, particularly the youth. Although the overall unemployment rate is generally low, this masks the high level of underemployment and high youth unemployment: generally two to three times that for adults.

Furthermore, Panth (2014, pp. 178–180) recommends six strategic areas to transform the skills ecosystem. These include: the substantial expansion of training capacity or investment in VET and HE sectors; establishment of a unified fund to target priority sectors and skill levels based on evidence such as regular studies and skills gap analysis; strengthening of leadership and institutional arrangements to ensure there is a coordinated approach to skills and human capital development that cuts across all government ministries, not only those with education and employment portfolios; substantial engagement of the private sector through training coverage and work placements incentivised through government funding and based on evidence-based data which targets priority skills and sectors; establishing national quality assurance systems inclusive of national qualification frameworks, competency-based training and assessment and mutual recognition agreements; and the establishment of sound and robust monitoring and evaluation system which tracks VET and HE graduates and their employment outcomes.

As demonstrated in the various country case study chapters, labour migration in and out of the ASEAN region is extensive (ILO 2013), and the issue of work-readiness is part of the labour migration flow (ILO 2016), with job seekers turning to other countries to find work suited to their skills, coupled with industry turning to international labour when they cannot find the skills they require nationally. The issue for graduates is that labour migration can fill jobs they might otherwise have obtained.

It is proposed that skills mobility for the ASEAN region can be improved through integrated Quality Assurance and Mutual Recognition Arrangement (MRAs) (Panth 2014). Between 2004 and 2014, the ten member states of ASEAN signed MRAs for the following professions: accounting architecture, dentistry, engineering, medicine, nursing and tourism (Batalova et al. 2017). Ease of labour mobility in the region will assist in sustaining regional growth and the demand will be for middle-level skills as opposed to low-level skills (McKinsey MGI 2012). The Asia Development Bank (ADB) and the Migration Policy Institute (MPI) have recently released three reports documenting the potential of labour mobility in the ASEAN region and in particular the use of MRAs to foster this movement amongst skilled professionals: *Open Windows, Closed Doors: Mutual recognition arrangements on professional services in the ASEAN Region* (Mendoza et al. 2016), *Reinventing Mutual Recognition Arrangements: Lessons from International Experiences and Insights for the ASEAN Region* (Mendoza et al. 2017) and *Firing Up Regional Brain networks: The Promise of Brain Circulation in the ASEAN Economic Community* (Batalova et al. 2017).

ASEAN regional and global partnerships

Internationalisation of higher education is tasked with the goal of integrating educational institutions into the emerging global knowledge economy, rather than trying to shoe horn international dimensions into existing institutional settings (Hawawini 2016; de Wit et al. 2017). To do this educational institutions are encouraged to reach outside of higher education, with calls for an approach that is internationally comprehensive and integrated, moving away from traditional disjointed and ad hoc strategies (Larsen 2016; de Wit et al. 2017). From an education delivery standpoint, the ILO (2013) highlights that it is not only a matter of matching skills between graduates and jobs that is important, but it is also imperative to weed out redundant and unused skills that may still be taught by educational institutions. Improved collaboration between educational institutions, industry and government will help to improve curriculum design to ensure learning opportunities are maximised. Having the wrong skills or not utilizing the skills that are possessed creates challenges for graduates and can contribute not only to graduate unemployment but also to under-employment.

Higher education research is increasingly moving its focus from narrow national initiatives to a more global focus, as evidenced by the creation of collaborations, such as, the Centre for Global Higher Education (CGHE) with ten partner institutions around the world, as well as the Global Centre for International Higher Education Studies (GCIHES) which collaborates with five other centers around the world and also the European Bologna Process, which seeks to strengthen quality assurance and provide easier recognition of qualifications (Bologna 2015). The ASEAN region, like other regions, has specific challenges unique to them. However, the skills mismatch is reported to be on a global scale (de Wit 2016). The ASEAN region can benefit greatly from learning what initiatives are being employed in other regions and indeed globally. Education networks of the future may include 'metanational' universities, which would be interconnected and integrated, providing a learning network spanning the globe (de Wit 2017).

Country-specific studies, undertaken for this book, reveal that many nations through their various educational institutions provide opportunities for graduates to improve employability skills, such as work-integrated learning and internships. In addition to this, some universities offer units and modules focused on employability skills, and these can act as a vehicle for graduates to learn the work-ready skills they need to gain meaningful employment. Partnerships between education institutions and industries with the ASEAN region have the potential to increase stakeholder involvement and open up more opportunities to improve graduate work-readiness.

The 2030 Agenda for Sustainable Development calls for improved vocational and technical skills to improve employment, decent jobs and entrepreneurship. The ILO (2016) proposes that skills mismatch will add to the problem of being responsive to labour market demands. The demand for high skills employment in ASEAN is projected to increase by 41 percent between 2010 and 2025 (ILO 2016). ASEAN governments will need to put in place initiatives to address the skills shortage challenge. The Asia-Pacific region accounts for around 40 percent of global trade, and this is likely to intensify in coming years (ILO 2016). The greater involvement of industry is essential to meet skill demands, and increased public-private partnerships are required to develop and agree on skills needs for the future. In recent years, substantial work has been done to develop competency standards and national qualifications frameworks throughout the region, and this needs to continue and increase momentum. Industry engagement with a demand-led approach will achieve the best results as employers are those best positioned to predict future skill demands (ILO 2016).

Inter-university collaborations, supported by macrolevel support through inter-governmental initiatives, along with immediate and continued response from industry to identify the skills demand for the future, will greatly assist the region to meet the challenges of the fourth industrial revolution.

Contributions of the book

This volume provides a detailed and rich picture of the key contextual issues and challenges being faced by the nine countries represented in the edition. The book presented a comprehensive review of the current literature on work-readiness and employability and presents a theoretical framework which remains central to the volume before detailing each country's unique economic, social and demographic contexts, respective tertiary education systems and policy initiatives. Country chapters are synthesised under the World Bank's (2016) GNI-based classification of low, lower-middle, upper-middle and high-income economies. Differing stages of economic development meant that service-oriented sectors provide the majority of jobs in high income economies, whilst agriculture and manufacturing employed the most people in low and lower middle economies. The book suggests a strong link between higher economic development and the maturity of HE/VET policies as well as lower economic development and the strength of influence of donor agencies in educational and employability initiatives.

These issues are not confined to any one stakeholder or any one nation, numerous reports highlight how increased labour mobility moves these issues beyond national borders and it is an issue for all stakeholders to take the initiative. This book serves to highlight how a concerted effort is required, by the three key stakeholders identified, to equip graduates with the skills they need to secure meaningful employment. Numerous universities were involved in the data collection for this book, and initiatives like this one help to raise awareness in regard to the urgency required to find measures to address skills deficits and mismatches throughout the region. The issue of graduate work-readiness and skill mismatches is a global issue, and the ASEAN region will want to look both inward and outward to work together to improve economic conditions for the region and increase global presence. From an education perspective, the growing internationalisation of universities and notion of 'meta-national' universities gives promise to the idea of universities helping to create new insights and create a stronger knowledge economy globally. From an industry perspective, recognising their important role in providing job opportunities for graduates and working with education providers to identify industry-specific employability skills is the only way the skill mismatch debate can move forward. Government initiatives that support a forward-thinking knowledge economy require a move away from bureaucratic and outdated education frameworks to a learning environment that is flexible, responsive and accessible to meet the needs and demands of contemporary graduates and employers (ILO 2016).

A range of actual and potential strategies and solutions to the identified issues are considered across the country chapters and include:

- The need for accurate and reliable evidence bases for decision making, planning, monitoring and evaluation
- National and regional labour market forecasting, skills gap analysis for priority skills and sectors and workforce planning for specific industries
- Linking funding to graduate outcomes based on national tracking systems for graduates and their employment outcomes
- More coordinated approaches across education and training institutions and across government portfolios
- Active engagement of employers/private sector in the provision, delivery and content of education and training which can be activated through incentives
- Up-to-date labour market and career information and services to students and graduates
- Priority funding to partnerships and education and training infrastructures and workforces
- Innovative employability initiatives within countries and regionally.

Future research

Areas that would benefit from further/future research lie within the examination and understanding of pockets of best practice in relation to:

- More effective and formal stakeholder partnerships;
- actively engaging the private sector/industry in having input into the curriculum and delivery modes of education and training;
- policy initiatives that take a hard look at existing education and training structures;
- investing in innovative teaching and delivery strategies;
- investing in the futuristic education and training workforces and infrastructures;
- exploring the effective use and utility of monitoring and evaluation systems or national data-tracking systems to assist in informing the effectiveness of education and training systems,
- improved focus on the links between education and employment in the context of social and environmental change.

The research can range from occupation, organisation and sector analysis; through to the examination of specific programs and transition arrangements offered by training/education institutions, employers and professions; and cover national and international evaluations.

References

ADB. 2011, *Higher education across Asia: An overview of issues and strategies*, Manila: Asian Development Bank [ADB].

Batalova, J., Shymonyak, A. and Sugiyarto, G. 2017, *Firing Up regional Brain networks: The Promise of Brain Circulation in the ASEAN Economic Community*, Mandaluyong City and Philippines: Asia Development Bank.

Bologna. 2015, *The Bologna process and the European higher education area*, European Commission. Available at: http://ec.europa.eu/education/policy/higher-education/bologna-process_en.

Brandenburg, U. and De Wit, H. 2015, 'The end of internationalization', *International Higher Education*, Vol. 62.

de Wit, H. 2016, 'Higher education research goes global', *International Higher Education*, Vol. 85, pp. 8–10.

de Wit, H., Gacel-Ávila, J., Jones, E. and Jooste, N. (eds.) 2017, *The globalisation of internationalization: Emerging voices and perspectives*, New York: Routledge.

Hawawini, G. 2016, *The internationalization of higher education and business schools: A critical review*, New York: Springer.

ILO. 2013, *Report on global employment trends for youth*. Available at: www.ilo.org/wcmsp5/groups/public/-dgreports/-dcomm/documents/publication/wcms_212423.pdf.

ILO. 2016, *Skills for the future: Background note for the special plenary debate*. 16th Asia and the Pacific Regional meeting. Balei, Indonesia December 6–9, 2016.

Available at: www.ilo.org/global/meetings-and-events/regional-meetings/asia/aprm-16/arabic/WCMS_534144/lang – en/index.htm.

Larsen, M. A. 2016, *Internationalization of higher education: An analysis through spatial, network, and mobilities Theories*, New York: Springer.

Mendoza, D. R., Desiderio, M. V., Sugiyarto, G. and Salant, B. 2016, *Open windows, closed doors: Mutual recognition arrangements on professional services in the ASEAN Region*, Mandaluyong City and Philippines: Asia Development Bank.

Mendoza, D. R., Papademetriou, D. G., Desiderio, M. V., Salant, B., Hooper, K. and Elwood, T. 2017, *Reinventing mutual recognition arrangements: Lessons from international experiences and insights for the ASEAN region*, Mandaluyong City and Philippines: Asia Development Bank.

MGI [McKinsey Global Institute]. 2012, *The world at work: Jobs, pay and skills for 3.5 billion people*, MGI.

MGI [McKinsey Global Institute]. 2017, *A future that works: Automation, employment and productivity*. Available at: https://issuu.com/fredzimny/docs/mgi-a-future-that-works-full-report_937f4a8b6a24f6.

OECD. 2016, 'Skills matter: Further results from the survey of adult skills', *OECD Skills Studies*, Paris: OECD Publishing. Available at: www.oecd.org/skills/skills-matter-9789264258051-en.htm.

Panth, B. 2014, 'Skills development for employability and inclusive growth: Policy dilemmas and priorities in South Asia', *Prospects: Quarterly Review of Comparative Education*, Vol. 44, no. 2, pp. 167–182.

Schwab, K. 2017, *The fourth industrial revolution*, London, Penguin.

WEF [World Economic Forum]. 2015, *Human capital index*. Available at: http://reports.weforum.org/human-capital-report-2015/.

WEF [World Economic Forum]. 2016, *The fourth industrial revolution: What it means, how to respond*. Available at: www.weforum.org/agenda/2016/01/the-fourth-industrial-revolution-what-it-means-and-how-to-respond/.

World Bank. 2011, *More and better jobs in South Asia*, Washington, DC: World Bank.

Index

Page numbers in italic indicate a figure and page numbers in bold indicate a table on the corresponding page.